UNLOCKED

About the Author

Eben Etzebeth grew up in Goodwood, a suburb of Cape Town. During his illustrious club career, he's played with the Stormers, NTT Docomo, Toulon and the Sharks. He has also represented South Africa more than 130 times, and is a pivotal part of the squad that has won back-to-back World Cups. He lives in Durban with his family.

UNLOCKED

Eben Etzebeth

HODDER &
STOUGHTON

First published in Great Britain in 2025 by Hodder & Stoughton Limited
An Hachette UK company

The authorised representative in the EEA is Hachette Ireland, 8 Castlecourt
Centre, Dublin 15, D15 XTP3, Ireland (email: info@hbgi.ie)

1

A CIP catalogue record for this title is available from the British Library

Hardback ISBN 978 1 399 73710 4
Trade Paperback ISBN 978 1 399 73711 1
ebook ISBN 978 1 399 73713 5

Typeset in Minion Pro by Hewer Text UK Ltd, Edinburgh
Printed and bound in Great Britain by Clays Ltd, Elcograf S.p.A.

Hodder & Stoughton policy is to use papers that are natural, renewable
and recyclable products and made from wood grown in sustainable
forests. The logging and manufacturing processes are expected to
conform to the environmental regulations of the country of origin.

Hodder & Stoughton Limited
Carmelite House
50 Victoria Embankment
London EC4Y 0DZ

www.hodder.co.uk

CONTENTS

Prologue

END OF THE WORLD

It is never just a game. Not when you're wearing a Springbok jersey. Not when failure ruins thousands of carefully planned parties and makes men weep and gnash their teeth. Not when losing is tantamount to a grave and mortal sin.

There are reasons why confession in church is anonymous. For one, owning up to wrongdoing can be embarrassing and make you cry. But here in a hotel meeting room in Brighton, we don't have the luxury of a confessional. One by one, some of the finest players ever to wear the Springbok colours trudge to the front and repent, before explaining how they will make amends. Shame radiates from every one of them. Some are unable to hold back tears. Huge men, tall as trees and wide as houses, blubbing like toddlers.

It's an ugly sight, and you can't accuse any of us of faking it. When it's my turn, I say I wasn't good enough, didn't put everything on the line, didn't take the opposition seriously enough. I'll be better next time. It's more like a military debrief after an operational debacle than a post-match review.

Losing to Japan in a World Cup isn't a disaster in the grand scheme of things – not when there's so much wrong with the world – but it is for a South African. I didn't know where to look at the final whistle, just wanted the ground to swallow me up. Thankfully, the TV cameras were more interested in the Japanese players – whooping, hollering, hugging, shedding tears of joy. Had someone shoved a camera in my face, viewers might have detected mortification, ignominy, guilt, disgrace and dishonour. That almost covers it.

Upsets like that aren't supposed to happen in rugby, so it's no wonder the crowd reacted like they did. All around me and my desolate teammates, 30,000 people celebrated the best thing they'd ever seen on a sporting stage. The bully-boy Springboks – brutes, ogres, Goliaths – cut down to size by a bunch of Davids. The Miracle of Brighton, as it would soon be known.

At least us players were able to escape down the tunnel. At least we've been able to avoid the flak that's been flying. I didn't look at my phone for 24 hours because I didn't want to know what anyone thought, not even family and friends. 'What do you mean, "what happened?" We lost! Didn't you watch the game?' I dread to think what our rugby reporters and pundits have been saying about us, or what people have been writing on social media.

As for the Springbok fans who travelled thousands of miles, confident of seeing their heroes crush any 'minnows' in their path, I can only imagine the abuse they've had to endure on our behalf. Walking the streets in green and gold – humiliated but still proud – they must have felt like sitting ducks.

Holed up in my hotel room, I wonder about the reaction back home. Springbok fans would have spent weeks organis- ing matchday parties, much like people in other countries plan for Christmas. Guests would have started arriving in the early afternoon, loaded up with salads, side dishes, beer and brandy, before hosts started throwing great slabs of meat onto the braai. By kick-off, such parties would have been in full swing all over South Africa.

Had the Springboks delivered as they were expected to, partygoers would have spent the rest of the evening boasting about how great their team were and who they might get in the final, or parking the game and discussing more trivial matters, all while getting ever merrier. But imagine a Christmas where everyone receives a present they hate, the in-laws fall out in a big way and the host gets drunk and burns dinner to a cinder. That's how those parties would have looked after the final whistle against Japan. Kids wailing, husbands getting darker and angrier, wives getting more and more irritable. Just a game? More like the end of the world.

1

DYING AND GOING TO HEAVEN

The Stormers had just beaten the Bulls away at Loftus Versfeld in Pretoria, which was immensely satisfying. It was pretty ugly. They smashed us up front and had far more of the ball, but our defence held firm and we ended up stealing it. Not even a sore shoulder, which meant I lasted only 50 minutes, could wipe the smile off my face. It was a good changing room to be in. Then it got better.

After congratulating us on the win, head coach Allister Coetzee cleared his throat and said, 'The following guys have been selected for the Springbok incoming tour: Bryan, Jean . . .' A pause. '. . . and Eben.' I tried to hide the tears – Springbok locks aren't really meant to cry – but I couldn't have done a very good job. My teammates exactly understood the emotions I was feeling and celebrated with me accordingly.

No wonder I got emotional, because my childhood dreams were suddenly coming true. When I was very young, I had a list of goals written on my bedroom door in chalk, and one of them was to become a Springbok.

I must have been one of the biggest Springbok fans in South Africa, and if you'd ever played rugby for the Boks, chances are that a picture of you was on my bedroom wall. Dad would bring home copies of *Huisgenoot*, an Afrikaans magazine, and tell me, 'You'd better not tear anything out before I read it, otherwise there'll be trouble.' Within seconds of him finishing, the centrefold poster (at least if it was a picture of a Springbok!) would be stuck up with the rest of them.

An image of the great Bobby Skinstad took pride of place on my wall, and the only foreign player to get a look-in was All Black phenomenon Jonah Lomu. I must admit, whenever I played *Jonah Lomu Rugby* on the PlayStation, I'd have to be New Zealand because his character was twice as big as everyone else and almost impossible to tackle. It was very realistic in that respect.

I was four, so I don't remember Lomu running riot at the 1995 World Cup in South Africa, when he destroyed the England defence. (I also don't recall the Boks beating the All Blacks in the final, although the image of Nelson Mandela presenting the trophy to Francois Pienaar while dressed in a Springbok jersey is seared into every South African's brain.) But I do remember Lomu's crazy try in the 1999 semi-finals, when he shrugged off six or seven French defenders, and I just loved the sight of such a big, athletic man beating people for fun.

I watched South Africa's quarter-final against England, in which Jannie de Beer kicked a barely believable five drop goals, at a campsite in Robertson. I thought De Beer was a superhero. Sadly, my most vivid memory of that 1999 tournament was the moment in our semi-final against Australia when

Stephen Larkham, who almost never kicked a drop goal in Tests, landed one from about 45 metres out in extra time. One minute I was dreaming of the Springboks winning the World Cup, the next was emptiness.

In the early 2000s, when the New Zealand backline included the likes of Lomu, Christian Cullen, Tana Umaga and Justin Marshall, I'd argue with my *ouma* (grandmother) whenever they played the Boks. She was convinced the All Blacks would win every game they played, including against us, and I'd say to her, 'Ouma, you don't know what you're talking about. We're better than them – and you must support the Boks.' I always wanted to believe the Springboks were the pinnacle, but Ouma was often proved right.

Of course, I never stopped loving the Boks, not even when England put 50 points on us at Twickenham in 2002. Around that time, my mom took me to Canal Walk shopping mall in Cape Town, where some Boks were doing a signing session. I stood impatiently in the queue for ages before hoovering up the autographs of my heroes (I remember being in awe of the sheer size of hooker Lukas van Biljon). It was as if I'd died and gone to heaven. And now, a decade later, I was set to be one of those men in green and gold.

I first met Victor Matfield before the 2011 World Cup in New Zealand. Victor's agent was trying to sign me up, and while I'd already committed to another agency, and loyalty is important to me, I stayed in touch and he asked if I wanted to meet Victor at his house.

Victor was one of my biggest heroes, a guy who had played 110 Test matches (at the time) for the Boks, one of the greatest second-row forwards in history, so I was in complete awe of him (despite being a few centimetres taller). I can't remember most of what he said to me, just that he thought I could be a Springbok within a year. I was only 19, two years out of school, and I hadn't even played for the Stormers. It was all a bit surreal. Me, playing for the Boks at the age of 20? Four years younger than Victor when he made his Bok debut? Surely not. But because Victor had said it, I felt almost obliged to go and do it.

You might imagine I was some kind of rugby prodigy, one of those kids who has stubble at 14 and is playing for the school first team a year later. Actually, I still didn't have any whiskers at 19, and I didn't make Tygerberg High School's under–16s 'A' team. I wasn't even a forward back then.

It all started at Goodwood Park Primary School in the northern suburbs of Cape Town. Normally at primary school, your teacher would be your rugby coach, but when Dad discovered that my teacher was a woman ('You can't have a *vrou* coaching you rugby . . .') he decided to take over. Dad was traditional about things like that, in common with most Afrikaner men of his vintage.

I was a massive Stormers fan and Dad wanted our under–8s team to play in replica jerseys. However, when the principal pointed out that Goodwood Park's colours were blue rather than black, as Stormers jerseys were at the time, Dad got hold of some sponsored blue jerseys with 'Stormies' emblazoned on a yellow stripe. And to be fair to Dad, we looked the business.

I had the number 8 on my back, because of Bobby Skinstad (we didn't actually have positions at that age). I was a decent enough player and won the *victor ludorum* for best athlete three years in a row, but after getting an athletics/rugby bursary to Tygerberg High, just down the road from Goodwood in Parow, I became an average-size fish in a much bigger pond.

Tygerberg wasn't known for its rugby and hadn't produced many notable players, but it had big ambitions to compete with the best schools in the Cape, such as Paarl Boys' High and Paarl Gimnasium, which have produced dozens of Springboks between them and whose under–19 derbies attract more than 20,000 spectators. (The whole week is devoted to the game, with flags appearing on front lawns, classes cancelled, and first-team players presented at assembly, lunches and dinners.) That meant Tygerberg had hoovered up all the best primary school talent in the area and suddenly I wasn't winning any races, jumping the furthest or the highest, or even playing A-team rugby.

I played for the B teams all the way from the under–14s (kids start high school at 13 or 14 in South Africa) to the under–16s, something the school wasn't thrilled about. I thought I was good enough for the A team but the one time I was given a shot, in place of our injured inside centre Anton, I fluffed my lines and was sent straight back down again.

I was just a half-decent back, not making much impact, but at least I looked the part: the bursary gave me a certain amount a year to spend on boots and other kit, and I splurged the lot on a scrum cap, shoulder pads, arm and leg skins and gloves.

It made sense to buy as much as possible because my parents couldn't afford that kind of stuff. Plus, I thought I looked like Waratahs and Australia back Sam Norton-Knight. But in hindsight, the other kids probably just thought I had all the gear and not much idea.

Halfway through grade 10, the school threatened to take my bursary away. Had that happened, I would have had to move to another school because my parents couldn't afford the fees. Thankfully, Mom and Dad had a chat with the principal and he gave me one last chance to prove myself.

It was around that time that I decided to hit the gym, and I'll never forget my first session because it was quite humiliating. I was trying to do bicep curls in front of the mirror and my brother Ryen, as well as his friend Edzard, were laughing at me. But I kept at it, all the time hoping the Etzebeth genes would suddenly kick in (Dad and my uncles were all tall, as was Ryen, so I'd always stuck out for being relatively stumpy). And at some point during my under–16 season, I had a big growth spurt. Having been average height at the start of the year, by the end of it I was a gangly winger.

I spent most of the off-season in the gym, having become hooked on pushing weights. I enjoyed the fact that I could see tangible results, that my muscles were growing. I was getting stronger and looking fitter. I hoped it might also make me play better rugby. By the time I returned to school for my grade 11 year, I was tall and broad rather than gangly. The coaches, Mr Page and Mr Beresford, didn't recognise me at first, then told me I'd have to start at lock instead of in the backs.

Playing in the forwards with the so-called matrics (in South Africa, matriculation is the qualification you get in your final year of high school) was scary enough, but when we suffered an injury crisis I found myself playing lock in the first game of the season. Outeniqua High in George was ranked in the country's top 10 rugby schools, so it was a big step up from playing on the wing for the under–16s B team. But while we lost by 30-odd points and I didn't really know what I was doing, the coaches seemed to think I played alright.

My parents had never really forced me to do anything – their attitude was always, 'You must decide if you want to push yourself or not' – and while I was naturally lazy, Mr Beresford did his best to kick that out of me. He pushed the boundaries – including having us tackling bags up and down the field before school and pushing ever heavier weights in the gym – and in doing so he toughened up the whole team physically and mentally.

Soon, rugby had become extremely important to me, and while I'd scored pretty good grades in my first three years of high school, mainly because I had a good memory, by grade 11 I was barely studying and missing a lot of classes because of my rugby commitments. My grades fell off a bit, not that I was too bothered. I'd found my calling and it didn't involve books.

Believe it or not, I still wasn't aggressive enough on the rugby field. After one of my school games, a father of another kid, who always watched me from behind the poles, told me, 'You played well but you're too soft, like a jelly baby. You don't have enough dog.' That stung a bit, which suggested it was true.

Around that time, Springbok eighthman Pierre Spies was held up as the model of the modern rugby forward – built like Hercules, quick and agile – and I thought I'd have to be like him to make it. I'd read about Pierre's prowess in the gym and tried to get as close as possible to the weights he was reportedly shifting.

I remained at lock for the whole of my grade 11 season, even though I weighed 117 kg and none of our props could lift me in the line-out. I was eliminated in the final round of trials for that season's Craven Week, which is a schools version of the Currie Cup, but made the Western Province (WP) team in my matric year (the WP team's props – future Boks teammates Frans Malherbe and Steven Kitshoff, plus Adriaan Botha – were strong enough to lift me but I refused to strap my legs, which meant they couldn't get much of a grip, and that probably didn't go down too well with the coaches).

After every Craven Week, a South Africa schools team is selected, and there are provincial scouts crawling all over the tournament, hoping to snap up a future Springbok or two. So while I didn't get selected for South Africa Schools, which remains one of my biggest disappointments, I did get selected for the South Africa Under–18 High Performance squad, plus offers from the Sharks in Durban, the Lions in Johannesburg and WP.

The Sharks and the Lions offered me about R6,000 a month, compared to almost nothing from WP. However, when WP's head of youth rugby, former Springbok lock Hennie Bekker, asked why I hadn't yet signed for them and I told him why, he came to my parents' house and told us that WP would match what the other unions were offering. And it was at the Western Province International Rugby Institute in Stellenbosch that any remaining laziness was rinsed out of me. Something clicked and I went up a couple of gears.

When I was little, I told Mom I wanted to be well known one day, although I didn't know for what. And when I was in primary school, a teacher asked me where I thought I'd be in 2010. 'I want to be a WWE [World Wrestling Entertainment] superstar,' I said, 'taking over from The Rock.' Now it was 2010 and the wrestling ambition had sailed. But the rugby dream was still on.

People were always asking me, 'What's your plan B?' And I'd always reply, 'If you have a plan B, that means you think your plan A might fail.' I was convinced that if I carried on working as I had been, I would be well known. I reckoned I'd be a Springbok.

WP gave me a two-year extension, while I also decided to play in the Varsity Cup, mainly to keep fit. I'd wanted to play for Stellenbosch, but when they didn't get back to me, the University of Cape Town's head coach, Kevin Foote, snapped me up instead.

I didn't have to study or even pretend to; I was there to train and play games. The joke was that I studied English, which was kind of true: after winning man of the match in one of my first games for the Ikeys, as UCT's rugby team are known, I gave probably the worst TV interview in history. My English really was that terrible. But it slowly improved, as did my rugby. The Ikeys won the Varsity Cup for the first time that year, beating the University of Pretoria in the final.

We had one hell of a team, including future Stormers team-mates Nic Groom, Demetri Catrakilis, Nick Fenton-Wells, Nizaam Carr (who also played for the Boks), Don Armand (who also played for England) and Marcel Brache (who also played for the United States). Slightly controversially, we also had Hilton Lobberts, who had played two Test matches for the Boks a few years earlier (Springboks were banned from the Varsity Cup a few years later). Fifteen thousand fans watched that final in Pretoria and you can still watch the highlights on YouTube, which shows you just how big university rugby is in South Africa.

During the Varsity Cup season, I had to be excused to play for the Baby Boks – the national under–20 team – in the Junior World Championship in Italy, and my first taste of competitive rugby in a green and gold jersey didn't pan out particularly well. We beat Scotland and Ireland easily enough before narrowly losing our final pool game to England, which meant we failed to make the semi-finals for the first time.

England had a pretty good team, including Joe Launchbury, Mako Vunipola, George Ford and Owen Farrell, but losing was still a source of shame for our boys, who included my future Springbok teammates Siya Kolisi and Bongi Mbonambi. We were officially the worst Baby Bok team in history.

*   *   *

I suffered my first major injury later that year, damaging my ankle playing for WP under–21s. And having been told I might make my debut for the seniors in the Currie Cup the following week, I was massively disappointed.

Some people think the Currie Cup has become less important since the inception of Super Rugby in the mid–1990s, but it still meant so much to South African rugby players. Every major name in Springbok rugby had played in it, including my uncle Cliffie Etzebeth, who was a Western Province stalwart between 1977 and 1981 and part of the side that shared the Currie Cup title with Northern Transvaal in 1979 (the final was drawn, which WP skipper Morné du Plessis likened to 'kissing your sister').

Instead of moping, I told WP's under–21s conditioning coach Charl, 'Listen, I don't care if I puke every day, just get me ready. I want to have a big season next year.' Whatever the conditioning coach told me to do, I did it, no questions asked. When I returned to action two months after the injury, for the under–21s Currie Cup semi-final, I was in the best shape I'd ever been. And after a good pre-season and two warm-up games before the start of the 2012 Super Rugby season, Allister Coetzee selected me for the Stormers squad.

I'd played with plenty of very good players before then, but nothing like this. When I walked into the changing room before my first Stormers training session, Bryan Habana, Schalk Burger and Jean de Villiers, all World Cup winners in 2007, were sizing me up. There too were Andries Bekker, a hero of mine since I switched to playing lock, and a guy who was 5 cm taller than me and had played 29 Test matches; Bok wing Gio Aplon; Bok centre Juan de Jongh; hooker Tiaan Liebenberg, who had been in the South African set-up for years; and loose forward Duane Vermeulen, who had long been earmarked for greatness.

A few years earlier, I'd come close to losing my school bursary because I wasn't cutting it as a rugby player. Now I was mixing with rugby royalty. Intimidating? Yes. Thrilling? Absolutely. And they were all very welcoming, especially Andries, whose dad Hennie played with Oom Cliffie for WP. Hennie had probably told his son to look after me.

It helped that I already knew some of the younger guys in the squad, including Nizaam Carr, Siya Kolisi, Frans Malherbe, Scarra Ntubeni and Steven Kitshoff. I discovered what a talent Siya was at Craven Week, where WP played against his Eastern Province (EP) team. Before the game, my teammates kept telling me to watch out for EP's eighthman, whom they'd seen playing for South Africa Schools the previous year. And every time we kicked the ball, he'd retrieve it and run it straight back, usually past three or four defenders, before someone managed to drag him down. We put almost 50 points on them that day but Siya was named man of the match.

Not long after that, Siya switched to WP's high-performance programme, which was the start of a beautiful relationship. My high school was Afrikaans-speaking, and while I had quite a few coloured classmates, including one of my best friends, Seth Pienaar (who was one heck of a singer!), I'd never really interacted with black kids before (for international readers, 'coloured' in a South African context refers to a specific, culturally distinct multi-racial people). But I loved Siya immediately. He was always laughing and joking, the life and soul of the changing room. And I'd always be asking him to smile for me because it was just so contagious.

I learnt new things from the Stormers veterans from day one. I had only one pair of boots, heavy duty ones with eight studs, and the first thing Schalk said to me was, 'Why are you training in those?' I didn't know what he was talking about, then he said, 'You must get yourself some *pantoffels* [slippers].' Now I was even more confused. Slippers? It turned out that Schalk called his multi-studded training boots 'slippers' because they were so light and comfy on his feet. In fact, everyone did. Including me from that day on.

I performed well enough over the next few months to be picked for the first warm-up game of the season against Boland. We had a lot of locks out injured, including Andries, Rynhardt Elstadt and Hilton, but we won comfortably with a young, experimental team. I thought I'd done okay but Andries called me in the following Monday and said, 'You had a good game, well done, but I'm going to take you through some clips.' He advised me on my positioning in the line-out but mostly he wanted me to hit people harder: 'If you'd tackled that guy like this instead, you'd have fucked him up much more.'

The following week, I was selected to start against the Lions, this time alongside Burger, Habana, De Villiers and the rest of the vets. The first time their scrum half got hold of the ball,

I picked him up, ran him backwards and dumped him on his back. Andries's words had obviously made an impression.

My first competitive game for the Stormers was against the Hurricanes at Newlands, where Western Province greats had been strutting their stuff since 1890. Andries had tipped me off beforehand, informing me that Rynhardt still wasn't fit and that I might play, but it was still a bit of a shock when Allister named me in the starting XV.

Schalk busted his knee after 15 minutes (he wouldn't play again for 18 months) but Siya was excellent in his place, scoring a try 10 minutes into his Stormers debut. The Hurricanes had World Cup winners Conrad Smith, Cory Jane and Victor Vito in their ranks, all guys I'd watched on TV plus a young Beauden Barrett, but Andries was such a calming presence and I knew that if the *kak* hit the fan, Andries and my other superstar teammates – Bryan, Schalk, Jean and Duane – would back me up.

Allister singled me out for praise to the media after the game, which we won 39–26. Not that I thought I'd arrived – if any youngster made the mistake of getting above his station, someone senior would soon put him in his place – and I still thought I'd be ousted from the starting XV as soon as Rynhardt was fit again. But when he did finally return, it was in the back row.

After beating the Sharks in week two of Super Rugby, I signed a contract extension alongside Siya and two more future Springbok teammates, Steven Kitshoff and Frans Malherbe. Three more wins followed, then another victory in my first tour game against the Highlanders in Dunedin. Six games as a professional, six wins. If I'd known it wouldn't always be such plain sailing, I'd have savoured it more.

Reality bit against the Crusaders in Christchurch, when I went off injured in the first 15 minutes and we ended up losing. I'd damaged the AC joint in my shoulder, and after 60 minutes against the Reds in Brisbane I couldn't lift my arm. That's not great for a rugby player, especially a lock.

At the end of April, Heyneke Meyer invited me to his first camp as the Springbok head coach. Twenty other Stormers were there too, so I wasn't getting ahead of myself, but I did get a bit excited when Heyneke said he would have selected me to start for the Boks if they had been playing the following weekend.

A few weeks later came that game against the Bulls at Loftus. I couldn't pass the ball to my left during the captain's run because my shoulder was so sore, and I needed an injection before the game. But I must have done something right for Heyneke to select me in his squad for the three-Test series against England. When Allister made that announcement in the changing room after the game, suddenly my shoulder didn't hurt anything like as much.

Before the first Test in Durban, the team stayed at the Beverly Hills Hotel. We were sponsored by BMW and the squad had 10 cars to share between us, but I got hold of one of the keys and spent the week driving to and from my family's hotel a few kilometres away.

I kept thinking about what Heyneke had said to me two months earlier, about selecting me to start for the Boks had they been playing the following weekend. But this wasn't April, it was now, and Heyneke had only five days to prepare us for the game.

He was new in the job and needed to get off to a flyer to keep the doubters at bay. The South African media and public aren't the most patient. Then again, Heyneke didn't have any choice but to experiment after the recent retirements of lock Victor Matfield and long-time captain John Smit. On top of that, Schalk Burger, Andries Bekker and Duane Vermeulen were injured, while two more World Cup winners in Danie Rossouw and Fourie du Preez, probably the best scrum half in the world, were plying their trade in Japan and unavailable for selection.

On the Monday before the game, Heyneke called me in for a one-on-one and told me I was starting, ahead of the Bulls' Flip van der Merwe. What a moment. For a South African rugby player, there's nothing bigger.

I couldn't wait to get out of the room and call my parents and brother. They were unbelievably proud, screaming and shouting down the phone. Mom was turning 50 that weekend, which made it even more special. And when Mom and Dad let the rest of the family know, my phone didn't stop beeping.

Jean de Villiers was named captain, and he told me, 'Make sure you take everything in, because it will go by so quickly.' I did my best, but it's not easy when you've been picked for the Springboks at the age of 20.

My shoulder still wasn't right but I didn't tell the coaches in case they had second thoughts about starting me. Besides, I became so swept up in the occasion that I almost forgot about it as the week progressed.

After being presented with my green and gold jersey, I sat with it on my lap and stared at it for ages. I couldn't believe I'd be playing a Test match in it the following day. I had goose bumps when they took the team photo. Slap bang in the middle of the back row, I'm wearing a slightly bemused smile, as if I'm thinking, *Is this really happening?*

With its five languages – Xhosa, Zulu, Sesotho, Afrikaans and English – you might think singing our national anthem is a tricky proposition. But since the end of apartheid, most South Africans have sung it throughout their schooling, which is why Springboks sing it so well. Our anthem really means something, being about reconciliation and unity in diversity. That's probably why I could barely get the words out when we sang it before the game at Kings Park. When I opened my mouth, nothing more than a squeak came out because I was so choked up. My whole body was vibrating and it felt like my heart was going to jump out of my chest. *Keep it together, Eben, there's a game to play . . .*

When my lock partner Juandré Kruger, also making his debut, called our first line-out to me, I could feel myself tense up. You don't really want to lose your first line-out when you're taking over from Victor and Bakkies in the second row. But I won an easy ball, which helped settle me. Even so, the rest of the game was a blur, just as Jean said it would be.

I vaguely recall giving away a penalty and Owen Farrell kicking the three points; changing into my old yellow boots at half-time because I preferred them to the new pair I'd been given; Jean and Manu Tuilagi beating seven bells out of each other; Morné Steyn dotting down in the corner early in the second half; Jean scoring another, just after I'd been replaced. But mostly I remember sitting on the bench and thinking, *I could have done more. I should have done more.* Strange, given that I could barely remember anything I'd done. But I don't remember feeling out of my league. England were definitely a different challenge, but I'd already played some Super Rugby and acquitted myself well against the best the southern hemisphere had to offer.

We beat England 22–17 that day, our eighth win in a row against them, and beat them again the following week in Johannesburg, before a draw in Port Elizabeth when Farrell fluffed a drop goal attempt after the hooter had sounded. After the series, a reporter asked Heyneke if I could be 'the next Bakkies Botha', to which he replied, 'I believe he can surpass that.' That meant a lot to me, but I did also think, *Jeez, that's ramped up the pressure.*

2

RELUCTANT ENFORCER

South African rugby was full of so-called enforcers back in the day. I should know because I had a few of them in my family.

Dad, his six brothers and two sisters grew up in Epping, an industrial part of Cape Town not far from Goodwood. All the brothers slept in one room and money was so tight that they bagged turtle-doves with ketties for dinner. When turtle-doves became scarce, they stole two of their father's racing pigeons and ate them instead. It was a rough and tumble upbringing, that's for sure.

Everyone of a certain age in Cape Town has a story about the Etzebeth brothers, and while all of them were hard as nails, Oom Skattie, the eldest, and Oom Cliffie were on a whole different level.

Afrikaner society was pretty macho in the 1970s and '80s, so it helped to be handy with your fists. And Skattie and Cliffie weren't afraid to use theirs, whether on the job as bouncers or on their own time. There's a famous family story about Skattie and a farmer called Appel (Afrikaans for 'apple', as you might have worked out) having a fight outside Newlands. Another guy had told Cliffie that Appel was going to give Skattie a hiding, to which Cliffie replied, 'We'll see about that.' After about 45 minutes, Skattie and Appel decided to call it a draw before sharing a few drinks in the bar and becoming firm friends.

Cliffie once inspired the newspaper headline, 'Springbok breaks farmer's jaw' (he wrestled for South Africa, hence Springbok, even winning a veterans' world title when he was 62). And when someone asked him what he did when nobody seemed up for some action in a pub, he replied, 'Someone is bound to get angry if you take their woman or their drink.' I think he was joking but I'm not entirely sure.

All the Etzebeth brothers played rugby to a decent level, and as I've mentioned, Cliffie was good enough to play for Western Province, slotting in at tight head prop or lock (which shows you how much the game has changed).

Cliffie was an enormous character, respected and beloved by many. He had such a good heart and would do anything for you if you were on his side. But there is a reason that most of the well-known stories about Cliffie involve fighting, and you didn't want to get on the wrong side of him, on or off a rugby pitch. He was WP's chief meanie, and every team in South Africa had two or three of those back then, guys well versed in rugby's darkest arts.

In a Currie Cup semi-final in 1977, Morné du Plessis knocked Northern Transvaal's star fly-half, Naas Botha, unconscious with a late tackle, which went down quite badly with the Loftus Versfeld faithful. Morné had to be escorted off the field by police, while WP legend Boy Louw, part of the management team, tasked Cliffie and Flippie van der Merwe (father of Flip) with guarding Morné that evening, because people wanted to kill him. Instead, they got roaring drunk, put Morné to bed around midnight, and instead of sitting with him for the rest of the night, as they were meant to, went back out again.

My dad was big like Skattie and Cliffie – about 193 cm and 105 kg – and a difficult customer in his day. But he became a police officer rather than a bouncer (he bailed out his brothers a few times over the years, though maybe that was why they were so casual about fighting in the first place!).

By the time I started playing for a living, you couldn't get away with being an old-school meanie, certainly not one of those guys who deliberately used his head, elbows and knees as weapons and nobbled opposition playmakers with late tackles. Not that South African rugby reporters seemed to have noticed, because they wouldn't stop going on about me being the Boks' new 'enforcer', the heir to Bakkies.

I understood why the media was so concerned about the Boks' void in the second row, because while quite a few players had called it a day after the 2011 World Cup, Bakkies and Victor were probably the best second-row partnership in history. Having played together for club and country for the best part of a decade, they'd won three Super Rugby titles with the Bulls, and a World Cup, a British & Irish Lions series and two Tri-Nations titles with the Boks. But I tried not to think about the size of the shoes that needed filling and kept telling myself that Bakkies and Victor were only two of 832 Boks who had come before me. I was just another guy in green and gold and I didn't need to be the next Bakkies or the next anyone. I just needed to be the best me.

I've never liked comparisons between old and new in rugby. They don't serve any purpose other than to make life more difficult for players in the present. Bakkies did one hell of a job for the Boks and revelled in his role as the team's enforcer, but the game had moved on since he made his international debut in 2002. It should be remembered that he received only four yellow cards in 85 Test matches and was never sent off. But he wouldn't have been able to operate the way he did in today's game, where there is so much scrutiny around head contact and flying recklessly into rucks and tackles.

I loved being part of an ultra-physical pack that dominated the opposition, and I always stood up for myself or a teammate if an opponent took a liberty, but the 'enforcer' tag made me uncomfortable. The term has certain connotations, suggesting a player does things outside the law. But if you habitually do things outside the law nowadays you'll keep getting suspended, which is no good for the team.

As well as that, claiming that I'm the team's enforcer would be disrespectful to the rest of the guys. How could I be *the* enforcer when there were other forwards like Willem 'The Bone Collector' Alberts, Tendai 'Beast' Mtawarira and Bismarck du Plessis, one of the most ferocious hookers ever to play the game, all working as hard as I was and trying to inflict the same amount of pain on the opposition?

In hindsight, stories about my performances in the gym probably fuelled all that 'enforcer' hype. The most famous was that the Stormers' conditioning coach, Steph du Toit, had to buy new dumbbells because the ones we had weren't heavy enough – which was true!

Steven Kitshoff and I were in the gym together during pre-season, and after four or five weeks we were doing bench press reps of 65 kg dumbbells too easily and needed something weightier. First, we tried to attach small weights to the top of the dumbbell, but that was as dangerous as it sounds. Then I pinched some brown strapping from the physio room and attached two 5 kg plates to each end of the dumbbells, making them 75 kg. Steph was delighted when he found out, and a couple of weeks later Steven and I turned up to find a pair of proper 75 kg dumbbells in the gym.

Steven and I enjoyed lifting heavy weights, but you could see some of the more senior guys weren't too impressed probably because they knew better than us that how much someone shifts in the gym has very little to do with how they perform on a rugby field – but the media loves that kind of stuff. And a true story soon became myth, with fans occasionally asking me if it was true that I could biceps curl a 75 kg dumbbell. For the record, I could never biceps curl that much, and after all the shoulder operations I've had since I certainly can't press that much today.

There was more enforcer chat with the Bismarck du Plessis incident in the Stormers' 2012 Super Rugby semi-final against the Sharks. Bismarck had a reputation as one of the game's hardest hitters, and to be fair to him, I think he just got his timing wrong that day. Two weeks after that game, we were back in Boks camp, Bismarck and I were sitting at breakfast together, and Frans Steyn came up to us and said, 'Are things okay between you two again?' Frans was only joking, but it made me a bit uncomfortable.

The media made a big thing about that carry and the clip pops up on my social feeds to this day, but I don't really like talking about it. First, Bismarck is a good friend; second, we lost the game, despite finishing top of the log and the Sharks only just scraping into the play-offs.

If we'd beaten the Sharks at home that day, the Chiefs would have had to travel all the way from Waikato in New Zealand to play us in the final at Newlands. Losing that semi-final was tough at the time and is still difficult to think about, probably because I never came close to winning a Super Rugby title after that.

Then there was the 2012 Rugby Championship game against Australia in Perth, when I was accused of headbutting their lock Nathan Sharpe. I'd never met Sharpe but he'd been on the scene for a hell of a long time and I didn't like the way he went about things on the field (exactly what I didn't like I couldn't remember). Before the game, I told my good friend Marcell Coetzee, 'I hope something happens between me and Sharpe'. And as if by magic, Sharpe grabbed Marcell from behind in the first half and I immediately joined in.

I can't remember if I meant to make contact with my head, but thankfully Bryan Habana and Willem Alberts were holding me back and I just missed his face. After the game, which provided my first taste of defeat in a Springbok shirt, I was cited and handed a two-week ban. It made me unavailable for our next game against New Zealand and I had to admit that I was too easily wound up. It's all very well standing up for a friend but you risk letting the whole team down if you allow your anger to get the better of you.

Watching the Boks play New Zealand in Dunedin, rather than being out there in the thick of things, was agony. And the game was an object lesson in what happens if you don't take your chances in Test match rugby, especially against the very best.

We only managed one try despite dominating territory and possession, and with 20 minutes remaining and the game in the balance, All Blacks scrum half Aaron Smith scored a brilliant individual try, just before our replacement prop Dean Greyling was shown a yellow card for diving recklessly into a ruck. The All Blacks ended up winning 21–11, mainly because they were far more clinical.

Something else I learnt during that tournament was that some teams are very different beasts in their own backyard than they are away from home. We beat Argentina fairly comfortably at Newlands, but the following week in Mendoza was the most physical game I'd played up to that point. The atmosphere was hostile, more like football than rugby, which made the Argentine players that much more up for it. And the more their players got on top of us, the louder the crowd became. It was like playing in the eye of a storm – 80 minutes of deafening noise and getting clattered from all sides – and we were fortunate to be down only 13–3 at half-time. We escaped with a draw only because of a late charge-down try and conversion from Frans Steyn.

In 2013, we put 70 points past Argentina in Johannesburg, only for the Pumas to almost beat us the following week, again in Mendoza (two late penalties from Morné Steyn gave us a narrow victory). How can a team transform from boys to men in the space of seven days? I can only put it down to the home crowd making their players believe, although all that passion can also make them do the craziest things. First, Francois Louw accused loose forward Pablo Matera of eye-gouging (he was later cleared of any wrongdoing), before eighthman Leonardo Senatore bit my forearm in a tackle. I knew that kind of stuff went on back in the day but it's not something I ever expected to happen to me on a rugby field. I'd rather Senatore had punched me – that would have been a lot more honest than using his teeth.

I was so upset that I pushed him to the ground and slapped him on the back of the head when he tried to get back up, which sent the crowd wild and gave Argentina a penalty. When I showed the referee the marks on my arm, he said his TMO couldn't see anything on the replay and therefore couldn't know for sure who'd done it. I replied, 'Flip, you saw who tackled me, and I haven't bitten myself!'

Senatore was later banned for nine weeks but his behaviour didn't stop me admiring Argentina's spirit on home turf.

They've always been my toughest opponents away from home, the ultimate physical challenge. And if you can keep your cool in that kind of atmosphere, you can keep your cool anywhere.

As time went on, I worked out that opponents were going out of their way to get under my skin and I learnt to laugh it off – you'll usually see a big grin on my face when pushing and shoving breaks out. Having said that, I'll always get upset if I see someone taking a liberty with a teammate.

John Smit once said that a Bok makes two debuts: when he plays his maiden Test match and when he faces the All Blacks for the first time. There is no bigger rivalry in rugby than New Zealand versus South Africa.

The All Blacks won the first Test match between the sides in Dunedin in 1921, before the Boks hit back to draw the series (the third Test match in Wellington ended 0-0!). South Africa won more than they lost in the apartheid era, but things had been quite different since South Africa's readmission to international rugby in 1992, the year after I was born.

The Boks took that famous victory over the All Blacks in the 1995 World Cup final but New Zealand had dominated the fixture since then. They won eight in a row between 2001 and 2004, which was agony for a young Bok fan like me, although those guys in green and gold on my bedroom wall never stopped being my heroes.

It helped that New Zealand kept coming up short in World Cups in the past, including in 2007 when they were upset by

France in the quarter-finals and South Africa went on to win the tournament for a second time. But the All Blacks side that won the World Cup on home soil in 2011 was right up there with the best in history, even though they limped over the line in the final. They got even better over the next few years, just as I was establishing myself as a Springbok. Between 2012 and 2017, the All Blacks just seemed to get better and better, and I was playing against them at least twice a year.

Having missed the chance to play against the All Blacks in Dunedin, I was back in the starting XV for the return in Johannesburg. And what an experience that was. Not everyone is a fan of the haka, mainly because they believe it gives the All Blacks a psychological advantage, but I flipped that theory on its head. By respecting their special challenge and staring it full in the face, I felt I was absorbing its energy. By the time they'd finished, it was as if I'd performed the haka with them. I was hyped up – breathing heavily, heart pounding, fists clenched – and desperate to wade into the fray.

That All Blacks side had every position covered, in some cases a few times over. In fact, if you were picking a greatest All Blacks team of all time, more than half of those guys would be part of the conversation.

The front row of Owen Franks, Tony Woodcock and Andrew Hore eventually played more than 300 Tests between them, while replacement hooker Keven Mealamu went on to win more caps than any of them. In the second row, Sam Whitelock had recently been joined by Brodie Retallick and they were on their way to establishing themselves as one of the best lock combinations in world rugby. Kieran Read was one of the greatest eighthman in All Black history, incredibly dynamic and skilful, while open side Richie McCaw was arguably the greatest All Black of all time.

Blind side Liam Messam, a future teammate of mine, was also a great player, while behind the scrum the electric Aaron Smith had taken over from Fourie du Preez as the undisputed best No 9 on the planet, and Dan Carter was probably the best No 10 ever. You'd have struggled to find a better midfield partnership than Conrad Smith and Ma'a Nonu, a perfect blend of courage, brain and brawn, while the back three of Israel Dagg, Cory Jane and Hosea Gear were all lethal finishers.

By the way, none of Sam Cane, Wyatt Crockett, Charlie Faumuina, Ben Smith, Julian Savea or Sonny Bill Williams, all very special All Blacks, were even on the bench that day in Johannesburg, while Jerome Kaino, their colossal loose forward who was voted New Zealand's player of the year in 2011, was on a break from international rugby.

To beat a team like that, we'd have to be at our very best. As it was, we had quite a few experienced players out injured and too many soft moments, while the All Blacks were ruthless as ever. It's not as if they would pound you into submission for 80 minutes – they've never tried to be the most physical opponents – but they were so clever and clinical, predatory even.

Their line-out and scrum were always rock solid but we more than matched them up front that day. However, despite spending most of the first 40 minutes in their own half, they still managed to score two tries, followed by two more just after the restart. Having grafted like maniacs to build a precious 16–12 half-time lead, we suddenly trailed by 10 points.

That game was like a scrap between a front-foot slugger and a skilled counterpuncher. We'd done most of the work while they soaked up the punishment on the ropes, but they'd struck with precision and done the more serious damage when our concentration lapsed. Every team will have two or three soft moments in a game, and that's all New Zealand needed.

We didn't score a point in the second half and they ended up beating us 32–16, with a few of their tries coming from quick plays and within one phase. Worse, they won yet another Rugby Championship and we finished third behind Australia.

The skill set of New Zealand's backs was on a different level from everyone else's, which is why they were able to create tries while seemingly on the back foot. They were big, fast guys who ran the sharpest lines and had the slickest hands. Carter gets the most plaudits, and he was a phenomenal player, but the two men outside him – Conrad Smith and Nonu – were just as important.

Smith wasn't the quickest but he was a great support runner, offloader and tackler, as well as being the man who marshalled their defence. Nonu had transformed himself from a direct ball carrier into one of the best distributors in the world. You never knew what to expect from him, which is what made him so dangerous. Often when you thought he was going to put a teammate into space, he'd step, tuck the ball under his arm and run over a defender.

Nonu was also a very hard hitter. In one of the first games I played against the All Blacks, I came around the corner, got smashed, and assumed it was one of their props. But when I looked up, Nonu was staring down at me. He wasn't a small centre but there's a lot more to tackling than just flying at an attacker and hitting him as hard as you can. It's an art, albeit a brutal one.

In terms of timing, good tackling is about reading the ball carrier and knowing exactly what he's going to do so you're in the right position to be as destructive as possible (and don't hit too high, which could lead to a card). In terms of technique, it's about making sure your shoulder connects correctly and your feet are planted in the right spot, creating a solid platform so you can explode into the tackle and not get bumped. Getting all that right takes a lot of practice.

It wasn't just their backs who could kill you with a pass, a burst of pace or some fancy footwork; they also had forwards who could do those things. Compared with opposition forwards with ball in hand, they were different animals. Retallick, for example, operated as a link between forwards and backs and would often pop up between the breakdown and No 10, creating different attacking opportunities which a forward would often finish off.

All the New Zealand forwards were smart in their own way but the cleverest of all was McCaw. He wasn't as eye-catching as other open sides but he had more influence on games than any of them.

McCaw knew the laws inside out and was a genius at judging how a referee would interpret the breakdown, which is why he was able to push the boundaries while not getting penalised as much as some people thought he should have been. He also had good people skills. He didn't complain about every little mistake because he knew that might irritate the referee and 50-50 decisions might start going against his team. And by flagging things only when he really needed to, always calmly and clearly, he made referees think, *He hasn't said much until now, maybe I did get that wrong.*

People who call McCaw a cheat don't know what they're talking about, I also learnt how important it was to know the laws (especially in my department), push boundaries, not pester a referee, and complain in a respectful manner only when I thought he'd really screwed up.

My perception of northern hemisphere rugby at the time was that it was inferior to the stuff we played down south, so it is fair to say that I was expecting less of a challenge when I toured Europe for the first time at the end of 2012.

England were still finding their feet after a poor World Cup in 2011, France were embroiled in an identity crisis, despite almost upsetting New Zealand in the World Cup final 12 months earlier, while Ireland and Scotland were nowhere near as good as they are today. Wales had performed brilliantly at the World Cup before going on to win a Six Nations Grand Slam, but as far as the Springboks were concerned anything other than a clean sweep in the end-of-year Test matches in the early 2010s was considered a failure. I expected the games to be tough.

Ireland pushed us quite close in Dublin, and while playing Scotland in Edinburgh we conceded the only try scored against us on that tour. Then we headed to London for a game we really had to win, against England at Twickenham.

I'm not sure why but for some reason the English weren't the most likeable team. Ex-Boks would tell me, 'You can lose to anyone else, just don't lose to them.' I assume the dislike is partly because of England's colonial history, partly because they're one of the richest rugby nations, and partly because English rugby players and fans are seen as posh and entitled. Whatever the reasons, it works for us, even though we know that stuff is myth and nonsense.

It's like the situation in South Africa, where the Bulls are stereotyped as this arrogant bunch from the north. It's true that some of the Bulls fans are intense and hostile, but when I got to know Bulls players they were *lekker ouens* ('nice blokes', as we'd say in Afrikaans). However, because most of us Boks didn't know any England players back then, we could use the myth and nonsense to our advantage.

Personalising the contest, believing the English had every-thing going for them and thought they had the right to beat everyone else, gave us an edge. We were from relatively poor South Africa with its identity of hardship and toughness, and we were going to fight tooth and nail against our more privi-leged rivals.

As it turned out, we beat them by only a point, although they let us off the hook by kicking a late penalty rather than going for a try that would have given them the win. That meant we hadn't lost to England in 11 games stretching back to 2006.

I don't know if Heyneke planned to bring old faces back when he took over in 2012 but there was a bit of uncertainty surrounding the team at that time. The media and fans were trying to work out if the new guys had what it took to be long-term Boks and if the old guys had enough in the tank to last until the 2015 World Cup. Also, more and more South Africans were playing club rugby abroad, so Heyneke's decision to consider everyone, wherever they plied their trade – even if he'd have preferred to pick home-based talent – made sense.

So it was that Fourie du Preez, who played under Heyneke at the Bulls, returned for the 2013 Rugby Championship, and by the end of the tournament he had replaced Ruan Pienaar as the starting No 9. I'd never played with or against Fourie, who left for Japan in 2011, but I soon realised his rugby IQ was off the charts. He is best described as a man who knew exactly what his job was. He wasn't in the team to make massive tackles (although he never shirked one) but his reading of the game was uncanny – he always seemed to know when to pass, when to kick and when to run. His game management was also second to none, and he had an uncanny calmness about him, the kind that comes with great experience.

Having a guy like Fourie in the matchday squad had its obvious advantages, but it was also great to have him on the training ground, especially for the younger guys. Fourie wasn't one for beers and stories but you could learn so much just from watching how he went about things. When Handré Pollard came into the side as a young fly-half in 2014, I remember thinking it wasn't possible for him to have a better person to learn half-back play from. It was like a young actor learning on the job from Robert de Niro.

However good Fourie was, the All Blacks were still ahead of us, and while coaches all over the world were studying their blueprint and trying to emulate it, the gap wasn't bridged for quite a few years. I always believed we had what it took to beat them during that period, but by the time I played my first game against them in New Zealand, in Auckland in 2013, we'd beaten them only once in the previous seven. And we hadn't beaten them at Eden Park for 76 years.

New Zealand crowds aren't particularly loud or hostile but All Black fans find other ways to get under your skin. As soon as you arrive in their country, they'll constantly be reminding you that you're playing against the best team in the world and there's no way they can possibly lose. Or people will come up to you and say, 'We're gonna put 50 points on you,' before adding, with a smirk, 'but good luck anyway.' The subtext being, 'Just the idea that you have any chance of winning this game is completely ridiculous.'

We did have a chance of winning that game at Eden Park, right up until the point Bismarck du Plessis was sent off in the 41st minute. His second yellow card, for a stiff-arm to the neck of Liam Messam, was debatable, but his first, for a tackle on Dan Carter, was highly controversial. It was a monstrous hit that sparked a scuffle, with everyone piling in, but replays showed Bismarck had done nothing wrong. I suspect the decision was largely because Carter had to go off with an injury.

It was very difficult to beat that New Zealand team with 15 men, so we were unlikely to do it with 14, and that turned out to be the case. A Sam Cane try put them out of sight, and while Bismarck's red card was rescinded after the game, that wasn't much consolation. At the time of writing, we're up to 88 years of hurt at Eden Park.

We were still in with a shot of winning the Rugby Championship before the return match at Ellis Park in Johannesburg, where the All Blacks had beaten us only twice since our readmission to international rugby, the last time in 1997.

When Ellis Park is packed to the gunwales it can be extremely intimidating for a visiting team, so we thought it was possible to do a job on them. Bryan Habana scored two first-half tries, Willie le Roux added another after the break, and when Jean de Villiers scored our fourth with 23 minutes to go – an absolute beauty that saw him run over the top of Beauden Barrett and through Nonu – we had a crucial bonus point. But then New Zealand did what they almost always did. First, Barrett slashed through our defence to score a bonus-point try, meaning we could no longer win the tournament, then Kieran Read finished off a brilliant sweeping move to put the game out of our reach.

The consensus in the media was that it had been an all-time classic and that it was evidence that the Boks were closing the gap. But the All Blacks had beaten us while playing with 14 men for 20 minutes, owing to two yellow cards, and we'd made too many defensive errors. Once again, we'd done most of the huffing and puffing but it was our house that had come crashing down.

New Zealand's 12th straight Rugby Championship win secured their second successive title and they'd now lost only one of their last 23 games. As for us, we'd posted a couple of healthy victories against the Wallabies (which was always sweet), including our biggest win yet in Australia, and hammered Argentina at home. But while finishing second in the tournament was an improvement on the previous year, we wanted to win trophies and we wanted to beat the All Blacks, so we couldn't consider it a success.

Bakkies, whom Heyneke had brought into the Bulls set-up in 2001, returned for our 2013 tour of Europe, and he was a very different character from Fourie – laid-back, and full of stories funny and serious. In other words, nothing like his on-field persona. Suddenly, guys were hanging around a bit longer at the table after dinner, listening to tales of the days when you could get away with a lot more on a rugby field and be lauded for it.

Because Bakkies played in the 2003 World Cup he was a link to another era. Guys would fire questions at him, about the famous names he'd played with and against, and he'd happily reel off stories.

Now I'm a senior player, I feel like the younger guys don't use the older guys enough, but I also understand why it might not happen. The older guys don't want to be too overbearing or come across as patronising, and when you're in your early '20s you feel like a boy next to men in their '30s, especially those who have won World Cups. Plus, I was raised to respect my elders, so I didn't feel it was my place to say a lot in a team environment.

But a young guy new to a team shouldn't feel comfortable anyway; he needs to earn respect, demonstrating that he's not just passing through and wants to become a fixture. And that doesn't come from talking; it comes from putting in the work on the training ground and performing in games.

It was only really in 2013 that I started to feel at ease in the Bok set-up. I'd got to know the seniors, guys like Pierre Spies, Bismarck and Jannie du Plessis and Beast, and having Jean de Villiers as captain really helped. Far from being one of those superior captains who shrug off the opinions of junior players, he was a mentor to everyone and I felt I could go to him with any issues.

I knew Bakkies's comeback meant more competition for the number 4 shirt – he was still doing great things at club level, having just won the Heineken Cup with Toulon – but I wasn't going to worry or get upset about it. I viewed it as a challenge, motivation to train harder and keep him on the bench. And lots of players fighting for every position in the team, in training and on match days, was exactly what we needed to improve as a group.

Other overseas-based players Heyneke recalled included the vastly experienced props Gurthrö Steenkamp (Toulouse) and Heinke van der Merwe (Leinster/Stade Français), while he continued to pick the likes of Bryan Habana, Zane Kirchner, Morné Steyn and Chiliboy Ralepelle after they signed for European clubs in 2013. Many said that wasn't great for domestic rugby but Heyneke thought it was essential for the Boks.

After we saw off Wales in Cardiff, I was rested for the game against Scotland, with Bakkies getting a chance to start. That was frustrating but only because I wanted to play every Test match, whether it was against the All Blacks or a smaller less competitive country.

I was back in the starting line-up for our final game of the tour against France, in which I suffered my first potential career-ending injury. We'd been playing for only 10 minutes when I tried to steal a ball, which was a stupid thing to do (I normally just get back on my feet and rejoin the defensive line). While my head was in the ruck, someone cleaned me out and my foot got stuck. I tried to play on but didn't have my normal power in the scrum, so I had to ask to be taken off, meaning I watched most of our 19–10 win from the bench.

My foot wasn't that sore, so when I went for an X-ray back in South Africa I wasn't particularly concerned. But after I was handed a weight and asked to stand on one leg, the X-ray revealed that the Lisfranc ligament had torn, creating a widening gap between my metatarsals. That usually happens when a vehicle runs over your foot or you drop something heavy on it, and while I was lucky that it was diagnosed quickly (left untreated, it can have serious long-term consequences), I'd still be out of action for at least six months.

I spent six weeks in a cast after the first operation, then six weeks in a moon boot with crutches and four weeks in a moon boot without crutches. I didn't have particularly big calves to begin with, but by the time I finally discarded the moon boot one was half as thick as the other. When I tried to do a calf raise, I could lift my heel only a few centimetres off the ground. I was shocked and quite scared, just hoping I'd play rugby again.

3

ONE STEP FORWARD, TWO STEPS BACK

People talk about my hometown of Goodwood as if it was one of the roughest places in the world back in the day, but it wasn't that bad. If you walked into the wrong pub when the wrong people were drinking there – some of my uncles, for example – you might not walk out unscathed, but mostly Goodwood folk were lovely, down to earth people, including my mom and dad.

Dad didn't care about status and treated everybody the same, namely with respect. But if someone didn't respect him, he wasn't afraid to let them know about it, and I have a similar approach to life. He was quite young when he retired from the police after 20 years' service, and he decided to turn his hand to debt collecting. That could be a dangerous job in the rougher parts of Cape Town – his eldest brother, Skattie, was killed collecting a debt in 1993, having given his life to the Lord and transformed his life only a couple of years earlier – but Dad was willing to do it to provide for his family.

When Dad wasn't working, he spent a lot of time with my uncles and friends in pubs and bars in and around Goodwood, so it was Mom who made sure everything at home ran smoothly. She was the rock, looking after us three men, and I sometimes think that if it wasn't for her the family would have fallen apart.

My parents set boundaries, and if Ryen and I pushed them too much they'd put us in our place. But I wouldn't describe them as overly strict. They didn't lay down the law like other parents, ordering us not to drink or smoke; they allowed us to make decisions for ourselves because they felt we'd learn quicker that way. I'm so thankful they did that because it made me self-reliant, which in turn better equipped me to navigate life's various challenges. And I never did drink or smoke as a teenager.

When the time came for me to sign my first professional deal, all the other players' dads were poring over contracts and making decisions for them. But my parents told me, 'Listen, it's your career, so you must decide. We'd love you to stay in Cape Town but if you think moving to Durban or Johannesburg would be better for you, then do it.' I decided to stay in Cape Town, but only because WP matched the offers from the Sharks and the Lions.

If you're wondering where my grit and desire came from, other than the Etzebeth genes, you don't have to look much further than my brother. Ryen and I were interviewed just after I was first selected for the Boks, and he said I was so tough because he bullied me so much. He was exaggerating, because we were extremely close, but there was some truth to that statement.

Being three years older than me and a decent sportsman, Ryen usually came out on top in any contests between us, and he gave me a fair few grazes, bumps and bruises along the way. Sometimes, that competitiveness spilled over into fisticuffs, and our last ever fight was over a beer that my Uncle Gerrit brought to our house for us to share. I didn't even drink at the time but still wanted my half – I was stubborn that way!

But the more he beat me, the more I didn't want to lose. And having spent my childhood constantly striving to beat my older brother, and believing I would do it one day, I started believing other outlandish things as well, including that I'd play for the Springboks. Without knowing it, Ryen was sharpening my competitive edge, as well as helping prepare me for the difficult things I'd experience in later life.

Ryen Etzebeth, Eben's big brother: I remember Eben's hopes of becoming a WWE wrestler, but by the age of 11 or 12 it was mostly rugby on his mind. We'd been watching the Springboks together since Eben was at primary school, and he loved Bobby Skinstad in particular. But now he was writing goals on his bedroom door, whether it was winning the 100 m at school sports day or playing for the Boks. And he achieved them all.

Our dad and his brothers were very sporty and could be quite rough. Dad wrestled for the province, was a decent pool player and played rugby for the police and Epping Rugby Club. And while he wasn't one to provoke trouble, if someone took a liberty with him there could be a big problem.

Before Mom and Dad were married they went to a dance one evening. Mom was nicely dressed up and in the pub afterwards a couple of guys kept leering and talking about her.

When Dad noticed what was going on he told them, in his weird English, that while he didn't mind them looking at his girlfriend, he didn't want to hear them talking about her. One of the guys replied, 'Fuck you,' which Dad didn't take that well. Mom tried to get Dad to stop fighting – she even threw an ashtray at him – but he ended up breaking one guy's arm. Mom was so upset with him but probably also relieved that none of his brothers were in the pub. Imagine going up against all seven of them.

It's no real surprise that Eben and I turned out to be so competitive. I won the victor ludorum for best athlete at primary school twice, before Eben won it three times, meaning it was in our house for five years straight. Goodwood was a chilled, safe place to grow up. We'd always be playing rugby on the streets or the rugby field near our house, and I wouldn't hold back when I tackled him. It's probably fair to say that I bullied him. And we fought a lot, but that's one of the reasons why he's such a hard man today!

However, after that scrap over a beer, when I broke my hand knocking him on his head before our uncle intervened, we never fought again. We were a bit big for it by then, especially Eben, who went from being quite a skinny boy playing on the wing for the B team to this enormous lock playing for the first XV. Mom puts his growth spurt down to all the peanut butter and syrup on bread he ate that summer, and she was particularly happy that our fighting days were behind us, because there wouldn't have been a winner.

Dad cared about us a lot but he didn't really get involved in *our schooling and liked hanging out with his friends in bars (that's probably why he was so good at pool), leaving Mom to run the show at home.*

Luckily for Mom, there was no social media back then and video games weren't as big, so the only thing Eben ever wanted to do was play sport, which is a far healthier addiction. Mom thought his first XV coach at Tygerberg worked him too hard – Eben would train before and after school, sometimes starting at 6 am and finishing at 5 pm – but she also admired her boy's determination and self-reliance. And he never once complained because he knew it was going to be his life.

Becoming a professional rugby player was a big dream for both of us, but while I played a bit for Western Province's emerging team I wasn't at Eben's level. But I never stopped being the older brother, however successful and famous Eben became, and it's impossible to describe just how close we've become since he made his debut for the Stormers and Springboks in 2012.

It's difficult to explain to someone who isn't from South Africa just how big a deal the Springboks are in our country, so seeing my younger brother run onto the field in that green and gold jersey and sing the national anthem felt otherworldly. Him realising his dream was also a dream come true for me, and I still get goose bumps thinking about that great day at Kings Park.

Eben had every right to be focusing on himself that week – he was only 20, after all – but he didn't forget that it was Mom's 50th the day after the game. Mom had been wondering how to mark the occasion, but Eben booked our flights to Durban and a hotel for the three of us. He even arranged for a cake to be delivered to Mom and Dad's room. She couldn't have asked for a better birthday.

The people of Goodwood were also incredibly proud to have a connection with Eben. A neighbourhood group on Facebook called him their 'Goodwood boykie', which means something like 'wonder kid'. Now and again, a random guy would come up to him and say something like, 'Do you remember me? I lived next door to your tannie (auntie),' *and while Eben wouldn't always know who they were, he was always friendly and polite. He even remained patient when people approached him while he was trying to have a quiet meal with his family, because he knew that was part of the package.*

In the early years of his Springbok career, sharing Eben with the rest of South Africa felt a bit weird. I'd see a gang of kids approaching him with pens and pieces of paper in their hands and think, Wow, that's my kid brother. *Some things still take me by surprise. I was in a restaurant the other day and a little boy came up to me and gave me a ball to sign, presumably because someone had told him I was Eben's brother. I can't even begin to imagine what that level of attention must be like for Eben, but he certainly hasn't allowed success to change him.*

Eben handles the weight of expectation that comes with playing for the Boks very well. In fact, it's that pressure that keeps driving him: the more he's under, the harder he trains. He's also able to put defeats behind him quickly and focus on the next game, although it probably took him a little longer than usual after the Boks lost to Japan in 2015.

Normally after a game his family members would get in touch to say well done, but we didn't after that one. We knew how much he wanted to win and how hurt he must have been, so it was better to leave him be.

It wasn't pleasant seeing a team that Eben was part of getting hammered by the All Blacks and losing to Japan and Italy, among other teams, but I was more philosophical than most. Most teams go through bad periods and look where the Boks are today, with Eben and the rest of the guys playing probably the best rugby the Boks have ever played.

As for me and Eben, we care about each other more than ever. He still asks for my advice about almost anything and I've pretty much evolved into his personal assistant. I no longer cook for him, like I did when we lived together in Japan, but I take care of most of his admin and I don't think I'll be stopping any time soon.

I sometimes say to him, 'I can't believe what you've achieved, it doesn't seem real,' but he's not that old, and imagine if he won another World Cup. But whatever else he achieves, he'll never stop being my dear little brother.

I'd been scribbling little notes about my rugby for years, but it was only after I started playing for the Boks, and at Heyneke's suggestion, that I started writing down my long-term goals. Whenever a reporter asked what I wanted to achieve in rugby, I'd keep my cards close to my chest. But sometime in 2012 I made a note that I wanted to win the World Cup.

The schedule for a Springbok was relentless. We'd go straight from Super Rugby to a home Test series, straight back to Super Rugby then straight into the Rugby Championship. Boks would then be expected to play in the final stages of the Currie Cup before heading to Europe for the end-of-year Test matches. We'd get a few weeks off in December before doing it all again.

No coach ever said to a player, 'You're looking a bit tired, have a game off.' That could happen in Ireland or New Zealand because they had central contracts, but our clubs were paying most of our salaries so it was understandable that they wanted to get the most out of us. In Europe, players could be rested for the odd league or cup game against a struggling team but there were no easy games in Super Rugby. Resting one or more guys for a game could mean the difference between winning and losing, which could tip the balance when it came to making the play-offs.

Unsurprisingly, all that rugby was taking its toll on my body. There was the shoulder injury I sustained just before my first Bok call-up, and I missed almost three months of the 2013 Super Rugby season after tearing ankle ligaments in a warm-up game. Now here I was, spending day after day and week after week with the Stormers' physio, desperately trying to get some strength back into this injured leg of mine.

I lived only 20 minutes away from the Western Province International Rugby Institute but I decided to stay there for a month and a half to get all the exercise and treatment I needed. It was mainly upper body sessions in the gym, including two 'mongrel' high-intensity sessions on Mondays and Wednesdays. But while my desire to get fit again in time for the Boks' home Test matches against Wales and Scotland was all-consuming, it was still a dark, lonely period. The fact that Andries Bekker had moved to Japan and the Stormers had another five or six locks injured made me feel even worse. One week, I saw the team running out for a game in New Zealand and had to Google who one of the locks was.

I was on track for the June internationals until my situation turned darkly comic. About four weeks before the first Test against Wales, I got out of the shower, walked towards a sliding mirror door and hit my toe on the concrete wall. I'd stubbed my toe plenty of times but this time the pain was off the scale. And when I presented the offending toe to the Stormers' physio, he sent me for an X-ray which revealed that I'd broken it.

I'd already been out for seven months, during which I'd done hundreds of hours of rehab, so you can imagine my reaction. Having felt like the Incredible Hulk, ready to be unleashed, now I just felt a bit pathetic.

The following day, it was all over the media that I'd broken my toe in the shower – why the doctor didn't just say I'd done it in the gym I don't know. There was a lot of good-natured ribbing from my teammates, who wanted to know exactly how it had happened and what exactly happened in the shower. The media also had a bit of fun with it, wondering aloud how a Springbok could injure himself in such a ridiculous way. But facing another six weeks on the sidelines, I wasn't really in the mood for jokes. I'd never get those three Test matches back.

Victor Matfield had also come out of international retirement in my absence, and he started all three Test matches in June 2014. So I knew that when I finally returned to action I'd be competing for a starting spot with the two greatest locks in Springbok history, plus new faces such as the Cheetahs' Lood de Jager.

No athlete ever wants to get injured, but missing nine months of rugby may have been a good thing. In a strange way, that time away from the training ground and competitive games was like a sabbatical, a long recharging of the batteries. Had I not been injured, I'd have played something like 20 matches, and who knows what toll they would have taken on my body.

I finally returned to action in August 2014, nine months after injuring my foot against France. The game was WP's Currie Cup opener against EP in Port Elizabeth, and I played only because Heyneke wanted me to get some game time before the Rugby Championship. Amazingly, that would be my last appearance in the competition.

Over the past decade, the Currie Cup has transformed into a development competition, mainly featuring young players who aren't in the Springbok set-up. The decision to restrict Boks from playing in the competition was understandable – it meant we could have a proper pre-season before the Rugby Championship then switch our focus to the end-of-year inter-nationals – but it frustrated the fans, especially as hundreds of talented South Africans were playing for clubs overseas. Back in Oom Cliffie's day, Currie Cup matches were played in front of packed stands, but nowadays stadiums are rarely a quarter full, even for play-off games.

I sometimes wonder what the Currie Cup might look like if the Boks were still involved, plus all those South Africans plying their trade in Europe and Japan. Imagine how good those seven or eight teams would be. For fans, it would be like watching a Test match every week. But it's still a great competition that produces stacks of talent, and it will always have a special place in my heart as the first senior trophy I won.

That happened in 2012, my first season as a pro, and one of the reasons it was so sweet was because we weren't given much of a chance. WP hadn't won the Currie Cup since 2001 and had gained a reputation as big-game chokers. Meanwhile, the Sharks, our opponents in the final, had beaten us in the last four of Super Rugby and were playing at home. They also had a load of Boks in their team, while the average age of our starting line-up was 23. Our chances weren't improved when Bryan Habana suffered an injury early on, but Demetri Catrakilis kicked a late penalty and two drop goals to secure the win.

Having come through that tune-up game against EP unscathed, I joined the Springbok squad for our Rugby Championship opener against Argentina in Pretoria. I replaced Bakkies at half-time and we secured a narrow win. A few weeks later I started my first Test match alongside Victor, playing Australia in Perth. I was in primary school when Victor made his debut for the Boks and he now had more than 100 international caps, so locking alongside him was very special.

That was also Bryan's 100th cap, although the fact we lost by a point took some of the gloss off the occasion.

In the return game at Newlands I played a Test match with Schalk Burger for the first time, Schalk having returned to the fold after a nightmare run of luck. Having missed the whole of 2012 with a knee injury, he strained his calf the following pre-season. We expected him to be out for a few weeks, but when he went under the knife they discovered a cyst in his back.

I was still a *laaitie* and I didn't know Schalk that well; it was only later that I found out how serious his situation had been. After an operation to remove the cyst he contracted bacterial meningitis, which almost killed him. He couldn't go outside for four months and there were rumours that he'd never play rugby again. But he made a remarkable return for WP in September 2013 and was back in the international fold the following June. And that was just the beginning of one of the greatest comeback stories in sport.

It's difficult to think of a player who was more different on the field than off it. Whenever Schalk crossed the whitewash he was as intense as it got, someone who grabbed games by the scruff of the neck and never let go. But as soon as a game was over he became a completely different animal. He was a fun guy to have around, loving nothing more than sitting back and chatting over a few beers. He was probably the most relaxed guy in the squad, someone who let life roll gently over him, which might explain why he won many more caps for the Boks after the docs told him he might be finished.

We inflicted New Zealand's first defeat for almost two years at Ellis Park, although we came close to losing a game we should have won comfortably. We were all over them that day and outscored them by three tries to one in the first half, with Handré Pollard, who had an unbelievable game, grabbing a brace. But that All Black side was like a horror film monster: almost impossible to kill off. First, Ben Smith scored a converted try to reduce the gap to four points, then Dane Coles went over in the opposite corner to make it 25–24 to them with 10 minutes left. Typical.

Luckily for us, Liam Messam had a rush of blood to the head at the breakdown with 3 minutes to go, catching Schalk with a high shot, and Pat Lambie knocked over the match-clinching penalty from inside our half and sent 60,000 fans wild. We celebrated on the pitch like we'd won the Rugby Championship, even though New Zealand had still won the tournament. Again.

People seem to think South African rugby players are like cyborgs, programmed to think about nothing but rugby, and it's true that we don't party together much. But that was our first victory over the All Blacks since 2011, we'd done almost nothing but train and play together for almost three months, and we weren't rejoining our clubs for a couple of weeks, so a massive night was inevitable. You can imagine what it was like: 30-odd players, coaches, all the backroom staff, most of them guys – a recipe for chaos.

I've no idea why, but in South Africa we call those after-match parties 'kontikis'. My maiden kontiki took place on my first Stormers tour, when I was told to stand on a chair, tell a few jokes and sing a song while teammates made out they were going to hit me. It being 2012, the fancy dress theme was the Olympics, and because my arm was in a sling, I went as a Paralympic athlete. In 2013, we had to go as superheroes, and some of the guys took it very seriously. Jean de Villiers arrived as the Silver Surfer, covered from head to toe in tinfoil. The Springboks also have a dress-up kontiki every now and then, including the times Jannie du Plessis dressed up as a WWE wrestler and Willem Alberts came as a traffic cop, a nod to the famous Afrikaner comedian Leon Schuster, who used to pretend to be a traffic cop and play pranks on people.

The guy in charge of the kontiki usually has the most caps without being the captain, so for a long time it was Bryan Habana, who would stand up front with the two next most-capped players and issue fines for various perceived crimes. When Bryan called it a day, Beast took over, with the likes of myself, Francois Louw, Frans Steyn and Duane Vermeulen taking turns to be his deputies.

Everyone puts their phone away during a kontiki, enjoys a beer and a laugh, and all the tension that has built up over the previous weeks or months hopefully clears. I don't think I'll miss the training when I finally retire, but I'll definitely miss the joy and camaraderie after winning a big game or trophy.

During every kontiki, the coach or captain will give a speech, imploring everyone to look after themselves and not get into any trouble. But you can't tell a guy who's had too many brandies what to do – all common sense has gone out of the window by that stage – and the best approach is to contain the revelry to the team hotel! When I played for Toulon, the French guys got far more out of hand after a big win, but that's not really an option for a Springbok because eyes are on us wherever we go.

At one of Heyneke's first team meetings he declared that we should aim to be consistently the best team in the world, and that winning the 2015 World Cup would merely be the cherry on top of the cake. Finally beating the All Blacks suggested we were heading in the right direction, then the end-of-year internationals made us think again. One step forward, two steps back.

The Springboks hadn't lost to a Six Nations side since Scotland beat us at Murrayfield in 2010, and we probably thought we'd go unbeaten again in 2014. If we could beat New Zealand, the best team in the world by some distance, what did we have to fear from England, Ireland, Wales and Italy?

Looking back, I think we focused too much on the England game, forgetting that Ireland were the reigning Six Nations champions and Wales had won the two tournaments before that.

Ireland were a good team in the 2000s, when Brian O'Driscoll was in his pomp, but they had weaknesses. However, their DNA was starting to change. Andy Farrell has taken them to a new level in the last few years but they were already playing a bit like the All Blacks under New Zealander Joe Schmidt. They were tough up front, could keep the ball for phase after phase, and had quite a few talented backs who could hurt you if you had a soft moment. They also had a dead-eyed goalkicker in Johnny Sexton, who notched 16 points from the tee as Ireland beat us 29–15 in Dublin.

There were signs before the England game that things weren't quite right in the Bok camp. Some senior players turned up late for a meeting and another guy was late for Friday's jersey presentation. We still won, stretching our unbeaten run against England to 12 games, but Heyneke remained furious the following week, telling the seniors he didn't want anything to do with them, virtually withdrawing his services for the Italy game and handing over the reins to his assistant, Johann van Graan. That was a strange time for me because I'd looked up to those senior guys since I was a kid and they could do no wrong in my eyes.

Bakkies announced his retirement from international rugby after the Italy game, even though we still had Wales to play. He wasn't in the squad in Rome and decided a victory over England at Twickenham, alongside his old mate Victor, was a pretty good way to bow out. Bakkies said some very nice words about us young locks, and while he was still effective (he'd win a third straight Heineken/Champions Cup with Toulon in 2015), he said in his final speech he can't see himself doing another World Cup pre-season.

Wales beat us in Cardiff for the second time in history and the first time since 1999. Worse, our captain Jean de Villiers suffered a bad knee injury (I vividly recall him being cleaned out at a ruck and screaming), making him a doubt for the World Cup. We headed home to South Africa looking nothing like the best team in the world, never mind the cherry on top of the cake.

4

DEVASTATION

Before the 2015 domestic season began, Allister Coetzee announced that he'd be leaving WP at the end of the year, which made me quite sad.

While his time at Newlands was good but probably not as great as the Newlands faithful wanted it, he didn't have a lot of luck. One season, he barely had a lock to choose from. In another, all the fly-halves were injured, while Schalk Burger was out for 18 months. Allister almost never had the luxury of picking from a full squad, and we always seemed to be down to our sixth- or seventh-choice player in a certain position.

I can't say for certain why that was – maybe there was too much full contact training, maybe some of our guys were playing too many games, maybe the resting periods weren't long enough; most likely it was a bit of everything – but whatever the reasons, you'll struggle to compete with the New Zealand franchises if your best players are regularly missing.

It shouldn't be forgotten that Allister steered Western Province to four successive Currie Cup finals between 2012 and 2014, winning two of them. And like every coach of a South African franchise, he was playing by different rules from New Zealand sides. Almost all of New Zealand's talent stayed in the country because All Black players were centrally contracted and didn't get selected if they played overseas.

The upshot was that five New Zealand franchises were always stuffed to the gills with the country's most talented players, minus a handful of former All Blacks who had decided to see out their careers overseas, versus five South African franchises missing a lot of players who were plying their trade abroad, including some of their best.

That's not the only reason New Zealand dominated Super Rugby (winning 17 titles between 1996 and 2019, to Australia's four and South Africa's three) but it obviously played a part. Imagine how good South Africa's Super Rugby franchises would have been if all those guys playing overseas had come home. Not that I blame our guys for going abroad. Most go for the money, and good luck to them. A rugby career is short and often brutal, so it's nice to have some cash in the bank at the end of it. Some go because they can't see a way into the Springbok team, such as Schalk Brits, who had John Smit, Bismarck du Plessis and Adriaan Strauss ahead of him at hooker and left the Stormers to try his luck at Saracens. Schalk missed a lot of Test matches he might otherwise have played in but he had a great club career in England and made a lot more money than he would have in South Africa (before returning to the Bok set-up towards the end of his career and winning a World Cup).

Then there are the players who look around, see how many guys are ahead of them and think, 'Maybe if I play for a few years in England or Scotland I'll be selected for their national team and get to play in a World Cup.' I don't view that last group as traitors; they make me even prouder of South African rugby. In fact, I love it when a South African tries his luck abroad and ends up playing for another country, especially if it's someone I know. For example, David Ribbans played a handful of senior games for WP before moving to Northampton in 2017, making a name for himself and winning 11 caps for England. And I was really pleased for him.

Heading into 2015, I hadn't played a Super Rugby game for something like 600 days. When I turned up for pre-season, I'd almost forgotten some of my teammates' names and some of them couldn't help joking that while I was often injured for the Stormers, I was almost always fit for the Boks. For the record, that's not how I planned it!

In his last season in charge, Allister led us to third on the log and a place in the play-offs, but we were poor against the Brumbies at Newlands and got blown away. That definitely wasn't the farewell Allister deserved.

Before he left, I gave him one of my Springbok jerseys. We get two for each game, one of which I sometimes swap and the other I keep for myself. But I only give jerseys away to those who I think deserve one, such as close family members and people who have done a lot for me in my career and life in general.

I'll always be grateful to Allister for giving me my first Stormers cap when I was 20 and coaching me to my first senior trophy. We had a great relationship, and while I didn't know it then, he'd be the Springbok coach soon enough, so giving him that jersey was probably a wise investment.

The Springboks' first game of World Cup year was a friendly against a World XV at Newlands, although it's never really a friendly when you're wearing a Bok jersey (and the other team contains eight South Africans). A few days before the game, Heyneke came up to me and said, 'You're going to score your first try for the Boks at the weekend.' This after playing for the Springboks for four years without once bothering the scorers. He'd say it every time he saw me, and lo and behold, I did, scoring under the poles after Bismarck passed to me from the back of a ruck. Marcell Coetzee was the first to give me a hug, just as I was the first to hug him when he scored his first try for the Boks. Me and Marcell made our debuts together for the Boks back in 2012 and since that time we've always had a special friendship. I will never forget the story my dad told me after the night we made our debut. My dad went to the toilet to find a familiar face in the toilet that he knew probably from the police or somewhere and my dad told the other guy that he's the proudest man in the stadium today, which the other guy replied to and said that can't be because he is. Soon my dad discovered it's the father of Marcell and to be fair they both had merit to who the proudest might have been but I would call it a draw.

Bakkies was captain of the World XV, and that was the first and only time I played against him. I hadn't expected to see him on a rugby field again after his international retirement, so that was a bonus. Predictably, we had one or two minor disagreements at the breakdown, but nothing too spicy. More importantly, Jean de Villiers returned to action that day after his knee injury, and a one-sided win against a decent side seemed like ideal preparation for a truncated Rugby Championship and the World Cup.

Before our Rugby Championship opener against Australia, Heyneke told me, 'I know I said last week that you're going to score your first try for the Boks, but this week you're going to score your first Test match try.' I thought, *This is getting weird – he'd never told me I was going to score before and now he won't stop saying it.* Things got even weirder when I did indeed score in Brisbane, sliding over in the corner on my knees. Jean, who liked to mock the younger guys, told me afterwards, 'Next time you score a try, do it properly.' What did he expect? A full-length dive? I'd hurt myself doing that – it's a long way down when you're my height.

Unfortunately, the Wallabies scored two late tries to win the match, and when I asked Heyneke if he thought I'd score against New Zealand the following week, he replied, 'Hmmm, I don't know.' I didn't score that day, Heyneke never predicted I'd score again, and I wouldn't score another Test match try for a long time. But more worrying than my try drought was another late mugging by the All Blacks, who trailed by three points with 7 minutes to go but ended up winning 27–20 at Ellis Park.

That game followed a familiar pattern, with us dominating for long periods and New Zealand doing what they always did, namely bouncing off the ropes and punishing us when we dropped our guard. We had a succession of scrums under their poles early in the second half but we came away with nothing when we could have taken the easy points. Then replacement tight head Vincent Koch went off injured, we had to go to uncontested scrums and we lost our dominance. Their winning try came from a training ground move: they made a big thing of lifting Kieran Read at the back of a line-out, Codie Taylor threw a wobbly short ball and McCaw ran through the middle of the line-out unopposed.

That defeat meant the Boks had lost three straight Test matches for the first time since 2011, and things were about to get considerably worse. We expected Argentina in Durban to be an easier game than the previous two – as I've already mentioned, the Pumas were usually less formidable away from home – but they were unreal that day, while we were miles from our best. Pumas winger Juan Imhoff scored a 20-minute hat trick and the scoreline would have been even more lopsided if Bryan Habana hadn't scored a late consolation try. They still won 37–25, the first time they'd beaten us.

That was one of those games that would have put a dent in the South African economy. Today, it can't be considered an upset when Argentina beat one of the so-called big teams because they *are* one of the big teams. But back in 2015 we weren't supposed to lose to Argentina, and not many Bok fans would have carried on drinking in the pub after the final whistle, that's for sure. As for the South

African media, they slaughtered us. One journalist called our performance 'utterly deplorable'; another said the result 'felt like the end of the world'. That was probably going a bit far but Heyneke still felt moved to apologise for our 'unacceptable' display.

Heading into the World Cup, we'd lost four Test matches in a row and five in seven. We were also the first Bok team to lose four consecutive Test matches to different opponents since 1965. Unsurprisingly, no one thought we had a chance of winning the Webb Ellis Cup, but we hadn't given up hope. Springboks never think like that.

After all, we'd almost beaten the All Blacks a couple of months earlier, and we had beaten them the previous year with pretty much the same group of players. So we knew that if we played them at the World Cup, and we were at our best and they were slightly off, we could beat them again. Of course, New Zealand were favourites to win the tournament, but they were almost always favourites and we'd won the World Cup as many times as them.

We won our only warm-up game against Argentina in Buenos Aires, albeit by two points, then we had five weeks to prepare for our World Cup opener against Japan. The senior players could see that Heyneke was feeling the pressure (as a youngster, I just wanted to focus on playing well rather than worrying about other things) and the media picked up on it. When you're head coach of the Springboks at a World Cup, the stakes are high and you know you're likely to lose your job if you don't at least reach the final. But it wasn't just the business of rugby that was causing him stress; he was also mired in political controversy.

On one hand, Heyneke was being criticised for having only eight players of colour in the squad, below SARU's target of 30 per cent; on the other, journalists and fans were criticising him for making so-called quota selections.

Transformation was the South African government's policy to redress racial inequalities in the country, and I could understand why people driving transformation in sport wanted to see immediate change. But when it came to major sports such as cricket and rugby, it needed to happen organically, at least if you wanted the Proteas and the Springboks to remain international forces. That's why there was only one player of colour, Chester Williams, in the Springbok side that won the 1995 World Cup final, and only two in the side that won the 2007 final.

Transformation had to start at grassroots level, with money going into improving coaching and facilities for less privileged kids, plus bursaries to bring the most talented of those kids into the schools system, which feeds the franchises, which in turn feed the Springbok set-up.

By the time I came on the scene, there still weren't that many players of colour in and around the Springboks but there were lots playing for domestic franchises. When Allister left the Stormers in 2015, almost half the squad were players of colour. Allister received praise for that but I think he'd admit that it was simply a reflection of the talent available in and around Cape Town. Guys like Siya, Gio Aplon and Juan de Jongh, who captained us a few times, weren't there because

Allister was operating a quota system, they were there because he desperately wanted to win games and they were the best players available.

It was the same for Heyneke with the Springboks, and I can honestly say that since I came into the national side I've never had a teammate who didn't deserve to be there. I can't think of a single case of blatant discrimination, either against white players or players of colour.

The bottom line is this: if you put 10 Springbok fans in a room and told them to pick a World Cup squad, no two would be the same. They might be arguing for eternity. Every squad a Springbok coach picks is controversial to some people and there will always be those who are convinced that certain players are there because of politics rather than merit. But the idea of some guy on his couch going on social media to criticise a talented young player of colour frustrates me. What does that guy even know about rugby? Has he done any research? Does he know how good that young player was at age-group levels? Does he understand that players aren't just picked on their club form or for their individual skills but also because they're the best fit for the team and the system? Of course he doesn't.

Not that I paid much attention to the chatter. I saw the odd video on social media, with people making jokes about there not being enough white or black players, but I was focused on the task at hand, which was about to get much harder. One day, we were asked to do a fitness drill that involved tying a length of elastic around our waists, with another guy holding the two ends, and running and crawling between cones placed at five-metre intervals across the field. I pulled my calf and was told it would take four to six weeks to heal. Our first game against Japan was in five and I wasn't ready in time.

While the matchday squad was doing the captain's run the day before the game, the rest of us were having a few beers in Brighton. But having cycled to another pub for lunch and a few more beers, I received a call from the team manager. 'Where are you?' he said, sounding slightly panicked. 'Having some lunch,' I replied, not mentioning the beers. 'Right, Willem Alberts has pulled out with an injury, so you're in.' With that, I wolfed down what was left of my lunch before jumping on my bike and cycling back to the hotel.

I can't remember the exact game plan for Japan but the general vibe seemed to be, 'Let's just get through it, then we can focus on the big games against Samoa and Scotland.' There were close to 900 caps in our starting line-up, including six World Cup winners, making it the most experienced Springbok side yet. It didn't seem possible that we could lose.

I could still feel my calf when I ran so I started the game on the bench. And it was a horrible watch. In fact, just thinking about that game still makes me wince. The Japanese came out like maniacs, tackling ferociously and forcing us to cough up the ball several times in the first 20 minutes. But they had only a single penalty to show for their efforts, and when Francois Louw went over for a try off the back of a line-out I thought we'd settle. However, 10 minutes later Japan scored in similar fashion, sending the crowd into a frenzy.

There were Japanese fans everywhere in the stands, waving flags and making a racket, and everyone in the ground was pulling for the underdogs, except for a few hundred nervous-looking Springbok fans, sticking out like sore thumbs in green and gold. But when Bismarck barrelled over a few minutes later, I thought, *Right, now we're going to run away with it*, and there was no sense of foreboding in the changing room at half-time.

Just after the restart, Japan full back Ayumu Goromaru slotted a penalty that restored their lead, before Lood de Jager broke the line off a ruck and crashed over for a great try. But within 10 minutes it was 19–19, indiscipline at the breakdown having gifted Japan two more penalties.

I thought we'd finally broken them when Adriaan Strauss scored but they just wouldn't go away. Still, when I went on with 11 minutes remaining I couldn't sense any panic in our ranks. We obviously knew they weren't the adversary we thought we were going to face – they were a proper international rugby team – and that we were going to have to dig really deep to see them off, but it still seemed the most likely outcome. However, less than a minute later Goromaru went over in the corner after an intricate training ground move then knocked over the conversion to make it 29–29. Cue more hysteria.

Handré Pollard kicked us ahead again with 7 minutes left on the clock, and the score remained 32–29 with a minute to go. The Japanese kept coming and very nearly scored another try, Fourie du Preez holding up one of their attackers over the line. They won a penalty from that and I assumed they'd go for the points, which would have secured a draw. Instead, they opted for a scrum. They didn't want the draw, which would have been embarrassing enough for us, they wanted the win – and they were confident of getting it.

First, the ball went right and we managed to snuff out the attack. But when they slung the ball back the other way, we were light in defence (we'd just lost Coenie Oosthuizen to a yellow card). Amanaki Mafi handed off a defender, spun it wide to Karne Hesketh, and JP Pietersen tried his best to stop him touching down in the corner, but it was basically impossible to stop him from scoring. An inspired Japan had pulled off the biggest upset in rugby history.

For the Springboks, calamities don't come any bigger, although at least we'd given the world an important lesson: if you assume the opposition are not on your level and make the mistake of looking past them, you can end up looking very foolish indeed.

Not much was said in the changing room afterwards. It wasn't the time for ranting and raving and recriminations, it was more a case of pack your bags and get out of Dodge as quickly as possible. I felt for Heyneke and Jean de Villiers, who had to speak to the media. Heyneke said we'd let the country down, while Jean insisted it wasn't all 'doom and gloom'. But the bus ride back to the hotel was truly depressing, as if everyone had a family member who had just died and was trying to make some kind of sense of it.

Then we had that harrowing meeting where Heyneke asked

every player to come to the front and explain what they were going to do to rectify the situation. That was fair enough, because while it's always the head coach who gets the most flak after a bad performance, the players are usually most responsible. Japan hadn't beaten our second-string team, they'd beaten a team containing some of the greatest Springboks. It wasn't nice seeing players cry and I really felt for everyone involved, but we were the ones who'd let our country down.

People soon forget if the Springboks lose against one of the bigger countries, but no one was ever going to forget that game. It wasn't *just a game of rugby*, it was one of the most momentous games of rugby of all time. We'd been woven into the tapestry of the sport, or, from our point of view, we'd made a permanent stain. Whatever else we did in our careers, it would never be powerful enough to erase the embarrassment and shame of that day.

I remembered how I felt when Australia knocked us out of the World Cup four years earlier. Western Province under–21s had just played in Johannesburg and we watched the game at the airport before flying back to Cape Town. Losing in the quarter-finals was a disaster for South African rugby and it felt deeply personal to me. I said that day, 'Hopefully I'll play in the next World Cup and be part of a Bok side that does a lot better than this.' But we'd somehow managed to do even worse, and our media and fans couldn't even be angry at the referee (New Zealand's Bryce Lawrence got much of the blame for our 2011 exit). That's why I avoided any coverage of our Japan defeat, especially on social media. It would have been like putting my head in a fire.

Only later did I discover how savage some of the commentary was back home. One paper called it 'the darkest day in Springbok history'; another called it 'South African rugby's Pearl Harbor.' Other words used to describe our performance were 'embarrassing', 'abysmal' and 'humiliating'. Former head coach Jake White, who led the Boks to World Cup glory in 2007, called us 'disgraceful'. The sports minister said he'd phoned Heyneke to express his dismay.

But we had to keep in mind that we were still alive. We had three more pool games, and if we lost any of them we were going home. While we were on the precipice and everything felt bracingly real, it was possible that the Japan defeat would work in our favour: future opponents might underestimate us, just as we'd underestimated Japan. Nobody back in South Africa gave us a hope but maybe – just maybe – we'd pull off one of the maddest reversals of fortunes in the history of sport and win the whole thing.

The week before our game against Samoa was one of the tensest in my Springbok career. Heyneke said in a press conference that he'd cried for 24 hours after our defeat by Japan and even considered suicide. He was joking, but the pressure on him must have been immense.

Samoa hadn't beaten the United States by much in their first game, but they knew we were vulnerable. If Japan could beat us, why not them? If you're not at your best physically against Pacific Island teams, they'll give you hell and it's going to be a tough and tight game. But from the first whistle our guys were in a different frame of mind than the week before. Samoa had some superb athletes, big, fast guys with great broken-field skills, but they didn't like to be boxed in. So the plan was to keep it structured, dominate them at the set piece and not kick it long, which would give them space to run into. JP Pietersen scored an early settler and Handré kicked four penalties to give us a healthy half-time lead. After the break, JP completed his hat trick and we scored three more tries for a comfortable win.

Our next opponents, Scotland, had beaten Japan with surprisingly little trouble, but someone somewhere made the mistake of producing a commercial for an energy drink that made fun of the South African rugby players, which added fuel to our fire. A good coach will use that kind of thing to motivate his team and Heyneke played the commercial throughout the week while telling us, 'This is what they think of you, they think you're dumb.' As a result, we were quite angry going into the game, although thankfully we had a few comedians in the squad to cut through the tension.

A squad of 30-odd intense, serious guys constantly thinking and talking about rugby doesn't work when you're away together for months. That's going to get very gloomy very quickly. True, you need some of those guys to keep the rest on their toes and drive standards, but you need others to provide levity.

Before I started playing for the Boks I expected Morné

Steyn to be quite straightlaced, but he turned out to be a funny guy and the perfect foil for Willem Alberts. Willem was one of the hardest tacklers I'd played with, a destructive blend of brute strength, technique and timing, but off the pitch he was hilarious. Whenever he saw a situation he thought might tickle his teammates, he'd produce his phone and record it. Before the Scotland game he recorded himself stalking and catching a pigeon, like Rocky Balboa in that scene with the chicken, and he was always sharing ridiculous videos like that. Whenever and wherever Willem and his sidekick Morné were around, there was sure to be laughter.

Jean de Villiers broke his jaw against Samoa and announced his retirement from international rugby shortly afterwards. That was a sad way for a Springbok legend and a good man to go out, especially as he'd also missed most of the 2007 World Cup with injury. Luckily, we had a ready-made replacement captain in Fourie du Preez, and we put in a decent performance in Newcastle, scoring three tries to one and winning 34–16.

Besides the win, the most heartening part of that weekend was the journey back to London. When we pitched up at the station we were swamped by South African fans, most of whom were taking the same train south. A few weeks earlier they might have heckled us but now all they wanted were autographs and selfies.

If we beat the United States at the Olympic Stadium, we'd finish top of the group. And suddenly I was thinking, *Maybe the Japan game was just an aberration and we can go on to win the tournament?*

We already knew we wouldn't be playing England in the last eight because they'd become the first host nation to exit at the pool stage. The reaction in our camp was probably the same as the rest of the world, a mixture of shock and amusement. But there was also a bit of relief, first because people stopped mocking us for losing to Japan and started mocking England instead, and second because you expect any host nation to be dangerous in a knockout game, especially England at Twickenham.

We hammered the United States, running in 10 tries to none, including a hat trick for Bryan Habana, who equalled Jonah Lomu's record of 15 in World Cups. That set up a quarter-final against Wales on neutral ground. And while there were sure to be plenty of Welsh fans at Twickenham, it would be nothing like playing them under the Millennium Stadium roof in Cardiff, with 70,000 fans screaming them on.

Wales had beaten us for only the second time in their history the previous year, and as their skipper Sam Warburton said, 'Why would we think we can't beat them again?' Wales had a good all-round team, including an excellent tight five, a bull of a centre in Jamie Roberts (his usual partner Jonathan Davies was injured), big wingers in George North and Alex Cuthbert, and one of the best goalkickers in the world in fly-half Dan Biggar.

Wales played a similar brand of rugby to us – focus on the set piece, very direct, lots of kicking – so no one expected it to be pretty. Good job, because it wasn't. The first half was a grim arm wrestle, with the only try scored by Wales's scrum half Gareth Davies after a nice chip and chase by Biggar.

Wales led 13–12 at the break but we started turning the screw after the restart. We led 18–16 with just over an hour gone, but after I was penalised for being off my feet at a ruck Biggar stepped up to make it 18–19. I had to watch the last 12 minutes from the bench, which is far worse than still being on the field.

You feel calmer when you're still out there because you have some control. But when you're on the sidelines it's completely out of your hands. You don't know what the players are saying or what the plan is. You feel more like the fans do, just having to sit there and see how things pan out. But while it was tense, I wasn't crossing my fingers, or anything like that. I knew we had a lot of depth in our squad and I trusted the guys who were still out there to get the job done, however ferocious the Welsh defence was.

Biggar went off with a head injury with 6 minutes to go, and from the next scrum Duane Vermeulen broke blind and gave a sneaky back-hand pass to Fourie du Preez, who scored in the corner. That wasn't a planned move – the scrum just skewed slightly, Duane picked up the ball and Fourie noticed there was no one defending the blind side.

Some people thought Wales were unlucky but that's not how I saw it. Winning games is always a team effort but some games come down to individual brilliance. And great players produce those X-factor moments when they're needed most, just as Fourie and Duane did that day. It wasn't just that Duane produced that back-hand pass, it was also that he read the situation while holding off a defender at the back of a wheeling scrum. As for Fourie, he had the IQ to know Duane was going to pass the ball, and he was deft enough to run that line without any Welsh defenders picking him up.

It's comforting to know you've got guys like that on the pitch, players who aren't just going to keep battering on the door, to no avail, but have it in them to pick the lock instead.

Coaches always want us to be good team players first and foremost, but they also tell us never to forget about the circus act we have up our sleeves, which can be different for each player. For example, Willie le Roux isn't going to step defenders but he's very good at seeing space where others don't and putting in chips and passes that put teammates away. Even props and locks are expected to have a circus act, for example, a prop scrumming for penalties or being good at counter-rucking, or a lock being good at disrupting exit line-outs or putting pressure on their kickers.

I should add a bit more on Duane, who wasn't appreciated by the rest of the world as much as he should have been (I knew that he was respected and rated by everyone, but other number eights seemed to be talked about a bit more). Maybe you only really understood how good Duane was when you were in the same team as him, because I thought he was the best eighthman in the world and certainly the best I'd played with.

He gave teammates tremendous confidence because he knew exactly what his role was and fulfilled it to the letter, game in, game out. He carried hard, often damaging defenders, and when you see a teammate doing that it puts a spring in your step. He wasn't the flashiest eighthman with ball in hand – that pass to Fourie wasn't typical of him, although I knew he had it in his locker – but he was always a good offloader, and we didn't want flash moves from him anyway. He had a calm head in pressurised situations, almost never missed a tackle, was one of the best at jumping in the line-out and rock solid in the scrum – when he packed down, it felt like a jackhammer behind me.

It's not that Duane didn't do eye-catching stuff, it's more that his unseen technical work was every bit as important. For example, spectators might see someone scoring a try off a maul and heap praise on them for finishing the move, but they're likely to have missed the finer details of how that move was set up, which is where Duane often came in. A special mention needs to go to the man of the match that day, Schalk Burger for a mighty 80-minute shift in attack and defence. And to think he'd almost died a couple of years earlier.

Before our semi-final against New Zealand, Heyneke told the media they were the best team ever. Sometimes, when a coach talks up another team, he doesn't always believe what he is saying. It's a mind game, trying to get them to believe they're better than they are and lure them into a state of complacency. But in this case Heyneke was telling the truth. The All Blacks had lost only three games between winning the 2011 World Cup and demolishing France 62–13 in their 2015 quarter-final, which is a ridiculous record when you're playing the best teams in the world week in, week out.

Not that Heyneke had given up all hope. That week, he drummed into us that while we'd suffered the biggest upset in history against Japan, beating New Zealand would be almost as big the other way round, especially if we went on to win the final. And because we'd beaten them the year before with basically the same team, we could do it again. Heyneke presented a pleasing narrative, a classic zeroes to heroes story, but it wasn't a pipe dream, it was perfectly rational and eminently achievable.

It wasn't looking good when Jerome Kaino went over for a try after only 6 minutes at Twickenham, but we coped pretty well for the rest of the first half. We had the edge over them in the scrum, our driving maul was working well and we weren't giving Dan Carter much time to weave his magic. We weren't creating much ourselves, either, but Handré still kicked four penalties to give us a 12–7 lead at the break. And with Kaino in the sin-bin for the first 9 minutes of the second half, it felt like the game was there for the taking.

Unfortunately, we didn't make anything of our one-man advantage, and a couple of minutes after Kaino returned to the fray, we made an error a few metres out from our line, the All Blacks sent the ball left and Beauden Barrett scored in the corner. We huffed and puffed for the rest of the encounter and a Pat Lambie penalty made it a two-point game with 10 minutes left, but they were able to hold out in the pouring rain.

That game felt much worse than the Japan defeat. After Brighton we could still go on to win the tournament, but this was terminal and it felt like we'd missed a huge opportunity. I lingered in the changing room for ages because I knew that once we left the stadium our tournament was over. Even when I was the last player left I went and sat in a toilet cubicle and thought about what could have been. That was one of the worst moments of my life, not just my rugby career.

I didn't leave my hotel room for two days or answer phone calls, texts and knocks on my door. Only when Bismarck and Jannie du Plessis came calling on the Monday morning did I finally open up. 'You can't stay cooped up in your room,' said Bismarck, as if he was talking to a sulking child. 'Come, we're taking you out.' Thank goodness for those two because instead of stewing in my own company, torturing myself by going over the game again and again, we spent that day exploring London. And after a few beers I might even have raised a smile.

We still had to play the bronze medal match against Argentina, who had lost to Australia in their semi-final. We started training again on the Wednesday. And while we weren't exactly excited to be playing for third place, it would be the last Springbok game for a few guys, including Victor, Schalk and the Du Plessis brothers (Fourie was injured in the semi-final and announced his retirement a couple of months later), so there was some emotion involved.

We beat the Pumas comfortably and I scored a try, but I was still smarting from the New Zealand game. Waiting for our plane home to South Africa, I went for a coffee with Johann van Graan, and I recall saying to him, 'I never want to feel like that playing for the Boks again. I'll do anything to help the team win the next World Cup, train harder than I've ever done, play harder than I've ever done.' But things would get worse before they got better.

5

NO WAY BACK?

Before the World Cup I'd signed to play for Japanese side NTT Docomo, so I was back in South Africa for only a couple of weeks before heading to Osaka. It was a three-month deal and I wouldn't miss any Stormers games, which is why they were happy to let me go.

I still couldn't see myself playing in France, despite the continued interest. French club rugby at the time was a lot slower than it is now, which is why most South Africans who went over were closer to their thirties, and I didn't think it would improve me as a player. I didn't expect playing in Japan to improve me either but it surely wouldn't make me any worse, and I'd heard that it wasn't as physical as club rugby elsewhere, and they paid good money and looked after you well. All in all, the move made perfect sense.

I had no girlfriend at the time and didn't want to go on my own, so I asked my brother to come with me and put him on a salary (let's be honest, I basically bribed him). It almost felt like I had a personal assistant for three months and he came in particularly handy in the kitchen. It's not easy to find food that you're used to in Japan, and everything is packaged differently, making shopping quite tricky, but Ryen would stock up on meat, vegetables and other home comforts at the international supermarket and would have dinner ready on the table on the nights we weren't feeling like going out.

Also at the club were my Boks teammates Handré Pollard, Jesse Kriel and Heinrich Brüssow, as well as former WP flanker Wimpie van der Walt (the league was brimming with South Africans), so Ryen would also cook for them some evenings. It was amazing to have Ryen there with me, and our bond became even stronger. In fact, whenever we talk about our time together in Japan, we agree that it was probably the best brother time we ever had.

Japan is an alien culture and hardly anyone spoke English, but the hospitality was out of this world. When Mom, Dad, my friend Corne and Ryen's girlfriend came over for Christmas (it was the first time my parents had been overseas), people went out of their way to help, and while some of the differences took a while to get used to (and I'd never wrap my head around the language), the fact that everything worked and was on time suited me down to the ground. I like things to be in order, which isn't always the case back home.

The Top League attracted lots of global stars (former Springbok Jaque Fourie was reported to be the world's highest-paid player when he signed for The Kobelco Steelers in 2012, and it was particularly popular with former All Blacks, including Dan Carter, Ma'a Nonu and Sonny Bill Williams) and there was a big emphasis on improving standards before Japan hosted the 2019 World Cup. Most of the Japanese players were amateurs, meaning it wasn't as physical as Super Rugby. The players were generally smaller and more agile, and games were faster. That meant I had to be a bit fitter, but my body wasn't sore until the following Wednesday, which made for a nice change.

Meanwhile, back in Cape Town, Eddie Jones, who masterminded Japan's upset of the Boks in Brighton, was named head coach of the Stormers. He phoned to tell me how excited he was to be taking charge and that he was looking forward to having me back. Then he gave a press conference where he said he'd woken up that morning, seen Table Mountain through his window and thought, *I'm very happy to be here.*

At his first meeting with the players, he'd told them he wanted to create an environment that was so good that they'd never want to leave. A week later, he was on the plane to take over as England's head coach, and in early 2016 former Stormers and Bok centre Robbie Fleck got the Stormers job instead.

When it was announced that Argentina's Jaguares and Japan's Sunwolves had been added to Super Rugby, my first thought was that it meant even more travel. Visiting teams would have to fly in, play the game and fly out within a week, which led to some grumbling among Stormers players. But it was obviously great for rugby overall, and Argentine and Japanese rugby in particular, because it meant most of their best players would be playing together week in, week out (before then, Pumas were scattered all over Europe).

The Jaguares at home proved to be every bit as tough as the Pumas at home – we only just beat them in Buenos Aires in 2016 – and they got better every season, finishing runners-up in 2019, the last time they competed in the tournament. (I didn't play against the Sunwolves in Tokyo that first season because I was resting after international duty.)

As for the Stormers, we qualified from our group quite comfortably in 2016 and were quietly confident going into our quarter-final against the Chiefs at Newlands. But that was one of those games where nothing went our way and we lost 21–60, the Chiefs scoring eight tries to one.

That was a sobering experience and we had a markedly different mindset when we played them in Cape Town the following season – up for it and very physical – which led to quite a few scuffles and a 34–26 scoreline in our favour. Sadly, they rumbled us again in the quarter-finals, also at Newlands, this time pipping us 11–17. Another chance gone, and I was beginning to wonder if I'd ever win another trophy at club level.

Heyneke wanted to stay on as head coach of the Boks and I texted SARU president Oregan Hoskins to let him know that he was a very good coach and well capable of taking the team forward. Oregan thanked me for my input and said he'd take it into consideration, but the writing was already on the wall.

The media was brutal in its assessment of South Africa's performances in the World Cup. Two ex-Boks even wrote an open letter titled 'Heyneke must fall', lamenting 'archaic' tactics and claiming South African rugby was 'going backwards'. Meanwhile, it was reported that several provincial unions had objected to what they viewed as the Boks' limited style of play and lack of transformation.

Some players weren't fans of Heyneke either, but they were usually those he wasn't selecting. I had a lot of respect for him. He gave me my first cap at 20, said some nice things about me to the media, and kept selecting me even after Victor and Bakkies came out of retirement. He could be quirky, no doubt. He always had to have his green Energade before a game and would get irritated if there were any scraps of paper or tape in the middle of the team huddle. He also enjoyed telling stories, which always included a lesson. But he was a great coach, a perfectionist who loved the planning side of things. And he was an even better person away from rugby, an absolute gentleman.

Then again, if you go a four-year cycle as head coach of the Boks without winning a World Cup or Rugby Championship, win only one out of eight games against the All Blacks, and lose to Japan and Argentina at home, people for whom rugby is a religion are bound to come down hard on you. Having said that, I hope that in retirement I'll never be like one of those guys who wrote that open letter, and that if I'm asked for my opinion I'll focus on the positives rather than trying to tear the team down.

I still thought Heyneke should have been given the chance to make up for the calamity in Brighton but he resigned in December 2015, presumably having been told his contract wouldn't be renewed beyond the end of the year. And while I felt for Heyneke and the rest of his coaching team (professional sport is brutal but I never forget that the people involved are humans, and I still speak to Heyneke), I was delighted when I heard that my old Stormers coach, Allister Coetzee, had been appointed in his place.

It can be stressful for players when a coach they don't know comes in. Will he see things the same way as the previous coach? Will he want to go in a different direction? But I knew Allister coached me before and selected me for the Stormers at 20, so he definitely rated me. Plus, he had one of my Springbok jerseys in a frame on his wall (just joking!).

For all the pessimism swirling around the Springboks, I didn't think we were too far away from New Zealand. In 2014, we'd narrowly lost to them in Wellington and beaten them in Johannesburg, then almost beaten them in a World Cup semifinal the following year, so I thought we'd be fine going forward with Allister.

We'd played a certain way under Heyneke and many thought we'd become too predictable. He'd brought in his Bulls assistants, Johann van Graan and Ricardo Loubscher, to coach the forwards and backs respectively, and they had a very structured approach to the game. It was all about systems, running lines, and forwards carrying hard and straight. But while Allister thought we needed to be a bit more expansive, that was easier said than done.

Different teams have what South Africans call their 'big rocks', and the Springboks' big rocks had always been a good defensive system, a solid set piece and a physical pack. I was still young and my understanding of the game wasn't what it would become, but in hindsight we should have just improved those big rocks and fine-tuned as we went along. Instead, we neglected them, thinking we could suddenly be like the All Blacks. If only sport was that simple.

New Zealanders play rugby the way they do because they were raised in a certain culture. Playing expansive, attacking rugby is in their DNA, and even it was no longer paying dividends they'd never dream of playing like the Springboks. Instead, they'd work hard to improve on what they did best. In the same way, it would be madness for a country like Fiji to try to play like the Boks because their rugby DNA is speed, athleticism and flair. Yes, they need to work on their set piece and game management, but the most important thing for them, and any sporting team, is to adhere to an identity.

Allister's first game in charge was against Ireland in June 2016, and he handed a debut to spiky Lions scrum half Faf de Klerk and a first start to Siya. Siya had been in the Springbok set-up since 2013, and while we had a lot of back-row talent (Francois Louw, Duane Vermeulen, Willem Alberts, Heinrich Brüssow, Marcell Coetzee) and I'm not suggesting he should have been starting ahead of them, I was surprised it took him so long to crack it.

I think Siya lost a bit of confidence when he was in and out of the team under Heyneke, but when Allister took over he became the Siya I remembered from Craven Week. His confidence came flooding back and he was more inclined to laugh and joke, which was the Siya I loved the most.

On the field, I'd always thought Siya was underrated. He was a big ball carrier at the start of his career, but as he matured as a player he got better at the unseen work in defence and attack, the sort of stuff that is unappreciated by the layman. Siya wasn't the best at everything but you could feel that the team was slightly stronger when he was on the field than when he wasn't. He added value that few others could emulate, which is the sign of a great player.

Ireland had been talked up before the 2015 World Cup, only to get blown away by Argentina in the quarter-finals, and when CJ Stander (who was born and raised in George, South Africa, but had recently qualified to play for Ireland) was sent off after 22 minutes for a late hit on Pat Lambie, I thought we'd put them away. But it didn't turn out like that. They defended like demons to stay in the game, Paddy Jackson kept knocking over kicks and we trailed by 13 points with 12 minutes left. Pieter-Steph did get a try back but they hung on for their first win over the Boks in South Africa.

Sometimes you have to concede that you were under par and the opposition played brilliantly, but for some South African fans almost every Springbok defeat is a stain on the country's reputation, as was hammered home after that defeat. When we left the hotel the next morning for a recovery walk around Cape Town a taxi driver started shouting at us, 'How can you lose to Ireland at Newlands? You're not fit to wear the Springbok jersey. You're a disgrace to South Africa!' I should have ignored him but instead I told him to shut his mouth. There was more back and forth and eventually some team-mates had to tell me to leave it.

It wasn't a good look but that kind of thing really got to me back then. I'd think, *Jeez, what do these people actually know about rugby?* Whether it was that taxi driver or a guy who spent his evenings drinking brandy and furiously typing scathing social media posts, I couldn't understand their way of thinking. But as time went on I became more empathetic. Even when a lot of things weren't up to par – politics, the economy, the social fabric – the Springboks were meant to be one of the things in South Africa that worked well.

People loved being part of our successes – the Boks were often the only source of national pride – and it was like a dagger to the heart when we lost, which is why they were so judgmental and gave us so much *kak*. If South Africans ever stop complaining about the Springboks, that's when we should worry because it will mean they don't care any more. Even harsh criticism is support of a kind, and as for that taxi driver, the fact he was slagging off the entire Springbok squad in the street showed he cared an awful lot!

If our defeat in the first Test upset the South African public, the first half of the second Test at Ellis Park must have sent some of them half crazy. Having been absolutely terrible – a lack of energy, an inability to make anything happen – we trailed Ireland 19–3 and were booed off the field, which I'd not experienced before. Again, I didn't understand the reaction at the time – *We aren't trying to play badly, screw them* – but I get it now. We were their heroes, whether we liked it or not, and they'd paid their hard-earned money to watch us play. They had the right to boo us when we let them down, just as they had the right to cheer us when we made them proud.

I can't remember what was said in the changing room at half-time – no doubt stuff about disgracing the jersey, embarrassing our country and deserving all the flak we were getting – but it seemed to work. Our bench injected greater energy and urgency, and a late converted try by Damian de Allende, our fourth of the second half, secured a 32–26 victory.

There was a lot of pressure on us to win the third Test in Port Elizabeth – no team from the British Isles had won a Test series in South Africa and it would have been a stain on the history of South African rugby if Ireland had been the first – and we managed to do so, albeit narrowly. Still, rugby writers weren't exactly glowing about us in their match reports.

The 2016 Rugby Championship was an even more chastening experience for Springbok players and fans alike, and by the end of it some people would be claiming that South African rugby was in terminal decline.

Having scraped past Argentina in our first game in Mbombela (formerly Nelspruit), courtesy of two late tries, the Pumas edged us the following week in Salta. That was their first win over the Boks on home soil.

Our next game was against Australia in Brisbane, when I reached the 50 Test match mark. New Zealand had hammered the Wallabies in their first two games of the tournament and it looked like they might fold again when we scored two early tries. But what might have been a nice occasion personally soon turned into a bit of a nightmare. Before that day my jersey had never been torn, I'd never needed stitches and I'd never been yellow-carded, but all three happened in that game. On top of that, Wallabies No 10 Bernard Foley didn't miss a kick, and when he went over for a try with 20 minutes left, our goose was cooked.

Next up were the world champions in Christchurch, and as was often the case against the All Blacks I felt like we had their number in the early stages. But a Bryan Habana try was soon cancelled out, we kept making mistakes, and before we knew it they were over the hill and far away. We barely laid a glove on them in the second half and they ended up putting 40-odd points on us.

We managed to beat Australia in an ugly game at Loftus, with Morné Steyn kicking all our points, but that result just papered over the cracks. Discipline in the squad wasn't great and some guys on the periphery of the first XV decided it would be a good idea to have a *jol* a few days before our game against the rampant All Blacks in Durban. South African reporters found out about that, which created bad feeling within the squad. There was a sense that we lacked an effective leadership group, experienced heads who had no qualms about telling younger guys how proper Springboks behave.

A year or two earlier, Schalk Burger had taken me aside at the Stormers and told me he wanted me to show more leadership. This icon of South African rugby telling me that felt weird, but I did try to be more involved. With the Springboks it was different. Guys like Schalk, Jean de Villiers and Victor Matfield were bona fide legends. What could I possibly offer in an international environment that they didn't already know? Plus, I was in complete awe of them and didn't want them to think I was a know-it-all.

Now those guys were gone it felt strange being one of the senior players. I was only 24 and still felt I was finding my feet within the Springboks leadership group. And there were still experienced guys in the team – Bryan Habana, Morné Steyn, Beast, and skipper Adriaan Strauss, who were all in their 30s – so it didn't feel natural to give my opinion in their presence.

While our preparation for the All Blacks at Kings Park wasn't ideal, I didn't think the game could be any worse than the Test in Christchurch. Unfortunately, it was. Once again, we kept a lid on them in the first half and they led only 12–9 at the break. But they couldn't stop scoring after that, running in seven second-half tries to win 57–15. I don't remember any boos that day but the silence was probably worse. When your fans boo they still have hope; silence means they've given up on you.

That was the All Blacks' biggest margin of victory against the Boks in South Africa and the most points the Boks had conceded. And while we finished third on the log with two wins from six games, the All Blacks won the tournament at a canter, equalling their own record of 17 wins in a row.

That defeat in Durban represented a crisis point in South African rugby, though some of my teammates didn't seem overly bothered. A few of the guys who'd gone out drinking before the game went out again afterwards, returning to the hotel a bit the worse for wear.

How a player handles losing tells me a lot about them, and I'm always frustrated with teammates who don't seem as hurt and angry as me. I've certainly never understood the philosophy of 'on the booze, win or lose'.

Maybe I'm not empathetic enough and some people cope with losing differently from me, but I've always thought that if you lose a game of professional rugby, especially a Test match, you shouldn't be acting as if you've just lost a friendly game of table tennis, laughing and joking over a few beers. If you're not hurt and angry after losing, you don't care enough and losing again won't bother you. Accepting a loss makes you a loser, which is why I've sometimes told teammates, 'You don't look like you're hurting enough.' But with the Boks in 2016, I didn't think it was my place to say that.

We had a couple of weeks off after the Rugby Championship but I didn't want to leave the house. If you don't perform for the Boks you can forget about trying to live anything resembling a normal life, especially if you're as tall as I am. I could just about get away with popping to the shop for groceries, but if I'd dared to visit a restaurant there would have been people giving me funny looks or telling me how shit me and the rest of the Boks were. No thanks.

*   *   *

It was one thing shipping 50 points to world champions New Zealand, but what happened in Europe at the end of 2016 was something else entirely.

Having almost been embarrassed by the Barbarians at Wembley Stadium – a last-ditch try by Rohan Janse van Rensburg salvaged a draw – we headed to Twickenham, having not lost to England for 10 years. But England under Eddie Jones were a very different proposition from the side who were eliminated early in their own World Cup. Not only had they recently won their first Grand Slam for 13 years, they'd also whitewashed Australia down under and were on a nine-game winning streak.

After an even first quarter, England proceeded to blow us away, scoring four tries to two, kicking goals from all over the park and eventually winning 37–21. To make matters worse, I suffered a concussion after 30 minutes, ruling me out of the rest of the game and our next fixture against Italy. Billy Vunipola was the guy who did the damage, as he did to quite a few opponents down the years. I tried to tackle him with my head on the wrong side and his elbow caught me against the side of my head.

We'd played Italy 12 times and never beaten them by fewer than 16 points (in 1999 we put 100 points on them). Moreover, they were on a terrible run, having shipped 224 points in the Six Nations on their way to winning another wooden spoon. They also lost 68–10 to New Zealand's second-string side the week before. To put it politely, it wasn't a vintage Italian outfit, which made what happened that afternoon in Florence even harder to swallow.

I'm not sure I've been more horrified watching a game of rugby. The first half was deeply frustrating, with Dries van Schalkwyk (born and raised in Bloemfontein) scoring for Italy from a rolling maul, Bryan Habana and Damian de Allende scoring for us, but the Boks also wasting a stack of opportunities. And after the interval, they scored a try when down to 14 men, matched us up front, defended their line ferociously and won 20–18.

The consensus in the South African media was that defeat by Italy was an all-time low for the Boks, and certainly as bad as that defeat by Japan, which no one who was in Brighton that day would ever have thought possible.

Afrikaans newspaper *Rapport* awarded every Springbok 0 out of 10. Another newspaper said of our performance, '[It was] woeful, embarrassing, incompetent, putrid, pathetic, sorry, miserable, wretched . . . [but] none of those words begins to do justice to the feeling that currently accompanies what was a once-proud Springbok brand.' Everyone seemed to agree that Allister's days as head coach were numbered. SARU called the Springboks' form 'extremely disappointing and deeply worrying', and while it ruled out a knee-jerk reaction, that was probably the first time I could feel Allister's pain and anxiety, however hard he tried to hide it.

Before our game against Wales in Cardiff, Italy lost to Tonga, which wasn't a great sign – there had been a lot of talk about a new dawn for Italian rugby, but now they presumably realised that beating us meant almost nothing. I was forced to watch from the stands again, and sure enough

Wales – who had been hammered by Australia a few weeks earlier – won quite comfortably, 27–13. We looked weary and completely out of ideas; we struggled to do the basics right and botched chance after chance. It was their second win in a row against us at the Millennium Stadium and their biggest winning margin.

Looking back on our squad for that tour, it seems incredible that things went so badly. Loads of those guys are now considered to be Springbok greats – Beast, Willie le Roux, Damian de Allende, Pieter-Steph du Toit, Lood de Jager, Vincent Koch, Bongi Mbonambi, Steven Kitshoff, Franco Mostert, Faf de Klerk.

We were a mess, light years away from being the best in the world. Some pundits claimed we were the worst Springbok team in history. We'd lost eight Test matches in a calendar year for the first time, and in almost every game our opponents set some new record against us: our first defeat by Ireland at home, our first defeat by the Pumas in Argentina, our biggest defeat by the All Blacks, our first defeat by Italy, our biggest defeat by Wales.

The whole Springbok organisation was probably to blame – players, coaching staff, management – because nothing was aligning. A South African optimist might have pointed out that England were in the middle of a long winning streak and Wales had one of their most experienced sides. And it's true that they were both very good, well-coached teams playing on home soil. But most South African fans weren't interested in any of that, especially those who had shelled out thousands of rands to watch their heroes play 13,000 km from home. I even heard stories about people burning their green and gold jerseys in disgust. Sometimes, I forget exactly how bad that period was, probably because I've tried to scrub it from my memory, although there were one or two moments of dark comedy, albeit only in hindsight.

Partly because of the team's poor performances and partly because so many marquee players had moved overseas, sponsors started deserting us. Early in 2017, SARU announced that it had lost millions in sponsorship money and space on the Bok jersey was being sold at discounted rates. As a result, the team could no longer fly business class, and economy isn't really designed with rugby players in mind.

Being the two tallest players in the team, Lood de Jager and I had to pay for upgrades out of our own pocket – if we'd flown the 11+ hours to Europe in economy, we probably would have only just got rid of our stiffness just before the game – but the rest of the guys just suffered it. I'll never forget turning round and seeing the bigger forwards, some of them over 115 kg, squeezed into their seats like giant horseshoes, sad looks on their faces. When the passengers in front put their seats back, some of them looked like they were about to go crazy.

Before the 2017 Super Rugby season got under way, Stormers head coach Robbie Fleck called me and Siya into his office and asked us if we'd like to take over the team leadership. He hadn't decided who would be captain or vice-captain, but after leaving the meeting Siya and I promised to back whoever got the top job because we both knew we couldn't do it by ourselves.

The idea of being captain really appealed to me and I was disappointed when Siya was handed the gig. But I wasn't angry. I couldn't be because I'd never captained a team before, not even at school level, and I thought Siya would make a fine captain anyway. He'd never been a know-it-all, so I knew he wouldn't try to do everything by himself. He'd ask other people for their opinions, not just me, and he'd take his responsibility seriously.

Siya was excited and I think he appreciated the matter-of-fact announcement from Robbie that didn't mention the fact that he was the team's first black captain. Siya didn't want to be remembered as a black captain, just as a good captain. Of course, the media made a big thing of it, and while most outlets simply commented on the momentous nature of the appointment, there were inevitably those on social media who suggested it was a political decision, a sop to transformation. Siya would prove that theory to be absolute nonsense over the coming years.

Bryan Habana retired from Springbok duty after our disastrous tour of Europe, while JP Pietersen moved to Leicester, reducing the number of World Cup winners in the squad to one. (Frans Steyn, who had been plying his trade overseas since 2009, returned to the fold in 2017 after a five-year absence.) Beast had the most caps with 87 and I was all of a sudden second in the group with 54 and we had a lot of inexperienced guys in the squad for the three-match series against

France, including eight uncapped players. So having been given the chance to hone my leadership skills with the Stormers, it now felt a lot more natural to be a leader for the Boks.

It seemed like a good time to be playing France. They hadn't won a Six Nations title since 2010 and were far from being the French team of today. They were in transition, not knowing which direction to go in – should they abandon their traditional flair game and go for all-out brute force? – and got stuck between two stools.

We easily beat them in the first two Test matches, outscoring them four tries to two on both occasions, but my highlight of the series, and one of the highlights of my career, was yet to come. Adriaan Strauss had retired from international rugby at the end of 2016, leaving Lions eighthman Warren Whiteley to take over. But he was struggling with an injury before the third Test at Ellis Park, and on the Wednesday Allister told me, 'Warren's not going to be ready, you'll be captain this weekend.'

I was quite emotional. I'd dreamed of playing for South Africa when I was a kid but those dreams never stretched as far as captaining the Springboks. When Allister said I couldn't tell anyone because Warren would be in the team photo as captain (presumably because he didn't want the French to know Warren wasn't playing until the morning of the match), I replied, 'I have to tell my family!' Allister reluctantly agreed but made it clear that they weren't to tell anyone else.

When I called Mom and Dad, they started screaming. I can't imagine how they must have felt, although I reckon it must have been quite surreal for them. They'd always been big Springbok fans and knew all about the history, and now their own son was on the same list as Francois Pienaar, Corné Krige, André Vos, Joost van der Westhuizen, Bobby Skinstad, John Smit, Victor Matfield, Jean de Villiers and all the other great leaders of men stretching back to Herbert Castens in 1891. I know Mom told her brother and I suspect Dad told a few people down the pub. To be honest, half of the Western Cape probably knew before my captaincy was officially announced.

There was some chatter in the media about why Siya hadn't got the job, and that was understandable – he was my captain at the Stormers, after all. Before that series, a psychologist working with the team had devised a personality trait test for the players, and apparently based on that, Siya or I was best suited to lead the side. But I assume Allister also accounted for the fact that I'd been with the Boks longer and had more caps. Whatever the reasons, Siya was as happy for me as I'd been for him when he got the Stormers captaincy. And I knew he'd support me every step of the way.

I also had Beast to rely on, and in case anyone was wondering, no one ever calls him Tendai (except when they're trying to get a laugh, and maybe his wife when she's angry with him). I didn't know what to expect when I first met Beast. He was called Beast – and he looked like a beast! – so I probably expected him to be quite beastly, a bit gruff and intimidating.

In fact, he was one of the nicest people I'd ever met – gentle, kind, unassuming – to the extent that I felt the need to keep telling people. I've often thought Beast is the wrong nickname for him – 'Gentle Giant' is far more appropriate.

Tendai 'Beast' Mtawarira, South Africa teammate: *I first became aware of Eben when my Sharks team played the Stormers in early 2012. Despite being only 20 he was massive, with the biggest biceps I'd ever seen.*

We had our first proper conversation when he made his debut for the Boks that June and I immediately knew he was an outstanding guy: very solid in his beliefs, a true team player and a family man, always speaking about his mom, dad and brother. But it was what he did to my friend Bismarck du Plessis when the Sharks met the Stormers again a couple of months later that told me he was destined for greatness. Bismarck was a serious operator and in his prime, but Eben gave him the big brush-off. Wow, what a moment.

There were a lot of older heads in the changing room when Eben started out with the Boks, established legends who had won the World Cup in 2007. I'd been in the set-up for four years already but I could feel the aura of those players and I can understand why Eben might have felt intimidated. But while he was very quiet he was also observant and soaked up informa- tion like a sponge.

Props always have a favourite lock, a guy they like to have behind them when they're packing down, and Eben became that guy for me. We developed a special connection in that most of our on-field conversations would be silent, but away from rugby we spent an awful lot of time chatting in Nando's, our go-to restaurant all over the world. I dread to think how many chickens we consumed between us over the years. He'd ask a few questions, and whether or not the advice I gave him was useful, we soon grew very close.

It was tough to stay positive during that bumpy period from 2015 to 2017. The Japan loss at the 2015 World Cup was a bitter pill to swallow – it felt like somebody had died in the changing room afterwards – and even though we almost beat New Zealand in the semi-finals, which would have been one of the greatest comebacks in sport, things deteriorated from there.

It got us all down, including Eben, but we stuck to our guns and held ourselves accountable – the one thing we could control was our own performances – and Rassie [Erasmus] taking over in 2018 made anything seem possible.

Eben became more and more influential as those old legends slipped into retirement. He was always focused on the task in hand and set a good example for the younger guys, whether he was turning up first for meetings or spending hours analysing videos. I wouldn't describe him as outspoken but he chose his moments well so that when he did speak, people listened. He was especially effective in difficult moments, such as when we were under the pump in big games, when he knew exactly what to say to rally the troops.

Eben is the epitome of what it means to be a Springbok. He cares so much about the jersey, he's taken physicality to another level and he's an extremely intelligent rugby player, far more than just a brute. He's the ultimate competitor who gives absolutely everything of himself in every game he plays.

Eben is among the crème de la crème of Springboks, probably the greatest of all time, a back-to-back World Cup winner, the most-capped Bok ever, someone who has never had a bad game in green and gold. The scary thing is, he's not even done yet. He could easily play another 20–30 Tests, and judging by his demeanour he's determined to win another World Cup in 2027.

But contrary to popular belief, Eben isn't a rugby machine. Like me, he's able to switch his aggression on and off and he's a gentleman away from the sport. Every time we speak, a braai is on the cards, and he loves nothing more than hosting friends and family and telling stories around a bonfire.

He knows my wife, kids and dogs very well (my French bulldog took a particular liking to Eben the first time he met him, if you know what I mean!) and we share a big love of sushi. Eben, Siya and I have probably broken loads of sushi eating records, from Cape Town to Japan, and we've had situations where we've hoovered up almost all the sushi available and the other diners have been fighting over scraps.

I like to live in the here and now rather than dwelling on South Africa's past, but we've certainly come a long way. I've always believed everyone should be treated the same, whatever their background, and there were never any barriers in the Springbok teams that Eben and I played in. We might have looked different but we embraced our diversity, we all felt like we belonged and we cared for each other. And whenever me and

Eben's families are out for lunch together, that's another pleasing snapshot of modern South Africa.

I'm so proud of the man Eben has become. Besides being an amazing family man, he's inspired the next generation of young South Africans. Kids of all colours and backgrounds idolise him, which is why he'll be remembered as a very powerful human being who strengthened bonds and bridged divides.

I normally ran onto the pitch fifth, behind the captain and the front row, so leading the team out felt strange. I actually thought, *I hope the guys are following me.* I sang the national anthem with more gusto than ever and I could really feel the extra responsibility. Besides my normal job I was now making decisions on behalf of the team and I didn't want to make the wrong ones. I also wanted to win even more than I'd wanted to win before.

We gave France another hiding that day, and as a bonus I scored one of our four tries. But while that series whitewash suggested we'd turned a corner, it's possible that it gave us a false sense of how good we were.

South African fans are quite a forgiving bunch and they'll soon forget about any recent failures if you string a few wins together. So when we beat Argentina quite handily in our first two games of the Rugby Championship, including in Salta where we'd struggled in the past, they probably assumed the crisis was over. Then we battled back from 10 points down early in the second half to salvage a draw against Australia in Perth, making us unbeaten in six Test matches in 2017.

I'd never heard of Albany before we played New Zealand there that year. Most of us were just disappointed not to be playing at Eden Park, the All Blacks' spiritual home, because Albany's North Harbour Stadium in the suburbs of Auckland holds only 14,000. In hindsight, that was a blessing in disguise.

Everything seemed fine in the camp before the game and we thought we had a decent chance of beating them. We certainly didn't think we were huge underdogs in need of a miracle. The early exchanges were all too familiar. We were matching them up front, our forwards were getting over the advantage line with almost every carry, and when loose forward Jean-Luc du Preez ran over Kieran Read, I assumed it was going to be an arm wrestle. But they got a penalty after 15 minutes, Aaron Smith put a quick kick through and Rieko Ioane touched down unopposed. All our hard work had been undone by one soft moment, namely not filling the backfield. Then again, it was just one try.

A few minutes later we were attacking in their half when Nehe Milner-Skudder intercepted a pass and carried deep into our half before passing to Beauden Barrett. Barrett then came up with a moment of absolute genius: a back-of-the-hand pass back to Milner-Skudder who finished off an incredible move.

Standing under the posts, I still didn't think we were out of it at 17–0 down. But things soon turned very black indeed. First, Barrett put up a cross-kick that our defence failed to deal with, allowing Scott Barrett to score in the corner; then Ioane shrugged off some weak tackling and Dane Coles put Brodie

Retallick in for a try under the poles, which made it 31–0 at half-time.

Locks dancing down the wing unopposed, defenders falling off tackles, hookers setting up locks to finish off brilliant sweeping moves – it had become a humiliation. And being a man who deals in reality, I didn't gather the guys together in the changing room and say, 'Come on guys, we can still beat them!' It was now just a case of trying to save face.

However, because saving face meant scoring at least a couple of tries, we had to chase the game – and the more we did that, the more open we became. Two more tries made it 43–0 with 17 minutes remaining and all I could think was, *Jeez, I hope they don't put 50 or 60 on us.* There was no chat whatsoever under the poles by that point; we were too shell-shocked.

Unfortunately, the humiliation was far from over. First, Lima Sopoaga scored under the poles after a barnstorming run (aided by more weak tackling) from Anton Lienert-Brown, before Beauden Barrett kicked the extras to bring up 50 points. And right at the death, Codie Taylor scored from a line-out drive – the ultimate insult for a Springbok team – making the final score 57–0. It was South Africa's biggest defeat and our biggest losing margin against New Zealand, surpassing our 42-point deficit in our previous match-up in Durban. At least the horror show had been watched by only 14,000, rather than the 60,000 who would have been at Eden Park.

After the excruciating handshakes with our opponents – they at least had the good grace not to look too triumphant –

I gathered the team into a huddle. I had tears in my eyes when I told the guys, 'What happened here today was unacceptable and must never happen again. No individual was to blame, we all let the jersey down, every single one of us. But we mustn't let it define us.' I'm not sure how much they were listening. Most were gazing at the ground and those who were looking at me had nothing behind their eyes.

Occasionally you play a game where everything goes the opposition's way and nothing goes yours, and that was certainly the case in Albany. At the same time, the All Blacks were ruthlessly efficient at turning lucky breaks into points. And like a batsman who can score all around the wicket, they accumulated points almost without you noticing, so that you'd look up at the scoreboard and think, *How the hell did that happen?*

They weren't necessarily spectacular (although they did score a few outstanding tries), they just made the most of every scoring opportunity. And the more we felt the game slipping away from us, the more desperate we became, and suddenly we were doing things we didn't normally do – running everything, trying risky passes and offloads, making more and more mistakes. And instead of the mistakes being in their half, they were in our half and the All Blacks gleefully seized on them. In the end, the only sensible option was to batten down the hatches and hope it didn't get too ugly and humiliating. But we left it too late.

Because it was only a small ground, their changing room was virtually next door to ours and it was impossible not to hear their celebrations. To be fair to the All Blacks, they've always been good winners, probably because they're so used to it – 'Whatever, another Test match to add to our 85 per cent win rate' – and most of our team went in and shared a beer with them. It was important they did that but I just couldn't. It's not that I'm a bad loser per se but I do wear my heart on my sleeve. I wouldn't have been able to chat and share a joke with them as if everything was normal, because the Springboks losing 57–0 to the All Blacks is very far from normal. Losing 57–20 would still have hurt me but I would have been able to exchange a few words through gritted teeth. But this was the biggest hurt of my rugby career, even worse than the Japan game.

I can't remember much about the post-match press conference except that it resembled an inquisition. But when you've just lost 57–0 to the All Blacks, reporters can get away with asking you anything. Someone could stand up and spend 10 minutes explaining how *kak* you were and you'd just have to sit there and take it. I know I was asked if I deserved to be captain and Allister was asked if he deserved to be coach, and we couldn't get angry, not least because I was definitely doubting myself and Allister probably was too.

I then had to talk at a function, which was tough (there weren't many jokes), before we flew home to prepare for our game against Australia in Bloemfontein. And although we drew with the Wallabies for the second time in the tournament, the flak from the media was becoming more personal.

Having been involved in a scuffle against the Wallabies – I came to Dillyn Leyds's defence after Israel Folau had grabbed him by the hair and dragged him into touch, before Kurtley Beale also got involved – some journalists, seemingly still obsessed with this 'enforcer' tag, had decided I was perhaps too much of a loose cannon to lead the side. And at a press conference before our next game against New Zealand, a journalist asked if I planned to tone things down a bit and suggested I shouldn't be getting yellow cards now that I was captain.

A coach who was sat beside me quickly pointed out that I'd received only one yellow card in 60 Test matches, which shut the guy up. And while he was sitting there looking slightly embarrassed, I couldn't resist adding that I'd been sin-binned only once in 50-odd games for the Stormers, I'd never been shown a red card and I wouldn't be toning anything down for anyone.

Yes, I was involved in the occasional altercation, but if that's not happening when you're a lock, you're not competitive enough. There was the headbutt that never was on Australia's Nathan Sharpe and I had a bit of a set-to with Scotland's Jim Hamilton in Mbombela in 2013. Jim had been chatting quite a bit early in the game, and when he was down getting treatment from the physio I said to him, 'Get up, you're scared,' except in slightly stronger terms. There was a bit of shoving at the next line-out, Jim pushed me in the face, I lost my temper and went for him. But people seem to forget that Jim was sin-binned for that incident, not me! (Jim jokes that when his kids type his name into YouTube, that's the first thing that comes up.)

Oh, I shouldn't forget my wrestling match with my Bok lock partner Lood de Jager, which happened when the Stormers played the Cheetahs in 2016. Lood pushed me from behind, I took umbrage and we ended up grabbing each other and rolling around on the ground. But the referee seemed to find it quite amusing, gave us a bit of a talking to, and we were in international camp together the following Sunday. Allister said before the first session, in front of the whole group, 'Eben, Lood – are you two guys okay now?' and everyone laughed. That made things less awkward and I reckon that disagreement brought Lood and I closer than we had been.

But that's what happens with the media: a narrative takes root and having done no research themselves, rugby followers believe it. As far as some of them were concerned, if some rugby writer said I was an out-of-control lock with anger issues and a poor disciplinary record then it must be true.

I tend to avoid the views of rugby writers and pundits, but if I do happen to read a negative article about me, I don't get angry and think, *Who the hell wrote this? I need to track them down and give them a piece of my mind.* Instead, I rationalise it. With one or two exceptions, whoever wrote the article might not have played rugby at all, let alone at a high level. And if you interact with them, whether in person or via social media, you're giving them power and legitimacy. Even if I read a glowing article about me, it still doesn't matter because they probably don't know what they're talking about. I know what's real, how hard I train, how hard I work in a game, whether I perform as expected or could do better.

I remember sitting at the back of the team bus once when someone was scrolling through comments on social media. Duane Vermeulen said to me, 'One of the things I've learnt is that however good you are and however much you want to help people, 20 per cent of people still won't like you. That's just human nature, and the day you accept it you'll be much happier.' He was bang on, and while some players do take the negative comments of the 20 per cent to heart, I never let negativity from people I don't even know dampen my mood. I find it best not even to pay attention to the positive 80 per cent because if you start believing the hype you'll become complacent and lose your competitive edge.

I did a lot of soul-searching before the game against the All Blacks at Newlands. Was I doing something wrong? I did my best not to read or listen to the criticism – people saying how terrible the Springboks were and how the team must be lacking in leadership – but it was impossible to avoid it completely. I could feel the negativity in the air, and while I'd never have said I didn't want to be captain any more – I couldn't just give something like that up, however bad things got – it was a tough time.

I suggested to the coaches that we should do something to relieve the tension, otherwise the guys would go crazy holed up in their hotel rooms. So I invited all the forwards to a spit braai at my house on the Monday, with a live band and instructions to relax and not talk about rugby.

As the week progressed, I knew I had to do everything in my power to give the team an edge. To that end, I wrote a note for each player, telling them they were going to play great at the weekend. And on the day of the game, I left a note on each player's locker, letting them know that I still backed them and honestly believed we could beat New Zealand, despite what happened in Albany.

I already knew from my experiences at the 2015 World Cup that a couple of weeks is a long time in rugby, but I'm not sure anyone thought we had a hope of bouncing back from a 57-point deficit against the All Blacks, especially since neither team had changed much in terms of personnel. But this time we were able to snuff out a couple of early try-scoring opportunities and gain a foothold.

We were leading with 12 minutes to go, until a magical try by All Black full back Damian McKenzie and a late penalty by Sopoaga. Malcolm Marx barged over for a try at the death and the conversion made it 24–25 but they managed to hold on for the win, their sixth in a row against us. The All Blacks had won all six of their games for their fifth title in six years, while we'd finished third behind Australia, with two wins, two draws and two defeats.

I knew it was going to take a miracle in our end-of-year internationals for Allister to keep his job, such as putting 50 points on Ireland, France, Italy and Wales. As it was, the Irish drove the final nail into his coffin in Dublin.

We were up against the best Ireland team yet, by some margin (they'd beaten New Zealand in the US the previous year, their first victory over the All Blacks in 29 games stretching back 111 years), while our planning wasn't what it should have been. We didn't analyse them in enough detail, so they were able to expose us on the edges with their kicking. That wasn't some secret tactic on their part, they'd done it before. And while we stayed within touching distance of them for most of the game, we never really looked like scoring a try and they ran in three in the last 10 minutes for a 38–3 victory and yet another national record score against the Springboks.

There had been some dark periods for the Springboks since our readmission to international rugby. In 2002, for example, we lost 53–3 to England after big defeats by France and Scotland. But this had to be the darkest. We dropped to seventh in the world after that game, our lowest ranking, and I'll never forget one pundit saying there was no way back for South African rugby. One journalist even likened the Springboks to the West Indies cricket team, who rose to dominance in the 1970s, were almost unbeatable in the 1980s, went downhill in the 1990s and were struggling to beat anyone by the 2000s.

We beat France by a single point the following week (they were also on a miserable run) but I still needed reassurance before the game against Italy. The man I sought out was Francois Louw, who felt like one of my seniors even though I was captain. Francois was six years older than me and made his Bok debut two years earlier, and I respected him a great deal. I asked him if he thought I was leading the team well and whether there was anything I could do differently. He replied, 'Listen, don't be too hard on yourself. We all need to do better but you're doing just fine as captain.' That Saturday in Padua we won 35–6.

The following weekend, Wales were missing seven players who toured New Zealand with the British & Irish Lions a few months earlier, so they should have been there for the taking. But they had two converted tries on the board after only 7 minutes and we trailed 21–10 at the break.

I couldn't come out for the second half because of an injury – just before half-time, I took the ball into contact, someone tackled me, and it felt like my neck and head were being torn away from my shoulders. I wanted to play on but had lost all power in my left arm and couldn't even pick it up in the changing room. We somehow managed to gain the lead through a couple of tries before a late Leigh Halfpenny penalty gave Wales a 24–22 victory, their third in a row against us in Cardiff.

One pundit said the game had a 'second division' feel about it and he was probably right. But was there really no way back for the Springboks?

6

JUST GETTING STARTED

When I heard that Allister might be sacked, I thought, *Shit, would that be wise two years before a World Cup? Who's going to be able to implement a plan and turn the team around in that time?* Actually, whoever they hired would have just over a year because his first game would be in June 2018.

SARU finally put Allister out of his misery in February, and while it wasn't exactly a bolt from the blue and I could see why the decision was made, I don't have a bad word to say about him.

Allister gave me my Stormers debut when I was only 20, just three years out of school, and trusted me enough to make me the Springbok captain. He was a great rugby man, a lovely person, and I'll be forever thankful to him. Unfortunately, he had lots of things going against him as Bok head coach. He took over just after the international retirements of a raft of truly great players. When a bunch of guys with more than 500 caps between them walk out the door, that's going to be difficult to overcome. And when Bryan Habana, JP Pietersen and Willem Alberts also left the picture in 2016, Allister was left with a squad that contained just a handful of guys with more than 30 caps, me being one of them, and quite a few guys with none.

Allister still had plenty of talent to choose from but young players need time to come to terms with international rugby. And it should never be forgotten that Allister blooded a lot of players who went on to win two World Cups. Faf de Klerk, Bongi Mbonambi, Steven Kitshoff and Franco Mostert all made their Springbok debuts during our series against Ireland in 2016, while Malcolm Marx and Lukhanyo Am were introduced within the year. Others were tried and discarded, some after just a couple of games, some after a couple of years, but that was to be expected of a team in flux.

Allister was further impeded by a rule SARU introduced in 2017 requiring overseas-based players to have at least 30 Test caps to be eligible for selection. It was designed to stop players leaving the country but it further reduced the Springbok talent pool.

While the likes of Duane Vermeulen (Toulon), Francois Louw (Bath) and Willie le Roux (Wasps) did have 30 caps and were often overlooked by Allister anyway, hundreds more South Africans, many of them playing at top European clubs, were unavailable for the Springboks. For example, the new directive ruled out Marcell Coetzee, who joined Ulster in 2016 (although he struggled with injuries in his first couple of seasons), and would soon rule out Faf de Klerk and electric Stormers wing Cheslin Kolbe, who signed for Sale and Toulouse respectively in 2017.

I understood the thinking behind the rule but it was quite muddled in practice. SARU didn't have the funds to keep all the players who had moved overseas in South Africa anyway. Meanwhile, a Stormers player could double his salary by joining a European team and a Springbok could earn three times as much or more.

Playing rugby is a wonderful way to make a living but it's still a job, and a dangerous, short-lived one. If you can do it for 15 years you're lucky, and many are able to do it for only a few. People have to think about their futures beyond rugby, especially if they have families, because no one from the rugby world is going to give them handouts when they hang up their boots.

It was a strange situation all round. On one hand, people were talking about the death of South African rugby; on the other, stacks of guys were good enough to play for some of the best club sides in Europe while being ineligible for the Springboks. Sometimes when we were struggling for depth in certain positions, I'd think, *We've got two or three guys playing overseas who could fill that role*, but I kept those thoughts to myself. There was nothing I could do to change the rules and griping about them might have jeopardised my own place in the team.

A month after Allister's sacking, former Bok captain Rassie Erasmus, who had been South Africa director of rugby since the previous summer, was named as his replacement. It was an appointment that would change the course of South African rugby forever.

Rassie was a great player who won 36 caps for the Boks between 1997 and 2001 but coaching seemed to be his true calling. In his second season in charge of the Free State Cheetahs in 2005, he led them to their first Currie Cup title since 1976, repeating the trick the following year. That's what you call an impact. He joined the WP set-up in 2008 and was senior professional coach when WP and the Stormers finished runners-up in the Currie Cup and Super Rugby respectively in 2010.

After various coaching roles with the Boks, Rassie joined Munster in 2016, leading them to the semi-finals of the Champions Cup and the final of the Pro12 in 2017. He landed the job of South Africa's director of rugby that June, and he and his long-term assistant Jacques Nienaber were in the stands when Ireland hammered us 38–3 in Dublin. Apparently, Rassie turned to Jacques and said, 'Flip, we need to save South African rugby.'

Other than his achievements I didn't know much about Rassie. I had heard that when he played for Free State in the 1990s he took it upon himself to be the team analyst, even though there wasn't much video to analyse back then. But the most famous story about him concerned his time as Cheetahs head coach. Having experimented with coloured cards to communicate messages to his players, he installed coloured lamps on the roof of the Free State Stadium for the 2006 Currie Cup season. They called him 'DJ Rassie' after that, but while some people thought he'd lost his mind he was really just thinking differently – and people who think differently, trying things others wouldn't dream of, are often pioneers.

Rassie had 18 Test matches to make the Springboks mighty again, but I wasn't around for his first phase of rebuilding. Having thought my injury against Wales in Cardiff was just a knock that would soon improve, it turned out to be quite serious. When I asked the specialist when I'd be back, he looked a little bit worried and replied, 'There's no timeframe. You'll just try to keep the nerve in your neck alive every day and you'll return to playing when it decides to work properly again.' That wasn't really what I wanted to hear because I took it to mean it might never work properly again.

For the first three weeks I couldn't raise my left arm up beyond 90 degrees. I had to drink beer right-handed, which meant I did a lot of chugging when playing the drinking game Buffalo. When I returned to the Stormers the muscle in my arm had wasted away and my biceps weren't much thicker than my wrist. The early days of rehab were dispiriting because there was no improvement whatsoever. I've spoken to the physio since and she admitted she didn't really know what to do and thought it might be the end for me. I was doubting myself some days, but had to stay confident and positive.

My main concern was if I'd be able to still be as physical as before, so seeing myself wither away and not being able to do anything about it wasn't *lekker*. Even when some movement finally returned, after about two months, I had to start with 1 kg dumbbell curls and I couldn't even bench press the bar.

Thankfully, my power eventually started returning and I thought I might be ready for Rassie's first game in charge, against Wales in Washington, DC. However, when I asked the Stormers if I could play one game for them to prove my fitness, they told me my arm still wasn't strong enough. I was quite upset with them but they argued that they had a duty of care and I could sue them if anything happened to me. So back I went to rehab and more dark times.

My family knew when I was going through a rough patch but the Etzebeths aren't big on sharing their worries, unless it's about something really big. I care about my family deeply but I never want my problems to become their problems and I'd certainly never phone my mom and say, 'Oh, things are going terribly, woe is me.' And while my family will ask how I am and maybe assure me that everything will come good with time, they know I'm resilient.

For much the same reason, I've never spoken to a mental health professional. Psychologists are a normal part of professional sport nowadays and good luck to anyone who sees one – if it helps, it makes sense – but I've always believed that if I'm playing at that level I shouldn't need someone to prepare me for a game, especially someone who isn't part of the team and doesn't really know what's going on. The Springboks don't even have a team psychologist under Rassie, although you could argue that Rassie is such a brilliant man manager that he *is* the team psychologist.

The main topic of media discussion before the international season started was who Rassie might appoint as captain.

Warren Whiteley was also injured and not expected to be fit for the Wales Test and the three-Test series against England. Duane Vermeulen was mentioned as a possibility, but while he and Rassie went back a long way – they were together at the Cheetahs and the Stormers – he played his club rugby overseas and lots of people expected Rassie to plump for a home-based captain.

Siya was also said to be in the frame, although he didn't think that was likely. However, on the Monday before the Wales game, SARU announced on its Twitter account that Pieter-Steph du Toit would take charge of an experimental side in Washington before Siya took over against England, making him South Africa's first black captain.

As soon as I heard the news I phoned Siya to congratulate him. At that moment I wasn't thinking in terms of colour or symbolism, I was just delighted that a very good pal – and a very good captain – had landed the job. He was still in a state of shock. Apparently, he'd been sitting in a team meeting, twiddling his thumbs, when Rassie said, in a businesslike manner, 'Right, Siya, you're going to captain this side.' Afterwards, he went to Rassie and said, 'Me, captain? Really?' I could just imagine Siya doing that.

Rassie was quite clear that he had picked Siya as captain because he was the best man for the job and that the colour of his skin was merely 'a bonus' for South Africa. And only later did I contemplate the significance of Siya's appointment.

Everyone remembered Nelson Mandela handing the Webb Ellis Cup to Francois Pienaar in 1995. Now Siya, who wore the

No 6 jersey like Pienaar but was black like Mandela and grew up barefoot poor and often achingly hungry in the Port Elizabeth township of Zwide, was the Springbok captain. And a team that for many years was the sporting embodiment of white minority rule was now truly a team for every South African.

There was racism on social media, which was as inevitable as it was dispiriting, but Siya's appointment was mostly well received. Having said that, one of the first questions Siya was asked at his first press conference as captain was, 'Do you think it was a political decision?' The journalist probably just thought it needed to be asked, and maybe he was looking for a reaction from Siya or Rassie, but whatever the reason, Siya was really hurt by it. He was tremendously proud and wanted to be a leader for everyone in South Africa, whatever their background, and here was this person suggesting, in a public setting, that maybe he only got the job because of his skin colour.

If that journalist had bothered to ask me, I'd have told him that Siya was able to unite a team because he got on with everyone; that he was comfortable in his own skin and never tried to be someone he wasn't; that he'd say what was on his mind and in his heart, but never talk nonsense; that he led through his actions in training and in games rather than with motivational speeches. Not that we needed a Churchillian captain anyway because we had Rassie for that sort of stuff. All things considered, Siya was the perfect choice.

We narrowly lost the game against Wales in Washington

but it was actually an encouraging outcome given that 13 players were making Test debuts for the Boks, including Kwagga Smith, Ox Nché, Makazole Mapimpi, André Esterhuizen and Thomas du Toit, all of whom would go on to win at least one World Cup.

More cause for optimism was SARU's decision to scrap the 30-cap overseas rule. Instead, home-based players would get top-up payments from SARU according to a new ranking system. Players could still earn more overseas, which is why even more left in 2018, including Franco Mostert for Gloucester, but at least there was some incentive to remain in South Africa and Rassie now had hundreds more players to choose from.

There were only five foreign-based players in Rassie's first 43-man squad, but that number would rise over the next few years, with the likes of Cobus Reinach (Northampton), Faf de Klerk (Sale), Willie le Roux (Wasps), Vincent Koch and Schalk Brits (both Saracens) being brought back in from the cold.

I thought I was ready to play against England but the Stormers' medical staff still weren't budging so I had to watch Siya's first game as captain from my living room. Still, I was confident we'd do well in that series because we had a battle-hardened core of players and plenty of leaders. Apparently, Rassie had made it clear that the captain was mainly just the guy who runs out first and talks to the referee. That wasn't him trying to undermine Siya, it was him emphasising that we needed the whole leadership group mucking in, including guys like Duane, Beast and Handré, who has an unbelievable rugby brain, continually comes up with different ideas and makes a lot of calls on the field.

Siya was given a rapturous reception at Ellis Park, but other than that his introduction as captain couldn't have gone much worse. Jacques Nienaber had introduced a new defensive system because he wanted more line speed, and we kept getting our reads wrong, defending too narrow, and England just had to pass the ball over our heads to find space. Mike Brown scored after 3 minutes, Elliot Daly added a second 9 minutes later, and when Owen Farrell added a third after 16 minutes we already looked dead and buried.

When you're not in the squad you're just like any other fan: you don't really know what's happening on the field and you're thinking, *Oh shit, England are going to put 50 on us.* I also wondered what Siya said under the poles after their third try. I later found out that he asked a couple of the senior guys to speak up and I assume their response was, 'Let's stick to the plan, go harder and things will turn at some point.'

Some people think a leader asking for help is a sign of weakness but it's actually one of Siya's big strengths. Sometimes as a captain you don't know what to say, but if you've got players like Duane Vermeulen and Handré Pollard beside you in the trenches, you'd be a fool not to tap into their knowledge.

We scored four tries to lead at half-time, and it was Faf de Klerk who started the comeback, belying his diminutive stature to barge over from close range. Faf had been a very good player for the Lions and put in some fine performances for the Boks. But while people were excited to see him back in the fold, not a lot of people would have predicted how excellent and what a fan favourite he would become. But Faf had transformed into a different beast since moving to Sale, improving technically and becoming one of the most competitive 9's on the planet, a fizzing ball of energy who feared nothing and no one.

The higher you go in rugby, the more important 'dog' becomes. In fact, I'd go as far as to say that it's usually the team with more dog that wins. You either display more dog or you get pushed around, and that's especially true of scrum halves, who are often the smallest guys on the field.

Faf was the epitome of dog: the rougher a game got, the more he seemed to be enjoying it. Sometimes, he looked like he'd be up for fighting any man on the pitch. He also won a lot of penalties, not because he was dirty but because he wound opposition players up so much, without really meaning to.

Faf was always getting slapped and having his hair pulled, and England appear to particularly dislike him because he seems to have won more penalties against them than any other team. He put in a man-of-the-match performance in that first Test, and although England came back at us hard in the final stages, the guys hung on for a heartening 42–39 victory.

The second Test in Bloemfontein was Beast's 100th game and I watched it at home with a bunch of friends. Of all the guys in that squad, Beast probably had the most respect from the group. He didn't speak a lot, but when he did speak, everyone listened. He was also such a good friend, so it was sad for me not to be there for such a momentous occasion, and when the anthem struck up, I started crying. At least we won again, and as England slumped to a fifth straight defeat they were now in crisis instead of us.

England did beat us at Newlands, although the thing I remember best about that game is Faf driving back England eighthman Nathan Hughes, all 196 cm and 126 kg of him, and almost dumping him behind his own try line.

By the time of the 2018 Rugby Championship my left arm was still noticeably thinner than my right but I had enough power to return after nine months out. I'd been speaking to Siya quite a lot and hearing only good things about the new regime, but nothing could prepare me for my first proper sit-down team meeting with Rassie at Kings Park. For the previous few years, journalists and pundits had been imploring the Boks to develop a more sophisticated game – play more like the All Blacks, in other words – and here was Rassie saying physicality was the very essence of South African rugby; and rather than doing something different, he thought that we needed to double down.

As far as Rassie was concerned, we could spend lots of time working on other parts of the game and still lose more matches than we won, but if we focused on making our big rock more solid we'd win more games than we'd lose. Then, once we'd nailed the physical stuff, we could start thinking about adding bells and whistles. As you can imagine, all this talk of physicality was great to hear for us as players, and I left that meeting thinking, *This guy is the real deal.*

Rassie made it clear that he'd never select someone he didn't think was willing to put his body on the line for the Boks, and the training session that followed that meeting was savage, just players smashing into each other. That was the way it was going to be because that was the way Rassie thought we were most likely to win.

Before the Rugby Championship we had a pre-season camp in Stellenbosch. The Stormers guys arrived early because we'd failed to reach the Super Rugby play-offs, and Jacques Nienaber, who had been my defence coach at the Stormers for a couple of years, kept shouting at us on the training ground, 'You guys must work harder! You're 58 points behind New Zealand!' In the end, I couldn't help saying back, 'We didn't lose by 58, we lost by 57!'

Of course, I knew that one point didn't make any difference – 57 or 58, we were miles behind the All Blacks, at least on paper. That's why Jacques kept reminding us and why Rassie's big goal for 2018 was to beat them in New Zealand.

He'd been handed a six-year contract and his grand plan was to create the best team on the planet and win the World Cup in 2023. He wasn't thinking about the 2019 World Cup but he knew that if we could beat New Zealand in their own backyard we had it in us to beat any team, anywhere.

Rassie didn't do one-on-one meetings with players. Instead we'd turn up to a meeting early in the week and the team would be on the board. He'd go through it, explaining why such and such a player was starting, why such and such a player wasn't starting and maybe why he would be starting in two weeks' time. It was an open, honest way of doing things, preferable to explaining his reasoning to individual players behind closed doors, which can breed suspicion.

Rassie was very much the man in charge but he wasn't a dictator. He didn't want an environment where some players felt more important than others, he wanted everyone to feel equal. There was still a slight separation of older and younger guys but the younger guys weren't expected to sit in the corner and be quiet. If a younger player had an idea, even if he'd never played for the Boks before, he could suggest it to a coach before a meeting. Not only that, but the coaching staff would also investigate it to see if it had any merit. In theory, players were even allowed to tell Rassie if they thought something should change or the plan needed some improvements, although in practice most of the guys were too scared to say anything of the sort.

Rassie seemed comfortable and relaxed in a team environment but he was quite reserved away from it. You wouldn't see him wandering around the hotel before games, which made him seem slightly unknowable, and I could understand why some players were a bit intimidated by him.

But I think a head coach should be slightly mysterious – it's certainly better than trying to be one of the guys – and I found him approachable.

Some people thought Rassie was mad to slot me straight back into the starting line-up for our game against Argentina in Durban, but I think he knew how much the jersey meant to me and how hard I'd trained while I was injured and it was a blessed relief to be back in green and gold.

I lasted 80 minutes, which I don't think many people expected after being sidelined for nine months, and we beat the Pumas at a canter, despite not being at our best. But after I spent the lead-up to the return game in Mendoza trying to explain to the younger guys that they'd be a far tougher proposition on their own patch, they posted their biggest win against us, 32–19.

Argentina edged us in the scrum and were more physical at the breakdown, which must have been quite alarming for Rassie. We also butchered a host of try-scoring chances and were porous in defence, while our discipline was poor, including a yellow card for me (for a cynical ruck infringement). Rassie called our performance 'embarrassing' and 'terrible' in the post-match press conference but that was tame compared to what he called it in the next team meeting.

Proof that there was a place for creativity and flair in Rassie's regime was Cheslin Kolbe's addition to the squad for our games down under. I'd played with Cheslin for the Stormers and knew what a special player he was, ridiculously quick and elusive. But while he'd gone up a few gears since joining Toulouse, dazzling crowds with those dancing feet of his, he was only 171 cm and 75 kg, causing many to doubt if he was big enough to be a regular for the Boks.

I understood the concerns because he'd be going up against wingers such as Julian Savea of New Zealand and Australia's Israel Folau, guys who were 194 cm, more than 100 kg and tough as teak. But French club rugby is quite brutal, so Rassie asked Siya one day, 'Listen, do you think Cheslin would fit in with us?' And Siya, who's a good friend of Cheslin's, immediately said yes.

I've seen lots of unbelievably talented club players down the years, guys who could step through a defence, produce beautiful cross-kicks and exquisite offloads but whose fundamentals weren't up to scratch: they bailed out of tackles, they didn't clean a ruck out when they should, they kept turning the ball over. And even if fans and journalists were purring over some guy who was scoring tries for fun in Super Rugby, Rassie wouldn't consider him for the Springboks if his nuts and bolts weren't tight enough. But I soon realised that Cheslin was different. Yes, his highlights reel was longer than most – he had a wicked step and could kick and chase with the best of them – but he wasn't just a highlights reel player. Pound for pound, he was one of the most physical guys in the team; he didn't shirk his defensive duties; he tackled forwards backwards; and when he got held up in a tackle he didn't cough up the ball.

Rassie made six changes to his starting line-up for the game against the Wallabies in Brisbane but we still came up short, making it four losses in seven games since he took over. Newspapers were already talking about a crisis, with Rassie's chopping and changing coming in for a lot of criticism. What people didn't realise was that he wasn't mixing things up for the sake of it, there was science behind it. Rassie's aim was to build combinations and find out what worked best for the team and he was putting players in tough situations to find out whether they belonged at that level. If they didn't, he'd weed them out.

Rassie was probably pleased he hadn't publicly announced his season's goal to beat the All Blacks in New Zealand. People would have died laughing and the pressure would have been immense. As it was, while the players were quite relaxed in the lead-up to the game, we could feel the coaches' tension.

Everything had been staked on that one fixture. If we won, the players' belief in their own capabilities, as well as in Rassie and his staff, would blossom; if we lost, there was a chance that some players would start to lose faith in themselves.

That week had World Cup vibes because it felt like a must-win game. It was all part of Rassie's plan to pile on the pressure and see if we could handle it. He even decided to heap some extra stress on himself, telling the media he might get sacked if we lost. That was the favourite result with the bookmakers, which wasn't surprising given our recent form, the fact that we hadn't beaten the All Blacks in New Zealand since 2009 (and never at Wellington's 'Cake Tin' stadium), and their 15–game unbeaten streak in the competition.

I'm sure Rassie's nerves were jangling when we went 12–0 down after 15 minutes, courtesy of two typically incisive tries by New Zealand. But Aphiwe Dyantyi scampered over for our first score a few minutes later, then the All Blacks gifted us a present: Jordie Barrett took a quick line-out throw and the ball bounced into the hands of Willie le Roux, who dotted down next to the posts. Malcolm Marx added our third try before a Handré Pollard penalty made it 17–24 at half-time.

Cheslin, on as a replacement, scored from a razor-sharp interception just after the restart, and Handré's conversion extended our lead to 14 points. When Rieko Ioane pulled back a try for the All Blacks, I'm sure a lot of people watching thought a comeback was inevitable. Aphiwe finished off a great team move to make it 24–36, but two close-range tries chopped our lead to a couple of points with 5 minutes remaining. I was on the bench and barely able to look when Beauden Barrett had a seemingly straightforward conversion that would have levelled the scores, but he sliced it and hit a pole. And after soaking up some more late pressure, the final whistle went, one of our players booted the ball into touch and we celebrated wildly.

My most abiding memory from that night is Pieter-Steph du Toit sobbing, while players were kissing and hugging each other and smiling with relief. That's how much that win meant to all of us. Even if we'd lost every other game that year, beating the All Blacks in New Zealand would have made it a successful one. It was the turning point for the Boks. All the good things that have happened since flowed from that game. It gave the players the necessary belief and it got our fans behind us again, exemplified by a video that did the rounds on social media of an old guy jumping up and down in front of his TV and roaring, 'Go Bokke! Go Bokke!' Plus, it made the rest of the rugby world think, *Shit, they're back.*

Pieter-Steph was one of a few players Rassie inherited who were now playing to their full potential. He was 21 when he made his international debut against Wales in 2013. He played lock for the first few years, usually starting on the bench (there was some talk in the media that we'd eventually be the next Matfield and Botha), until Allister tried him out at flanker against England in 2016. Unfortunately, he made one or two defensive errors in quite a heavy defeat and journalists and pundits crucified Allister for playing him in the back row. But Pieter-Steph didn't make those mistakes because he was playing out of position; they were mistakes that anyone could have made.

Pieter-Steph started the 2017 season back on the bench as a replacement lock, then Allister decided to trust his gut and start him at No 7 against New Zealand in Cape Town, a game we lost by a point. I reckon he's since developed into the best No 7 South African rugby has seen.

Like Duane Vermeulen, Pieter-Steph rarely has an under-par game and always stars on the biggest occasions. He's a workhorse, never takes a backwards step and chases everything. Against New Zealand in Wellington, he made 28 tackles, many of them in the closing stages when Willie le Roux was in the sin-bin.

Our hard-fought win over Australia in Port Elizabeth on the 100th anniversary of Nelson Mandela's birth wasn't enough to stop New Zealand winning their sixth Rugby Championship title in seven years with a game to spare, but we still had plenty to prove against the All Blacks in Pretoria. If they beat us handily there would be a suspicion that our win in Wellington was a false dawn.

As it turned out, we played our best rugby so far under Rassie in the first 50-odd minutes, dominating New Zealand up front, starving them of possession and territory, and scoring two quick tries early in the second half to lead 23–6. Aaron Smith scored against the run of play, but when Cheslin went over for our fourth try we were 17 points ahead again with 20 minutes to go.

If it had been a boxing match, we'd have won almost every round. Unfortunately for us, the All Blacks were the rugby equivalent of Muhammad Ali. Having been stuck on the ropes for most of the game, they suddenly came to life and started landing stinging punches. First, Rieko Ioane went over in the corner after a slick passing move. Then, with 5 minutes remaining, Scott Barrett bulldozed over and Richie Mo'unga's conversion reduced our lead to five points. Suddenly, it was us reeling on the ropes, and with a minute to go Ardie Savea scored from close-range and Mo'unga kicked the winning conversion.

Rassie was gracious in defeat, telling the media, 'I can talk about all the things that we did wrong in the last 10 minutes, but what about the things they did right? Hell, what a team they are.' And while we were bitterly disappointed not to have held on, that was another big learning game for us.

People obviously focused on New Zealand's ruthless precision under pressure but I kept thinking about the chances we had to close the game and also a small lapse of concentration at the end cost us dearly. And what should have been another psychological blow against the All Blacks ended up being yet another win for them.

By 2018, southern hemisphere sides no longer travelled to Europe for the end-of-year internationals expecting to win every game. Their club competitions had become more professional; their players were learning from and competing against high-class southern hemisphere imports; they'd gradually got bigger, fitter, more athletic, more organised, better technically; and national sides were being led by experienced southern hemisphere coaches – Eddie Jones at England, Warren Gatland at Wales, Joe Schmidt at Ireland.

We won two and lost two of our four Test matches in Europe that season, which probably led some fans to think we hadn't improved much. But unlike the previous year, every game was tight.

We dominated England in the first half at Twickenham but couldn't make the most of our chances and allowed them to come back and edge us by a point (although we might have won it if Owen Farrell had been penalised for a late no-arms tackle on André Esterhuizen).

I injured my calf in that game and had to watch the rest of the tour from the sidelines, all the better to see that we were heading in the right direction. We trailed France 23–9 early in the second half but showed tremendous resilience to snatch victory at the death. Francois Louw stole the ball near our poles and we reeled off four penalties to touch before Bongi

Mbonambi peeled off a driving maul and dived over for the win in the 85th minute.

We were gritty if unspectacular in victory over Scotland in Edinburgh, and while Wales beat us for the fourth time in a row in Cardiff, they were on an impressive winning streak and there wasn't much in it.

No doubt about it, that result against New Zealand in Wellington had changed everything. Every game we'd played since then we'd either won or been in with a shout. And Rassie was only just getting started.

7

RASSIE UNITED

While I was on South Africa's end of year tour in 2018, negotiations began with Toulon to join after the World Cup. I don't think the Stormers' hierarchy were happy that Toulon owner Mourad Boudjellal leaked the news to the press but I think they saw it coming.

A move to Toulon was on the cards after the 2015 World Cup – they contacted my agent and said they wanted me as a replacement for the recently retired Bakkies Botha – but it didn't feel like the right time. Back then, signing for a European club was something South African internationals did towards the end of their careers and I'd had only one World Cup cycle with the Boks. But I'd be turning 28 in 2019, when I'd have been at the Stormers for eight years, so it felt like the right moment had finally come.

I have mixed feelings about my time with the Stormers. It was a dream come true to play so many times for my home-town team but we didn't achieve anything like as much as we should have done. I'll never forget Jean de Villiers saying to me, 'If you win a trophy in your first season, you assume that it will always be like that. But you should make the most of any opportunity you get because it might be your last.' He was bang on, because after winning the Currie Cup in 2012 the trophies dried up.

The Stormers reached the semi-finals of Super Rugby that same year but we didn't reach the last four again during my time in Cape Town. That's why I tell my younger Springbok teammates now, 'I'm not saying it won't always be like this, but if you take it for granted, think you've arrived and stop working as hard, you'll start losing more games and the trophies will dry up.'

Me and my old Stormers teammates still talk about why we didn't achieve more. We had some unbelievably good players during that time: De Villiers, Habana, Burger, Kolisi, Vermeulen, Pieter-Steph du Toit, Damian de Allende, Frans Malherbe, Steven Kitshoff, Bongi Mbonambi, Cheslin Kolbe, Andries Bekker, Gio Aplon, Tiaan Liebenberg, most of them past or future World Cup winners. And while we had to deal with lots of injuries and untimely departures, maybe some of the young guys who later became Springbok greats didn't realise how good they were and how much potential we had as a team. No doubt about it, one Super Rugby semi-final in eight years was a poor return for the talent we had in our ranks.

As for my move to Toulon, of course money was a consideration. Southern hemisphere players who move to Europe often talk about wanting to experience a new culture and challenge themselves in a different rugby environment, but rugby is a business. And ask anyone, whatever line of work they're in, if they'd like to do the same job in another part of the world for almost twice as much money, and they're highly likely to give it serious thought.

You also have to bear in mind that top rugby players don't earn anything like as much as top footballers, and while a footballer going from £100,000 a week to £200,000 (R2.4 million to R4.8 million) will notice almost no difference in their standard of living, for a rugby player a chance to double his income is potentially life-changing, especially post-retirement. Playing for the Stormers in Super Rugby was the ultimate for me and I was surrounded by my nearest and dearest in Cape Town, but the three-year contract Toulon offered me was something I couldn't refuse.

I must have travelled around the world a hundred times by then but I hadn't seen much of it. Mostly, the plane would touch down, I'd head straight to a hotel, I'd train, play a game, then fly home again. So if I was going to live elsewhere for a couple of years I wanted it to be somewhere to write home about. That's why I phoned Bakkies, Bryan and Duane, who had all played for Toulon, before signing on the dotted line.

They assured me that Toulon was a proper rugby town with a nice stadium and passionate fans. Plus – and this was the kicker – they said it would be impossible to find anywhere else in Europe with better weather. (I don't like the cold, never have done, and playing for Toulon on the French Riviera sounded more agreeable than playing in the UK or Ireland, where many of my teammates play, none of whom have ever said anything good about the weather.) They also said the language barrier could be difficult and that the French were slightly set in their ways, but if I could cope with that I'd be fine.

I wasn't joining Toulon specifically to win trophies because I thought the Stormers had the potential to do that and I'd always wanted to win a Super Rugby title, but I did look at the squad and think it was a possibility. Toulon already had Julian Savea and Liam Messam, former New Zealand sevens star Bryce Heem, plus Italy legend Sergio Parisse, former Bok prop Marcel van der Merwe, Georgia loose forward Mamuka Gorgodze and a handful of past and present French internationals. (Nehe Milner-Skudder was set to join at the same time as me before an injury scuppered the move.)

I was desperate to finish my time at the Stormers on a high but we suffered a raft of injuries in pre-season, shipped 40 points to the Bulls in our Super Rugby opener and were never able to get on a roll. By April, journalists were already calling for Robbie Fleck's head, while I injured my hand playing against the Lions in the third-last game of the regular season: they took a shortened line-out, someone hit it up in midfield, they came back on a reverse play, Malcolm Marx ran a hard line with Kwagga Smith out the back, and somehow my hand got stuck between Malcolm and Kwagga when he received the ball. On the following Monday I was told it was broken, meaning I was in a race against time to make the Boks' Rugby Championship opener against Australia.

We were still in with a chance of making the play-offs heading into our final conference game against the Sharks at

Newlands, but I could only watch from the sidelines (along-side Siya, Pieter-Steph and a host of other crocked players) as my Bok teammate Lukhanyo Am scored the match-winning try in the 82nd minute. That meant the Sharks advanced to the quarter-finals at our expense and my final season with the Stormers ended in more disappointment.

My hand was still in a splint by the time the Rugby Championship came around but I was fit enough to play in our opener against Australia in Johannesburg. In the absence of Siya, who had been ruled out of the tournament with a knee injury, I was named captain for that game, Rassie having already sent what was effectively an A team to Wellington (albeit only 13 players) to prepare for the following weekend's game against the All Blacks.

Some South African journalists and fans thought that was a foolhardy move, given how few games he had to fine-tune things before the World Cup, while some Australian journalists and fans thought it was disrespectful. But I looked at my team-mates and thought, *Flip, this is a pretty good side.* The starting pack included me, Beast, Bongi, Pieter-Steph, Trevor Nyakane, Lood de Jager and Francois Louw, five of whom would start the World Cup final a few months later. Our backline, which included Sharks wing Makazole Mapimpi, Jesse Kriel, Andre Esterhuizen, Frans Steyn, Sbu Nkosi and Stormers scrum half Herschel Jantjies, who had come from seemingly nowhere, wasn't bad either.

When asked at the pre-match press conference if I was captaining a second-string Springbok side, I answered emphatically no. But I was singing a different tune behind the scenes. I said to the guys, 'Listen, the media thinks we're just a B team, the Australian team thinks we're just a B team, and we are a B team because there's another Springbok team already in New Zealand. Rassie might be telling you how important this game against Australia is but you're not the first choice. What are you going to do to prove him wrong?'

I don't know if that was a deliberate ploy by Rassie to motivate those players, get them to bare their teeth and prove that they shouldn't be anywhere near the B team, but it worked. There was definitely a bit of anger among the ranks in the build-up and we thumped the Wallabies 35–17. And while Rassie told the media that it 'wasn't close to a world-class performance' and that we'd been a bit lucky to win by as much as we did, he must have been delighted with some of the players, especially Herschel, who scored two tries on debut.

Herschel had been in the WP Currie Cup team just a couple of seasons earlier and my first impression of him was that he was a bit cocky, but once I got to know him we became good friends.

He hailed from the village of Kylemore outside Stellenbosch, which he's since described as 'not the worst place to grow up but also not the best'. There was quite a lot of rugby talent in and around Kylemore when Herschel was a kid but a lot of it was ruined by bad decisions. Herschel was lucky enough to have supportive parents who kept him on the straight and narrow, as well as a caring primary school teacher who recommended him to the exclusive Paul Roos Gymnasium in

Stellenbosch, a school which has produced more Springboks than any other and was wise enough to offer him a scholarship.

I can't imagine how small Herschel must have been back then because he was only 166 cm and 74 kg when he made his Bok debut, but he was obviously an extraordinary talent. Herschel starred for Paul Roos and at Craven Week before graduating to the senior WP set-up. And now, aged just 23, he was setting tongues wagging wearing the green and gold.

South African media outlets were running more and more of these kinds of fairy-tale stories, mainly because more and more players of colour were being selected for the Springboks.

As well as Herschel there was Siya, whose remarkable journey from Zwide to the Bok captaincy has been well documented; there was also Bongi, who grew up playing rugby with a makeshift ball made of an orange sack stuffed with newspapers on the streets of Bohlokong in the Free State; and there was Makazole Mapimpi, who was born in the desperately poor Eastern Cape village of Tsholomnqa. The late commentator Kaunda Ntunja once described Mapimpi as the player who had come from the 'most hopeless situation in the history of Springbok rugby', but no one doubted that he was as important a part of the South African story as anyone.

And I shouldn't forget Cheslin, who grew up in Kraaifontein north of Cape Town and made it as a Springbok despite almost everyone thinking he was too small for professional rugby. Cheslin has a heart as big as a lion and has never been afraid of running into a channel full of bony knees, sharp hips and swinging arms. I think a lot of people assumed he'd be found out defensively in his second season with the Boks and fade from the international scene, but that didn't happen. Instead, little kids from every conceivable background watched Cheslin tie defenders in knots and tackle guys almost twice his size and thought, *If he can do it, maybe I can, too*. He changed rugby for little guys more than anyone, before or since.

While the growing number of players of colour in the Bok set-up had nothing to do with quotas and positive discrimination on Rassie's part – he was going to pick the best talent whatever colour they happened to be – he was more open about transformation than any previous coach I'd played under.

Rassie had been in charge for just a few games when he sat us all down and brought up what he referred to as 'the elephant in the room'. He explained that there were people in South Africa who didn't like transformation but that we needed to embrace it.

'In this team,' he said, 'transformation is about more than certain guys playing because they're black or white, it's about accepting and respecting each other's cultures.' Because if we did that, he said, people would feel comfortable being themselves and play better on the weekend. As such, we'd be more likely to win together, and the more we won together, the quicker we'd transform the mindset of the South African public.

Rassie had a set of rules that every player had to abide by

but he also knew he couldn't treat everyone the same. An Afrikaner who went to a farm school in the Boland is likely to be different from a black guy who grew up in a township or someone from a wealthy family who attended an exclusive school in Cape Town. The coaching staff understood that they had to be empathetic to individual needs within a framework that applied to everyone.

Rassie homed in on the fact that black players liked to sing and dance before a game while white players preferred peace and quiet (in South African rugby, you don't really get guys who scream, shout and headbutt walls). He'd noticed that some players were irritated by the singing and dancing and realised that a compromise needed to be struck.

'If you want to sing and dance before a game,' he said, 'you can do that. And if you want to sit quietly and not talk to anyone, you can do that as well. That means guys who want to sing and dance might have to tone it down, and certainly will need to give guys who want peace and quiet some space; and guys who want peace and quiet mustn't get grumpy about guys singing and dancing and tell them to shut up. It can't be like the old days when the changing room was silent before a game or certain songs were played. We are a transformed team, different players come from different cultures and have different beliefs, and we must find a way that works for everyone.'

I hadn't really appreciated that singing and dancing was how black players got themselves up for a game. They weren't singing and dancing for the sake of it, they were doing it because it was deeply entrenched in their culture. As crazy as it sounds to some white people, black tribes would sing and dance before going into battle, and sport is a modern, less brutal version of war. As such, if they didn't sing and dance before a game, they'd be more likely to play badly. Nowadays, if I think Siya seems a bit subdued while leading us through the tunnel before a game, I'll say to him, 'Why are you singing so quietly?' At the same time, black players now understand that white players need some peace and quiet to focus.

Before Rassie, if transformation was discussed by coaches at all it was whispered about behind closed doors, presumably because they feared it would cause divisions. But Rassie wasn't afraid to mention it. For example, before we played New Zealand at Newlands in 2024, he asked Deon Davids to chat to the team about why so many coloured people still supported the All Blacks against the Boks.

All Black great Mils Muliaina has described the two Test matches he played against the Boks at Newlands as 'more like home games', with thousands of coloured fans decked out in black cheering All Black tries and even belting out the New Zealand national anthem. A lot of white South Africans simply dismissed those fans as stupid – 'They live in South Africa, they're South Africans, and apartheid ended 30 years ago' – but Deon explained why their support for the All Blacks made a lot of sense, because to them the Boks remained a potent symbol of apartheid South Africa.

The first player of colour to be selected for the Boks was

Errol Tobias in 1981 and only a few more players of colour were selected before readmission just over 10 years later. For many years, the All Blacks toured South Africa without Maori players, at the request of South African politicians, and when Maoris did start coming, many in the coloured community adopted them as heroes – comrades in the struggle against apartheid – while hating the Boks even more for denying such opportunities to their own people of colour. Whenever New Zealand played the Boks in Cape Town or Port Elizabeth, coloured fans, always penned into one corner of the ground, celebrated every All Black try wildly because they viewed it as a blow against their daily oppression.

Given the history, it's naive of white South Africans to think people of colour would suddenly start supporting the Boks once apartheid ended. It takes time to build trust and make the formerly disenfranchised and oppressed feel not only as if they're part of the project but also integral to it. But Rassie firmly believed we could transform people's opinions, and that one day in the not-too-distant future the Boks would truly be a team for all South Africans, whether white farmers or black kids from a township.

*　　*　　*

Pieter-Steph and I were the only two forwards to retain our places in the starting line-up for the game against the All Blacks in Wellington, and Mapimpi was the only back. Duane was named captain, while Herschel and Frans Steyn, a World Cup winner in 2007 who had played three Test matches in seven years and none since 2017, were on the bench, proving that Rassie put as much store in experience as youthful vim and vigour.

The game in Wellington was a tight one, and with a couple of minutes to go, we were down 16–9. But the players were aware that if we snatched a draw against the All Blacks and followed it up with a bonus point win against Argentina, we could win the tournament. So instead of kicking it out for a losing bonus point, our replacement front row of Beast, Bongi and Trevor Nyakane won a scrum penalty, the ball was shipped wide to Cheslin, and he chipped ahead for Herschel to gather and score in the corner.

Herschel was understandably elated but the first thing I said to him jokingly after the game was, 'Why didn't you touch the ball down under the poles?' He wasn't to know that he didn't have any defenders close to him. It was also immaterial because Handré stepped up and slotted the extras with the sound of the full-time siren ringing in his ears.

I've always joked with Handré that he's more likely to miss a straightforward kick in a relatively unimportant club game than one from a fiendish angle in the final seconds of a massive Test match. That's the sort of guy he is, someone who performs better the more pressure he's under.

I've played with guys who preferred to kick the ball to the corner late in games rather than go for goal from out wide, but Handré would have a go from almost anywhere. It's so reassuring to have a kicker like that in your ranks, especially in knockout games, which often come down to a point or two.

Every World Cup-winning team had had a dead-eyed goal-kicker – Dan Carter in 2015 and 2011, Percy Montgomery in 2007, Jonny Wilkinson in 2003, Matt Burke in 1999, Joel Stransky in 1995, Michael Lynagh in 1991, Grant Fox in 1987 – and I was convinced that Handré could be our man.

The guys jokingly called him KP, short for Kingpin. Some called him the GOAT, others called him Ice Man. If I ever had to choose someone to kick a goal from anywhere on the field to save my life, I'd pick him in a heartbeat.

We thought we'd need a bonus-point victory against Argentina in Salta to claim our first Rugby Championship title since 2009 (there were only three rounds that year because of the World Cup). However, when Australia pumped the All Blacks 47–26 in Perth, a result that no one saw coming (although the All Blacks did have a player sent off in the first half, and the Wallabies had a habit of producing fine performances against them out of nowhere), we only had to win. As it was, we got the bonus point anyway, scoring five tries to one in a 46–13 victory.

Success in professional sport often comes down to timing, and suddenly I was thinking, *Hang on a minute, we're looking pretty good here. We've won and drawn our last two games against the All Blacks in New Zealand and they've just suffered a record defeat at the hands of Australia. Maybe the pendulum is swinging in our direction at exactly the right moment.*

New Zealand had lost a lot of great players since winning their second World Cup in a row in 2015 and of the starting line-up for the 2015 final, only seven were still around, and trying to replace Dan Carter, Ma'a Nonu, Conrad Smith, Richie McCaw and Jerome Kaino was always going to be a tall order.

So much has been said about the greatness of the first four of those names, but I'm not sure people understood how important Kaino was to that team. Off the field he was a lovely guy, one of those opponents who would always come to our changing room for a chat, win or lose. On the field he was a bruiser, the kind of player who would take it upon himself to stop the other team's hardest guy. And when things got tough he'd always put his hand up and say, 'Give the ball to me, I'll get us going forward again.'

I'm sure it wasn't just the Boks who saw the All Blacks slipping up. They hadn't lost many games over the previous couple of years but Ireland had beaten them in Dublin, to add to their victory over them in Chicago, England had come close to beating them at Twickenham, and Argentina had done the same in Buenos Aires. They were no longer miles ahead of the pack and a knockout game against them at a World Cup looked a bit less of a daunting task than playing them the two previous tournaments.

One of the keys to our improvement under Rassie was the addition to his coaching staff of Welshman Aled Walters as head of athletic performance.

Like Jacques Nienaber, Aled had been with Rassie at Munster, and when he joined the Springbok set-up in 2018 he didn't think we were fit enough. I wasn't surprised he thought

Goodwood Park Primary School, where my rugby journey began. My dad was the coach and I am the lucky one in the middle holding the ball. The perks when your dad is the coach.

Having not even made Tygerberg High School's under–16s 'A' team (I wasn't even a forward back then), I finally had a growth spurt and became a first-team regular.

Siya and I became firm friends playing for Western Province's under–19s – he was always laughing and joking, the life and soul of the changing room.

I didn't study at the University of Cape Town, but I was part of the first Ikeys team to win the Varsity Cup, beating the University of Pretoria in the final.

I loved my time playing for NTT Docomo in Osaka – it helped that I had a few South African pals, including Springbok teammate Handré Pollard.

I enjoyed my time playing for Toulon in France, even though things did turn a bit sour. I didn't have the success I wanted on the pitch, but I made some friends for life.

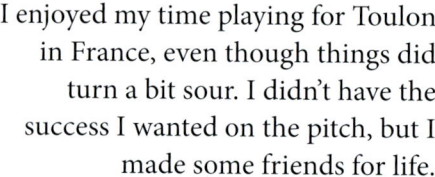

Siya and I spent many joyous years playing together for the Stormers – I just wish we'd managed to win some silverware.

Making my debut for the Springboks, against England in Durban on 9 June 2012 – it was an emotional day, we won 22-17.

Losing to Japan at the 2015 World Cup was painful, but narrowly losing to New Zealand in the semi-finals was worse – I never wanted to feel like that again.

My 50th Test match, against Australia in Brisbane in 2016 – my jersey got torn and we lost unfortunately!

Leading the team out against France in 2017 – being asked to captain the Boks was one of the greatest moments of my life.

Playing against the Lions in 2021 was a dream come true – Covid-19 made it a strange series, what with the lack of fans, but we recovered from losing the 1st Test match to win the series 2-1.

Winning my 100th international cap against Wales in Cape Town was a very emotional day – what made it even more special was my fiancée, Anlia, singing the national anthem.

(*From left to right*) Ryen, me, Mum and Dad – while rugby is very dear to me, I've always regarded family as the most important thing in life.

My brother Ryen is one of my biggest supporters – when the Boks won the 2019 World Cup, he felt like he was in my shoes.

Locks United – (*from left to right*) Franco Mostert, Lood de Jager, RG Snyman and me. We had a lot of fun together over the next week or so.

Anlia and I with our parents at our engagement party.

I had absolutely no doubt that I was marrying my soulmate.

On our wedding day, Dad presented our rings in a shell filled with sand from Plage de l'Almanarre, where I asked Anlia to be my girlfriend and my wife.

My life has been full of highlights, on and off the rugby field, but I'm sure nothing will ever top marrying Anlia, along with having kids.

We had to dig even deeper to hang on to our World Cup crown in France in 2023, winning our three knockout games by a point – this time Franco, RG and I were joined in the celebrations by Jean Kleyn and Marvin Orie.

As the bus drove through the township of Khayelitsha, I said to Siya, 'You know what, my brother, right here is transformation.'

A selfie with probably the best three trophies you can win as a Springbok (*from left*: British & Irish Lions, World Cup and Rugby Championship).

More than a decade after winning my first club trophy with Western Province, I finally won my second with the Sharks, beating Gloucester in the European Challenge Cup final in London.

Becoming the most capped Springbok in history, with my family by my side, made it such a special day.

On 16 January 2024, Anlia and I welcomed Elizebedi, soon shortened to Liv, into the world. The love I feel for both of them is indescribable.

that because if you've conceded 155 points in three games against the All Blacks, clearly nothing is up to scratch.

Rassie had tasked our forwards coach, Matt Proudfoot, one of only a couple of survivors from Allister Coetzee's regime, with transforming our scrum into a mighty weapon that could consistently win the team penalties, territory and points. We had the raw materials to achieve that – lots of big, strong forwards – but previously they hadn't been fit enough to dominate for long. However, with Aled whipping us into the best shape we'd ever been in, that changed in 2018. Aled's fitness sessions were brutal, as were Matt's scrumming sessions, and by the time of the 2019 Rugby Championship we were confident in our ability as a pack.

The policy of rotating the starting pack wasn't immediately popular with everyone – every player wants to start Test matches – but Rassie convinced us that naming someone on the bench didn't necessarily mean he was inferior to the guy starting ahead of him; it might mean that Rassie thought he'd inflict more damage later in the game, when the opposition was flagging, or that he'd be more effective against a specific opposition player at a particular stage of the game.

As the World Cup approached, it became clear that all those scrumming wars on the training ground had paid off and we had two or more players in almost every forward position who could do an equally good job, whether they were in the starting XV or on the bench. Furthermore, with 30 minutes remaining Rassie had the luxury of introducing an entirely new front row that was just as destructive as the old front row – a nightmare for the opposition.

When Rassie first selected a 6–2 forwards-backs split on the bench, it made sense to me. The forwards do the scrumming, mauling and most of the tackling, and a 6–2 split meant that only two of the starting forwards would have to play 80 minutes.

I'm sure some of the backs weren't as convinced by the tactic, because if you've got only two of them on the bench they're going to have to cover a few positions, which rules out certain players. But as far as I was concerned, rugby was war in miniature and a good leader selected his best soldiers to win specific battles. If that meant specialist fly-halves, centres or wingers missing out – which it did – so be it.

Did I think we'd win the World Cup? We'd prepared as well as we could have and we certainly had a better chance of winning it than in 2015. Then one night I walked into a nightclub and my world got turned upside down.

It was my last weekend in the beautiful coastal town of Langebaan before I was due to rejoin the squad and fly to Japan. I invited lots of friends and family to the yacht club for a braai and a couple of drinks. When I walked into the club-house, a guy sitting on the other side of the bar shouted at the top of his voice, 'Hey, Etzebeth, take off your cap!' I almost always wear a cap, but I would have removed it if I'd known it was a club rule. And I wasn't going to put up with some stranger being rude to me.

So I walked over to this guy and said, 'Who do you think you are? I'm not your child. If the club rule is no caps, come over and tell me politely rather than screaming at me from across the room.' It wasn't that I thought he shouldn't be speaking to me in that way because I was somehow important, but that he shouldn't be speaking to anyone in that way.

A couple of people I was with got very agitated but I calmed them down and got them out of the clubhouse before things turned nasty. And from the yacht club we went to a nightclub called Watergat, which means watering hole.

The incident at the yacht club was soon forgotten and we had a fun night – until it was time to leave. Seeing that a fight was happening outside, I decided to wait until things had settled down. But as I was walking to my car someone almost reversed into me. I shouted at him to be more careful, and as he drove off he swore at me. A group of friends saw the incident, and fired back with swearing, before a few coloured people surrounded the group. They probably knew the guy who was in the car, I'm not sure. My brother and I stepped in to make sure the situation wouldn't escalate any further. Things calmed down, but as I was driving out of the car park towards the traffic circle, something hit my car – a brick, I thought – so I circled back, lowered my window and said, 'Who the fuck threw that?'

It was a brand new car so I was understandably upset, and now we had a bit of a situation. I parked my car and climbed out to assess the damage, and while that was going on, my brother, cousin and friends, who were already halfway home, had realised I wasn't travelling behind them and turned around to find out what had happened to me. By the time they returned, a whole load of club-goers had been drawn to the commotion and there were so many people – most of whom we didn't know – that they probably just thought it would be fun to join in on the action. And suddenly, fights started breaking out all over the car park. I ran after my brother, to stop him from doing something stupid and make sure nothing bad happened to him, and we eventually managed to extricate ourselves from the situation, but as we were making our way to our cars, another missile – this time definitely a brick – went whistling past my friends' heads. That was our cue to get the hell out of Dodge.

The following morning, my brother knocked on my bedroom door. The first thing he said to me was, 'There's massive *kak* from last night.' Then he showed me a picture on social media: it was of a guy with a bleeding face and the caption, 'Etzebeth you racist fuck. You're gonna go to jail.' That wasn't the most pleasant wake-up call, and things got worse from there.

Another video emerged of the disagreement at the yacht club, with the poster claiming I'd used a racist slur. That made no sense at all. First, there were only white people in the club and the video showed me reasoning with friends and family when they took exception to the guy calling me out, in front of everyone, for my cap. Second, I never use racist slurs. It's simply not in my nature, no matter how angry I get. But this being South Africa, where race is a sensitive issue, I knew there was going to be trouble.

Rassie called that afternoon, asking if I'd done anything untoward. Even though I was innocent I feared he was going to say, 'Listen, we need to focus on winning the World Cup, we've decided not to take you.' But when I told him what had happened – that there had been a disagreement in the car park, missiles thrown, a few scuffles – and that I'd done nothing wrong, Rassie said he believed me. The entire conversation must have lasted less than a minute. Unfortunately, others thought they could benefit from the situation.

Some of the media reports were wild – they even said that I pointed a gun at a mother and child and assaulted a guy with it – and I had to put out a statement saying I hadn't done anything that I was accused of. (When the police came to my house in Blouberg to take away my gun for forensic testing, I was happy to hand it over because I knew it had been locked in a safe on the night in question.)

Then, a couple of days after the incident I heard that four people – who soon became known as the 'Langebaan Four' – were seeking compensation from me of more than R1 million and that they'd be represented by the South African Human Rights Commission (SAHRC). It also came out that the SAHRC legal chief had told a public meeting in Langebaan that I'd 'got away with murder'. So much for being innocent until proven guilty.

A few attention seekers were marching on the streets of Langebaan, calling for my conviction. That was tough because I loved that town so much. Meanwhile, journalists were demanding that I be axed from the Springbok squad and former Bok head coach Peter de Villiers said I shouldn't be anywhere near the team. I was upset about that because he was a big figure in South African rugby and didn't even know me. I saw him a few years later in Port Elizabeth, and while I wasn't planning to speak to him he approached me and apologised. I told him, 'Coach, you don't know what sort of person I am so how could you say what you did?' There wasn't much he could say to that.

That was a tough time for my family, especially my mom, who was active on social media and could see all the awful things people were saying about me. All I could do was tell them not to worry too much because I was innocent.

But that night in Langebaan definitely haunted me for a while. Most of the locals knew I did nothing wrong, but there will always be some that won't believe my innocence. In response, all I can say is that it was a crazy night, people did get beaten up (there were photos of it on social media), there was racism (I also heard it) and if I could have my time again, I would have just driven away when my car got hit. But I never assaulted anyone, and I'd never use racial slurs.

I didn't speak to any of my teammates about it, probably because none of us thought it necessary. I wasn't some isolated, bigoted white guy who never mixed with people of colour – my three best friends in the Bok team were Siya, Beast and Cheslin, none of whom are white. Still, it was a relief when I finally boarded the plane and set off for Japan. With Rassie in charge, we felt united.

8

COMPLETING RUGBY

We were the first team to arrive in Japan because our final warm-up game was against the hosts in Kumagaya. When we pitched up at our hotel there was a massive TV screen in the lobby next to the lifts showing their winning try against us in 2015 – over and over again. They obviously thought we needed reminding of that day, not realising that we'd never forget it for as long as we lived. And it was fair enough, especially as the welcome was generally magnificent. I can't think of a country that does hospitality better than Japan.

Not that I had much time to immerse myself in the culture. We got one day off each week, and while some of my team-mates played golf or visited the sights, I only really left the hotel for lunch and dinner and a bit of sightseeing. I've never understood how people can play 18 holes two days before a Test match, but they would say it allows them to switch off from rugby. Also, most of them hit the ball straight down the middle of the fairway, while my round of golf would involve a lot of hitting into the rough and twice as many steps.

Some training sessions we'd train in a 10,000-seat stadium

which would be packed to the rafters. I'd played matches in front of fewer fans in Super Rugby. We'd mostly practise defence so that we didn't give anything away in attack.

It was nice to beat Japan in Kumagaya, especially for the guys who played in the Miracle of Brighton, and everyone came through it relatively unscathed. We then had two weeks to prepare for our World Cup opener against New Zealand in Yokohama, which would probably decide who topped the pool (although with Brighton in mind and Rassie in charge we were going to prepare for Namibia, Italy and Canada just as thoroughly as we prepared for the All Blacks).

Before we left South Africa, Rassie told us, 'For you to win the World Cup you're going to have to win four of your five big games and make sure you win the last three of those games.' That was his way of saying that while we obviously wanted to beat New Zealand in the pool, it wasn't over if we didn't (even if no team before then had lost a pool game and gone on to win the trophy).

There was a bit of controversy in the build-up to our game against the All Blacks, with Rassie telling the media it was 'a well-known fact' that tight decisions often went their way. That was interpreted as Rassie trying to put pressure on French referee Jérôme Garcès, who had overseen five Bok defeats against them, including the 2015 semi-final, and earned him a rebuke from All Blacks head coach Steve Hansen.

We suffocated the life out of them in the first quarter, Faf's pinpoint box-kicking proving particularly effective, but one mistake allowed them to gain a foothold: we spilled a kick, the

All Blacks came flooding forward, and from the next recycle Beauden Barrett hit the line and offloaded to George Bridge, who went over next to the poles.

A couple of minutes later, Dane Coles – their hooker – found Anton Lienert-Brown with an overhead basketball pass, Lienert-Brown stepped past a couple of defenders, then Scott Barrett appeared on his shoulder and touched down unopposed. That was classic All Blacks, forwards and backs blending to devastating effect. But stunned as we were we didn't buckle, as we might have done a couple of years earlier.

A converted Pieter-Steph try and a monster Handré Pollard drop goal cut the deficit to four points with 20 minutes remaining and it looked like the comeback was on, especially since Cheslin was finding more gaps as their defenders tired. Alas, their set piece held firm and they killed us off with two late penalties.

Even so, the changing room afterwards wasn't a scene of devastation, and at Monday's match review errors were pointed out and fixes were agreed. Then it was time to start analysing our next opponents, Namibia, in granular detail – how they kicked off, how they attacked, how they defended, how they did absolutely everything – exactly as we'd analysed the All Blacks.

There was a poignant moment after the game that left some of us close to tears. Before the tournament, someone had the idea of having photos of loved ones superimposed on each players' number, and we were asked to send in six each. At the jersey presentation, some guys quickly realised that while most of us had photos of parents, siblings, children, close friends and mentors on our numbers, Mapimpi had six different photos of himself.

People thought that maybe he hadn't understood what they wanted. And at the post-match fines meeting Francois Louw stood up and proposed that Mapimpi be convicted of fancying himself too much. It was classic rugby banter and done in a light-hearted way, but things were about to get a bit awkward. It's always the case that the accused get to defend themselves, and when Mapimpi got to his feet and was asked, 'How do you plead?' he explained that he only had photos of himself because he didn't have any family left. Nobody was laughing any more and Francois was mortified. He paid the fine himself, in the form of a downed beer, and couldn't stop apologising to Mapimpi. Talk about a sobering moment.

I don't think many of Mapimpi's teammates knew his story before then, but he's since become a guy I have the utmost respect for because of where he's come from and what he's achieved. He's a Springbok great and a Springbok warrior with whom I'd go to war any day. Lots of people think their life has been hard but Mapimpi's life has been one of genuine struggle. He's a great example to everyone – not just black kids in townships – of what can be achieved through belief, hard work and having good people pulling for you. He never complains, he's never not in top shape, he always gives 100 per cent to the team and he motivates me to keep pushing.

I've never told Mapimpi how much I think of him – elite

rugby is a macho environment and you don't want to come across as soft – but I have told one or two other guys what he means to me. I reckon if we were more forthcoming about our feelings for our teammates, as long as they are positive, it might spur them to even greater heights.

We ran in nine tries against Namibia in Toyota, with only two players who started the New Zealand game and Schalk Brits captaining the team from the back row, rather than his usual position of hooker. Rassie mixed things up again for our game against Italy, selecting Beast, Bongi and Lood de Jager – who wasn't even on the bench against the All Blacks – to start. He selected me to start, too, even though he knew some people back home wanted me out of the team.

Confirmation that the SAHRC was going to initiate legal proceedings against me was all over the media and I was getting messages the whole time, asking me to pay lawyers' fees or linking to articles calling for me to be sent home (one story claimed the gun I'd offered up for forensic testing had been used to pistol-whip two men).

I didn't know what Rassie was thinking but I'd have understood if he'd taken me aside and said, 'Sorry, Eben, but your presence is too much of a disruption for the team.' Some coaches would have buckled under the pressure, even if they thought I was innocent, because race is such a sensitive issue in South Africa and the team is more important than any individual. But Rassie's attitude was, 'He didn't do anything wrong, why would I punish him?' I'll always be grateful to him for that because I'm not sure I'd ever have got over watching the Boks play in that World Cup from my living room.

One of Rassie's favourite phrases was 'We need to physically fuck the opposition up!' which perfectly captured the soul of South African rugby. We scrummed hard, we mauled hard, we tackled hard, we ran hard. If people didn't like it we didn't care, and when we got it bang on it was extremely effective. And against Italy we got things absolutely bang on.

The guys played angry that day, producing one of the best Springbok pack performances of my career (one journalist described it as 'spine-chilling', while Italy head coach Conor O'Shea said we might be the most powerful team ever to take to a rugby field). Beast saw off two tight heads in the first 18 minutes, and while that meant we had to go to uncontested scrums we just thought, *Well, if we can't scrum them off the park, we'll maul them off the park instead.* And while some in the media bemoaned what they perceived as an over-reliance on kicking and physicality, Cheslin pulled plenty of rabbits from his hat and we scored some eye-catching tries.

Sadly, our excellent 49–3 victory was overshadowed by more controversy. After the final whistle, TV footage showed Mapimpi walking over to a group of white players in a huddle and the players shooing him away. Soon, the clip was all over social media and some people decided it was evidence that racism was alive and well in the Springbok team, without understanding the context.

The guys in the huddle were what Francois Louw had dubbed the 'Bomb Squad', the six forwards and two backs who had been introduced from the bench in the second half. Francois came up with the nickname as a way of making the guys who weren't in the starting XV feel different from just a normal bench, to the extent that some players almost preferred being part of the Bomb Squad (a couple of the guys got Bomb Squad tattoos after the World Cup, that's what it meant to them). Francois became quite protective of the brand he'd created, which is why Mapimpi was told, 'No, this is the Bomb Squad', and while it just so happened that the Bomb Squad consisted of seven white guys and one coloured guy that day, it quite easily could have consisted of four white guys and four black guys, in which case there wouldn't have been any controversy.

That whole situation was very frustrating. Presumably, people were looking to destabilise the team because they wanted us to fail. These were clearly people with no joy in their lives, trying to find some by taking it from others. Still, I thought it would soon blow over, simply because it was so stupid. But our media manager decided that if we remained silent other people would fill the vacuum with more lies. So he put out a statement and poor Mapimpi, who isn't a fan of speaking publicly, felt the need to record a video for social media, denying that he had been the victim of racism and explaining the concept of the Bomb Squad, which was the first time the term had been heard outside the Springbok camp.

If a movie were ever made of that World Cup campaign, the writer would probably make a big thing of that situation and claim it brought the team closer together. In truth, we all just thought it was ridiculous and carried on as before. We beat Canada 66–7 in Kobe to secure second place in the pool and a spot in the quarter-finals, and managed to avoid any of the mayhem caused by Typhoon Hagibis, which wrote off New Zealand-Italy and Namibia-Canada.

I don't think any of us expected to be playing Japan in the last eight, especially after we lost our opener against the All Blacks, but they'd surpassed the expectations of even their most fervent fans by finishing top of their pool, beating Ireland, Samoa and Scotland along the way.

Ireland's reward for finishing second was a quarter-final against New Zealand, whom they'd beaten twice in their last three meetings. The Irish had been widely fancied coming into the tournament but their wheels had been rattling since their defeat by Japan. They finally came off against the All Blacks, who ran in seven tries to two in a 46–14 win. New Zealand were brilliant, in defence and attack, and having gone into the tournament as marginal favourites to win a third successive title, they were now red hot.

The Japanese had looked after us extremely well until then, but suddenly they weren't so helpful. Wives and girlfriends couldn't stay with us unless we paid extra for our rooms and they'd turn the floodlights off early at training so we'd have to finish earlier. But it was just the hosts trying to gain an edge, which I understood, and Rassie was good at personalising stuff like that. Just when you thought you'd heard it all from Rassie, he'd come up with something new and raise the intensity to a whole new level. He included all the Japanese funny business in his pre-match speech, and by the time he'd finished we no longer thought they were so nice.

As good as Japan had been in Brighton four years earlier, Eddie Jones's successor as head coach, Jamie Joseph, had made them even better. They had probably the most innovative and effective attacking shape in the tournament, they worked like demons without the ball, they had pace throughout the team and they were extremely fit. Plus, they were brimming with confidence after knocking off Ireland and Scotland, and they'd have 50,000 crazy fans cheering their every move. It wasn't going to be easy for us, that much we knew.

Mapimpi got us off to the perfect start with a great solo try, but Beast was sin-binned for a tip tackle after 10 minutes. Defending Japan's attack shape with 15 men is tough enough, so being down to 14 for even 10 minutes was a nightmare. That period while Beast was in the sin-bin was the most tired I've ever been in a Test match. They were throwing the ball around from everywhere, leaving us scrambling all over the field desperately trying to put out fires. Meanwhile, the crowd was getting more and more frenzied. How we managed to stop them from scoring a try was anyone's guess, but they did collect three points after mangling our scrum from our put-in, making it only 5–3 to us at the break.

There was a lot of pressure on us coming out for the second half, but there was also a lot of pressure on Japan because they were in a good position to upset us again, only this time in front of their own fans.

Luckily for us, they gave away a couple of silly penalties

early in the second half and Handré did the rest from the tee. That gave us some breathing space before we took the game away from them with what I thought was the most beautiful move of the match. It started with a line-out just inside our own half, which Lood caught cleanly. We then rolled a maul all the way into their 22 before Malcolm Marx burst through a gap and fed the ball inside to Faf, who scored next to the poles. When Mapimpi went over for his second try a few minutes later, we were home and hosed. We finally had our revenge, and maybe they'd stop showing that try in the hotel lobby.

Our matchday squad was pretty much nailed down by now, something Rassie had suggested would happen. His plan was for everyone to play two games in the pool stage, to give them a chance to prove themselves, before selecting the best performers for the quarter-final then sticking to his guns. But Rassie was good at making sure everyone felt wanted (which is difficult when players aren't getting selected for play-off games in a World Cup) and everyone saw the bigger picture.

I'm sure one or two were frustrated but Rassie would say, 'Please don't be negative if you're not in the squad for the knockout games. It's for the good of the team and everyone will get a medal at the end of it.'

Besides, he had already weeded out any guys he thought could be a virus. He'd say, 'The 31 guys in the squad aren't necessarily the most talented but they're the right guys for this team.' He understood that sometimes you had a player who was arguably the best in his position in club rugby but also sulked, moaned about game plans and facilities, talked *kak* about people and infected the whole environment. Other coaches don't notice those players but Rassie spots them immediately and never considers picking them again.

Our semi-final opponents, Wales, were our bogey team. They'd won their last four matches against us and had won the Six Nations Grand Slam earlier in the year, so we knew it was bound to be another arm wrestle. Like us, they had a simple game plan, the kind that tends to be effective in World Cups, with a solid set piece, lots of kicking and not much rugby played in their own half. We also thought of them as a tough rugby nation, full of players from testing backgrounds. They weren't a team you could blow off the park with pure physicality because they would stick in there and give it back to you. Having said that, Rassie's plan remained the same: fuck them up!

We'd have to beat Wales without our stick of dynamite, Cheslin, on the wing because he'd hurt himself against Japan. Rassie had a policy that if a player couldn't train on the Monday he couldn't play the following weekend, so it didn't matter that Cheslin was on fire by the Wednesday, making the starting XV look foolish with his hot-stepping. (Those who weren't in the matchday squad would study opposition players and mimic them in training so that the matchday 23 could better visualise how the game would pan out, but there was absolutely no chance of Wales having anyone like Cheslin.) Rassie must have thought long and hard about breaking his own rule and swapping him back in, but he presumably decided that by doing so he'd lose some of the guys' trust.

Going into the game, we knew they were going to kick

almost every time they got the ball and that we were just going to kick it back. Rassie said more than once, 'Don't get bored of the plan,' because he knew the team that ran out of patience first would probably end up losing. You have to be very disciplined to carry out such a simple, some might say limited, game plan. It's particularly difficult if you're a winger or full back whose first instinct is to run into space, and it takes only one have-a-go hero going off script to ruin things.

With neither team willing to take risks, it was an ugly, tense encounter. Wales had more possession than us in the first half but it didn't really mean anything because they kicked most of their ball to us. And, as instructed, we mostly kicked it back to them. It had more in common with two men trying to strangle each other to death than a ding-dong boxing match.

Try-scoring opportunities were few and far between, but when we won a penalty advantage inside their 22 in the 56th minute Faf switched play to the left and Damian de Allende somehow fended off four Welsh defenders and touched the ball down. However, Wales levelled things up 10 minutes later with a converted Josh Adams try. We already had five of the Bomb Squad on the field by then, and Francois Louw replaced Siya with 11 minutes to go. One of his first acts was to force Alun Wyn Jones to hold on at a ruck, which allowed Handré to boot the ball downfield for a line-out. That's when the hours and hours of mauling work paid dividends once again.

As we rumbled forward, one of their players was caught offside, giving Handré the chance to kick the match-winning penalty. It was from out left and the wind was gusting across the pitch, but as soon as Handré struck the ball I knew it was sailing straight between the poles.

The media reaction to our win over Wales was grudging, at least from outside South Africa. One prominent English journalist called it a 'mind-numbing, one-dimensional muscleman performance, all thud and wallop'; another described the game as 'so attritional you expected infantrymen to start writing mournful poetry about it'. Others pointed out that there had been a kick for every minute in the first half, while approaching the half-hour mark we'd kicked the ball more times than we'd passed it. But we didn't care a jot.

Our motto was, 'Do whatever it takes to win,' and we preferred to win games by one or two points playing simple rugby than lose games despite scoring a hatful of tries. Besides, beauty is in the eye of the beholder, so while some people watched that 50-metre maul against Japan and concluded we were ruining the game, I thought it was probably the best thing I'd ever seen.

We'd watched the England-New Zealand semi-final in the team room the evening before our game against Wales, and I was surprised by how convincingly England won. They started impressively, and while I thought their wheels might come off down the stretch, they kept piling the pressure on.

Beating favourites New Zealand must have given England so much confidence, especially as the All Blacks had beaten us in their opening pool game. But I thought that if both teams were at their best, New Zealand would have the edge. And while England had won their last two games against us, they'd never beaten the Boks in a World Cup and New Zealand had a much better record against us overall.

We started studying England on our laptops as soon as we got back to our hotel after the Wales game (alongside organising visas for our families), and Rassie announced the team on the Monday morning, which gave the guys who weren't in the matchday squad plenty of time to perfect their impersonations of England's players.

Most English journalists and pundits were confident their team would be too good for us. The prevailing view was that we were too one-dimensional and not clever enough to beat England, and I particularly remember one article explaining that England's Six Nations games the following year were already sold out because their fans were certain they'd be watching the world champions in action.

All week Rassie kept feeding us articles from English newspapers, which served as extra motivation. The more you hear that the English are going to match you physically, that they're going to be too smart for you, that they're going to do rugby a favour by beating you, the more you want to prove them wrong.

Rassie wasn't about to change tack for a World Cup final and his overriding message was, 'Keep whacking them and hopefully they'll yield as the game goes on.' In other words, fuck them up.

We did come up with one new line-out move, but because our training ground was overlooked by lots of buildings and people sometimes go to extreme lengths to spy on an opposition's preparations before a big game, we only ever walked it through in our hotel. We had lots of experienced forwards in the team, guys who could try something for the first time in a game and nail it. And to be honest, it wasn't a difficult move anyway, just a case of taking a shortened line-out, setting up a maul in the middle of the field and going from there.

I didn't feel too stressed during the build-up, probably because I'm the kind of player whose confidence stems from training as hard as possible. Other guys will require a bit of mental support to make sure their brain is ready for the game. They'll play the game over and over in their head, visualise where they'll need to be and what they'll need to do at certain points. There's no right or wrong way, it's whatever is best for the individual. But for me, preparing properly and nailing the technical stuff is more important than psychology.

I went out for dinner with a couple of guys on the Wednesday evening, just so we could forget about the game for a few hours. We knew what was coming and what we needed to do by then. And the following day my family arrived – Mom, Dad and Ryen – and things started to feel a bit more real.

On Saturday morning I decided to write down everything I did that day: what I had for breakfast and lunch, what time the team meeting was. And just before leaving my room to board the bus for the stadium, I wrote what time I thought the game would finish and 'WORLD CHAMPIONS' next to it.

Rassie's final speech wasn't what you'd describe as technical – we'd been together for 19 weeks by then so we knew our jobs.

He said we weren't allowed to walk off the field with any regrets. He said pressure for a South African isn't rugby, it's not being able to find a job, or having a loved one murdered. He said we had the whole of South Africa behind us, that we should throw ourselves into as many battles as possible and not think about any mistakes because that would be selfish; if we missed a collision, we should get straight back up and throw ourselves into the next one.

I don't know what the dynamics were in the England set-up but I was surprised that Owen Farrell started at No 12 rather than No 10 for England. He was physical, tackled hard and kicked well out of hand. And had he played at 10 it would have given England the option of a bigger, more physical inside centre. As it was, we suspected that if we could get to George Ford, who was starting at 10 instead of Farrell, and rattle him a bit, his decision-making would become a split-second slower and he'd be more reluctant to try things.

England had a good pack and we knew they'd come at us hard. Maro Itoje had a big game against the All Blacks, we knew Tom Curry never shied away from the rough and tumble, and I'd always rated Courtney Lawes highly – he was an exceptional player and a tough man. But we never really looked at individuals; it wasn't about me versus Itoje or Pieter-Steph versus Curry, it was about the Springbok pack versus their pack.

England's first big scrum problem was tight head Kyle Sinckler going off with a concussion after 3 minutes. That meant Dan Cole, who probably expected to play only 25 minutes, having to play 77. And up against him was Beast, probably the strongest loose head in the world, and Steven Kitshoff, maybe the second-strongest loose head in the world. That's a big ask, even for a scrummager as good as Cole.

We'd had a good scrumming outing against Argentina in the Rugby Championship and we were even better against Italy in Fukuroi. And after the first scrum of the final, when we shunted England backwards, I knew our front row of Beast, Bongi and Frans Malherbe were in a mean mood again.

When it comes to the scrum, there's nowhere a pack can go. It's not like tackling, where players can use different methods to get a guy to the ground; or mauling, where you can employ technical tricks to thwart the other team's advance. The scrum is eight guys locked in against eight guys, and no amount of tricks are going to match a pack which is massively up for it. Beast, in particular, seemed possessed. And after maybe the third scrum, I thought, *They simply can't deal with us.*

Handré gave us the lead from the tee after 10 minutes, Farrell levelled the score 12 minutes later, then Handré edged us ahead again after Cole was drilled out of a scrum. There was a huge period around the half-hour mark when England tried time and again to get over our try line but came away with only three points. Jacques Nienaber had done an incredible job of transforming our defence from leaky to watertight, and I think that particular defensive effort had a big influence on the final result. Throwing everything they had at us and still not scoring a try must have been a big psychological blow for England, and it was certainly a big shot in the arm for us.

Rassie often talked about the need for his players to be warriors. To successfully repel wave after wave of attacks, everyone in your team, from No 1 to No 15, must be up for the physical challenge, and no one can be scared of putting their head in dangerous places. A good example of that was Faf, because a little guy like him stopping a big guy in his tracks gives the team a bigger lift than a forward like me doing the same.

Having kept England at bay, we went down the other end and won a penalty, which Handré nailed, and he put us six points ahead after our scrum demolished theirs again. We probably should have been further ahead at half-time but Rassie was calm in the changing room. The only thing I remember him saying was that any signs of tiredness would give England hope, so we should get back on our feet as soon as possible after going to ground.

Of course, Rassie also knew that he still had four fresh forwards up his sleeve, Bongi and Lood having suffered injuries and been replaced before the break. I can't imagine what Dan Cole was thinking when he saw Kitshoff and Koch running onto the pitch just 3 minutes into the second half, but their first scrum was something ridiculous.

England replaced Vunipola with Marler a couple of minutes later and they soon won a scrum penalty, which shifted the momentum for 5 minutes or so. But at 15–9 we decided to unveil the line-out move we'd only practised in our hotel: a shortened line-out, a maul in the middle of the field which England collapsed, three cheap points. That was a tremendously satisfying moment and one in the eye for those who thought we lacked tricks.

Nevertheless, England were still very much in it and another Farrell penalty made it 18–12. That was too close for comfort. I was on the bench by then but I sensed that if we hit back quickly it might finally extinguish their spirit. And with 14 minutes remaining, England box-kicked, Willie le Roux caught the ball and was tackled, and we cleared the ruck. Faf played to the blind side and Malcolm Marx, showing great hands for a big man, fed Lukhanyo Am, who put Mapimpi clear. Mapimpi kicked ahead, Lukhanyo collected, then he passed it back inside to Mapimpi, who went over for South Africa's first try in a World Cup final. Handré added the conversion and I couldn't see England coming back from 25–12 down.

England huffed and puffed but couldn't find any way through our defensive line, and when they coughed up the ball in the tackle, Lukhanyo popped it up to Pieter-Steph, who swung it wide to Cheslin on the right wing. Cheslin glided past a couple of forwards, left Farrell for dead with a goose-step combined with a vicious swerve, before touching down unopposed. We all went crazy on the touchline because we knew we had it in the bag.

When something you've dreamed of for most of your life really happens, it's difficult to know how to react. What was I supposed to do when the final whistle went? Jump in the air? Tackle a teammate to the ground? Start crying? Say a prayer? What I actually did was run onto the field like a madman and grab the first person to cross my path, who happened to be Herschel (at least I think it was).

After being presented with my medal, I looked straight at my mom, dad and brother, who were beaming back at me. I then gave my medal a proper look, which is when the last few months of my life flashed before me: that night out in Langebaan, all the horrible lies that had been told about me, the hours and hours of gruelling training, the joyous camaraderie of my teammates. I looked up to the sky, said a thank-you prayer, tears poured down my cheeks and it felt like two big boulders had rolled off my shoulders.

When Siya came on stage to collect the Webb Ellis Cup, I wasn't thinking about symbolism or anything like that, and I suspect most of my teammates would say the same. We didn't think of Siya as a black captain, he was just one of the guys, a good friend to everyone, and we wanted him to lift the trophy as quickly as possible so we could start celebrating properly. When he did so, it felt like I'd completed rugby, like you can complete a computer game, because there was no bigger achievement. Where do you go from there?

Siya Kolisi, South Africa captain: I knew Eben was going to be a great player for the Springboks when we were together at the Western Province Institute as teenagers. I'd played with some very good players but before Eben I'd never met anyone who knew exactly what they wanted in life.

He worked incredibly hard and didn't party and drink like some of us, including me. But he loved it when I smiled and we had a close relationship from the very beginning. I'd stay at his house at weekends, his mom and dad would braai and it was obvious how much his family meant to him. Family meant a lot to me as well, so that really struck a chord.

We became roommates early on at the Stormers and have been ever since (apart from the odd time he's had his own room and I've shared with Cheslin, which makes him jealous). I've probably spent more time with Eben than anyone else, even his own family, and I've had the privilege of seeing sides of him that most people never get to see. He doesn't hide any of his emotions from me, which is one of the reasons I love him so much, and far from being simply a rugby machine, he can be soft and vulnerable.

We've been through so much together, good and bad, and it's the good stuff that brings friends closer for when the bad stuff happens. After Eben's dad passed away, I'd just lie next to him in our hotel room. There's not much you can say to someone in a situation like that, but just being present is something. And whenever I'm going through a tough time I'll see in Eben's face that he really wants me to feel better, which means so much to me.

Rugby-wise, Japan was tough for all of us, but the worst time was when Eben was captain and we lost 57–0 to the All Blacks. I felt for us as a team, I felt for our country, but I also felt for him as a mate. We didn't say much to each other afterwards, apart from that we never wanted to go through something like that again. Three weeks later, they beat us by a point.

When I was named Springbok captain he was one of the first people to congratulate me and tell me I had his full support. And because I don't talk a lot, he's the team's voice. He's the most *experienced guy in the group, like a big brother to everyone. It's obvious how much he loves playing for the Boks and everyone respects him. And while he has very high standards, he's never unreasonable. We have argued in the changing room but that's healthy in a team environment – it shows how much we care – and it was soon forgotten about.*

When I'm not sure what to do on the field, I look to Eben because he's technically brilliant and asks the referee the right questions. Rassie wants us to think for ourselves and Eben is always coming up with new ways of doing things. His research is meticulous, ridiculously so. He'll sit in a room with [Bok assistant coach] Felix Jones for hours, analysing opposing teams' plays, before sharing his findings with the rest of the guys. He'll do anything to give his team an edge.

Eben is incredibly physical, fit and athletic – he's faster than some of the backs over 40 m – and has got better over the years at channelling his aggression. But what really makes him unique is how much he cares.

One time, he thought he was ready to play after a long-term injury but wasn't selected. Everyone in the room could feel his hurt and he was almost in tears when I spoke to him afterwards. This was a guy who had already played more than 100 Tests but he was still desperate for more.

Whenever he's not on the team sheet I worry because he brings something most players don't have. He's obviously a formidable rugby player but a lot of what he brings most people can't even see – it's more of a feeling. I'm certain he'll be playing at the next World Cup, injury permitting, and maybe even after that.

Eben has a professional mode that he clicks into but I wish more people could see his fun side. He has the dumbest jokes and we have favourite coffee shops and restaurants wherever we play in the world, where we chat about life. We mostly like the same things but if he's not really into something I want to do, he'll do it with me anyway, and vice versa.

Even when Eben was living in France we stayed in close contact, and now that we live next to each other in Durban our families spend a lot of time in each other's company. We do trips together, go out for meals, have braais at each other's houses, and I can tell by the way he talks to my kids that he loves them dearly. Eben is simple like that: if he cares about someone he'll show it.

Eben and I don't think about our friendship in terms of what it says about modern South Africa, it's more about how the whole world should work. It's easy really: don't judge somebody based on the colour of their skin, take the time to get to know them properly and judge them on who they are.

Eben knows my story – where I've come from, my struggles, what I play for – and I know his story, and as such we've learnt to love and appreciate each other. I know he'd do anything for me, just as I'd do anything for him.

So while I'll always know him as one of the greatest Springboks of all time, if not the greatest, he'll also be one of the best mates I've ever had, more like a brother really. Hopefully we'll still be living next to each other in retirement because I want to continue our journey together to the very end.

Only later, after the dust had settled, did I think about the significance of the occasion. Throughout the tournament we'd been very aware that we were playing for the people back home in South Africa. Rassie was always showing us videos of supporters from all different backgrounds celebrating our wins, and he'd say to us, 'Look how much they want you to win, look how they're getting behind you, look how much you're changing people's lives.'

I love South Africa, it's a beautiful country, the best in the world despite its problems. And while I wasn't naive enough to think that us winning the World Cup would change the long-term fortunes of the country, I did think that rugby could do what politics couldn't, namely raise spirits and unite people, however fleetingly. If we made people happy and proud even for 24 hours, we'd achieved something.

Maybe there were black kids in townships watching Siya lifting that trophy and thinking, *I want to be captain of the Springboks*. Perhaps there were black kids who wanted to be Pieter-Steph, or white kids on farms who wanted to be Siya or Cheslin, or coloured kids from poor neighbourhoods who wanted to be me. That would be real transformation.

I wish I'd had a GoPro strapped to my head when my family joined me on the field because the emotion was so raw and beautiful. And after a lap of honour with the trophy we headed back inside for photos before retreating to the changing room for beers. Lots of them.

It was chaos in there, and when Prince Harry walked in most of the guys were in their undies (Faf was wandering around in a pair of South Africa flag Speedos). Someone gave Prince Harry a beer, he said a few kind words then made his excuses and left. The Webb Ellis Cup – gleaming, gold and beautiful – finally turned up in the arms of Frans Steyn, South Africa's second two-time World Cup winner, and we cranked the music up and got back to partying.

I've no idea what Rassie said at the meeting back at the hotel – I'd already had too many beers by then – and the party was still going when I left at 5 am. I grabbed two or three hours' sleep, got dressed, staggered downstairs for a function, then got straight back on it.

We flew home in different groups, which wasn't ideal, and I was on a plane with Rassie (whose 47th birthday it was), Jacques, Siya, Beast, Handré and the Webb Ellis Cup, which had its own seat. When we were two or three hours from home, one of the management team told us all to stop drinking and try to sober up a bit before facing the media, but I was still massively under the influence when we landed in Johannesburg. Still, I'll never forget the welcome home.

The airport was a wonderful sight, packed with well-wishers of all colours decked out in green and gold, waving South Africa flags and singing. There was even a choir to sing the national anthem. And once we'd scribbled a few autographs we were bundled straight into a room for a media conference, after which we continued our celebrations at an airport hotel.

I'd always said that if I won the World Cup, I'd get a tattoo, so a tattoo artist came to the hotel and a couple of us decided to get tattoos, which is when some tattooed Bomb Squad on themselves. I got one of the trophy, along with the date and a Bible verse I'd received on the day of the final from former Stormers forwards coach Russell Winter, Deuteronomy 20:4: 'For the Lord your God is the one who goes with you to fight for you against your enemies to give you victory.'

By the time the trophy tour began in Pretoria two days later, most of the guys had consumed a ridiculous amount of alcohol, but we weren't stopping any time soon. But despite all the revelry it was impossible not to be touched by the outpouring of happiness we encountered in cities across South Africa. Yes, there were so many things that needed fixing in our country, but at least we'd provided people with a small window of wonder and hope.

A week after the final was my 10-year school reunion, which I wasn't going to miss, then I went on holiday to Sun City with my family. I kept thinking, *I'm never going to win a World Cup for the first time again, so I should make the most of it.* And just when I thought I'd had enough, someone else would phone and say, 'No, no, no, you're coming out with us.' I'm sure some people were thinking, *Is this guy ever going to stop drinking?* But I wanted to share my success with as many people as possible.

I finally stopped drinking after about three weeks, and one of the first things I did when my head had finally cleared was get my jersey framed, alongside the England one I'd swapped with Itoje. My cap and boots are in the frame as well, as is the note I wrote describing my routine on the day of the final. Memories tend to fade, however great, but that's not a day I ever want to forget.

9

LION TAMING

So many guys from that World Cup squad had also experienced some of the darkest days of South African rugby, when we were regularly losing to the All Blacks, as well as teams that had never previously laid a glove on us. Hard times create strong men and that period of adversity made us so much flintier. And because we'd now experienced the best of times in a green and gold jersey, we never wanted to go back to the worst.

With the World Cup done and dusted I also felt strong enough to confront those who had accused me of terrible things before the tournament. I sat down with the four of them and said, 'I hear you want a million rand to make this thing go away. Well, if you each asked me for 10 rand now I still wouldn't give it to you. I know I'm innocent and you haven't got a leg to stand on.'

I could tell they were surprised by my bullishness. And when I asked why they were so sure they had the right man, their story unravelled. Two of them were certain I'd been wearing a red Nike T-shirt on the night in question, but I had a photograph that proved I was wearing a black Asics T-shirt

(I was sponsored by Asics at the time so never wore Nike). These guys were clearly opportunists looking to make money, just as the SAHRC were opportunists looking to make political capital from the situation.

The clouds started to clear after that, although it took a long time for them to disappear. SARU found me not guilty of racism the following year, while the courts finally dropped the case against me in late 2021.

After a few weeks unwinding, I packed my bags and headed for France, which was a big thing for me. I'd played club rugby in Japan but only for a few months. This was a three-year deal and I was going by myself – my brother and I are very close but I couldn't expect him to be my wingman for that long.

Thankfully, Toulon is a lovely little city on the Mediterranean coast with sandy beaches, a beautiful old town, lots of culture and, most importantly, lots of sun, even in winter. Liam Messam had been in touch before I left South Africa, offering to take me out for breakfast and show me around when I arrived, and I was made to feel very welcome by everyone at the club.

The side wasn't as good as the one that Jonny Wilkinson had led to three consecutive Heineken/Champions Cups between 2013 and 2015 but it was still decent. Toulon were fifth in the Top 14 table when I arrived and jumped to third after my Top 14 debut, a comprehensive defeat of Clermont in which I scored after 4 minutes. We easily qualified for the quarter-finals of the European Challenge Cup, winning all six of our games, but then we started hearing about something called coronavirus. Soon,

Covid-19 was sweeping across France, causing games to be cancelled. And on 17 March, President Emmanuel Macron announced a national lockdown.

That was a real smack in the face. I'd been playing well, I'd made quite a few friends, I was learning more and more French and I was loving the city, and suddenly I was cooped up in my apartment on my own with nothing to do.

A day or two after the announcement from President Macron, I explained my situation to the club and asked if I could go home, which they were very against. They said we'd be playing again in four or five weeks but I knew that wouldn't be the case and I didn't want to get stuck. They eventually agreed to let me go and I escaped on one of the last planes out of France. A few weeks later, with deaths from Covid rising exponentially, the Top 14 season was officially cancelled.

The pandemic was also ravaging South Africa, but holed up in my house in Blouberg with my mom, dad and brother, I was able to enjoy the break. We had plenty of space and a pool in the backyard. I also had dumbbells and an air bike delivered, which meant I was able to do two gym sessions a day. We cooked together every evening, often on the braai, and it was some of the best family time I've ever had.

I know a lot of rugby players look back on that period fondly because it was a break from constant travelling and staying in hotels. It made me think the whole world should shut down for a couple of months every few years so that people can spend quality time with loved ones and recharge their batteries (minus the pandemic part, obviously).

South Africa withdrew from that year's Rugby Championship and the end-of-year internationals, which meant I was back in Toulon for the start of the 2020–21 season. And while my good mates Liam Messam and Julian Savea hadn't returned, All Black great Ma'a Nonu soon did, two years after leaving the club. What a guy he was, one of the best I've met, as was fellow former All Black Isaia Toeava, who had joined from Clermont.

We still had to finish the previous season's Challenge Cup, and while I missed our knockout wins against Scarlets and Leicester with a rib injury, I was back in the starting line-up for the final against Bristol in Aix-en-Provence. The thousand Toulon fans who were allowed in had to wear masks but Bristol didn't have any supporters there at all. And despite it being a virtual home fixture for us, we were beaten quite comfortably. The wait for my second piece of domestic silverware went on, eight years after I'd won my first.

We were then knocked out of that season's Champions Cup by default, one of our players having tested positive for Covid before our scheduled game against Leinster, and we ended up finishing eighth in the Top 14. The top eight normally qualify for the Champions Cup, but unfortunately for us, Montpellier, who finished below us in the Top 14, won the Challenge Cup, which earned them automatic qualification for Champions Cup at our expense. Before joining Toulon I'd set myself the goal of winning two Champions Cups to make them a five-star team, and we'd been knocked out of that season's competition by a pandemic and hadn't qualified for the following season. It was all a bit deflating.

We weren't the superstar team they'd had a few years earlier but we had plenty of quality players from France and abroad. The Top 14 was very physical but I got the impression that teams didn't plan as well as some in the Pro14 or English Premiership. Maybe because the salary cap was higher in France, they thought natural talent would win the day, but whatever the reason, the Top 14 appeared to be more about feel than structure, with some teams seemingly just sent out to play. It was like nothing I'd experienced and I found some of it quite frustrating.

Anyone who says a British & Irish Lions series is bigger than a World Cup is talking nonsense – if you're a South African, Australian or Kiwi player and you could win only one during your career, you'd pick a World Cup every day of the week.

But a Lions series is definitely second in terms of importance, at least for me, because they only come around every 12 years. And being 29 when the Lions toured South Africa in 2021, I'd only get one shot (as much as I'd like to be, I don't think I'll still be playing when I'm 42).

Sadly, South Africa was in the grip of a third Covid wave, meaning there would be no fans in the stands and all three Test matches, plus the Lions' tune-ups against South Africa 'A' and the Stormers, would be played at Cape Town Stadium. Still, the fact that the tour went ahead in South Africa was a minor miracle. Earlier in the year there had been talk about the series being played in Britain and Ireland instead, postponed until the following year or cancelled altogether.

I was well versed in the colourful history of series between the Springboks and the Lions and had been looking forward to being a part of one for years. I was only six when the Lions toured South Africa in 1997, the year Jeremy Guscott won the series for the tourists with a late drop goal in Durban, but I obviously remembered 2009, when Morné Steyn clinched the series with a late, late penalty from inside his own half in Pretoria. I'd also heard all about the 1974 series, when the dazzling Lions went undefeated in 22 games, including four Test matches, and proved they were every bit as hard as the Boks in the 'Battle of Boet Erasmus'.

Such was the rarity of a series against the Lions that they had an almost mythical status in South Africa. But compared to all those legendary tales of yesteryear, the 2021 series turned out to be a bit of an anti-climax.

We hadn't played since the World Cup final almost two years earlier, so it wasn't ideal when a few of our players tested positive for Covid just before our scheduled warm-up game against Georgia, which meant the whole squad had to isolate. The Test match went ahead, and while we were understandably rusty and there was hardly anyone there to see it, it was just a relief to run around in the green and gold again. It must have been an even bigger relief for Jacques Nienaber, who had been appointed head coach 18 months earlier (Rassie switched to director of rugby, although he was still very much involved with the team).

A second warm-up game against Georgia had to be cancelled because of Covid outbreaks in both squads' ranks, while the Lions had also been hit. At that point, the smart money was on the Lions series being scrapped altogether.

The situation was borderline farcical: if one guy tested positive we'd all have to isolate in our rooms for five to seven days, then we'd emerge to train in small groups before heading back inside and crossing our fingers. Two weeks before the first Test, we hadn't had a proper team session, which is why Rassie decided to select the best team available for South Africa 'A's game against the Lions, effectively turning it into a four-match series.

Inevitably, there was another Covid outbreak in the build-up, which ruled Siya out of the game and meant Jacques had to coach us remotely from his room, with Rassie flying solo on the training ground. Meanwhile, Steven Kitshoff had to drive 1,300 km from Johannesburg to Cape Town and arrived only on the Thursday evening. He slept that night, did the captain's run on the Friday and started the game on the Saturday.

For a bunch of players who had spent a big chunk of the previous month cooped up in a hotel, we did well to win that game, even though we flagged down the stretch because of our lack of conditioning. But perhaps the main talking point was Rassie's water boy role, which some in the British and Irish media seemed to think was mischief-making or even cheating but which was actually just another sign of his genius.

Rassie had the choice of sitting in the box, miles away from the action, or, because he wasn't the head coach, taking on the role of water boy and being able to speak to the players on the field. And of course he was going to choose the latter. He'd been a player, so knew that it was better to relay messages in person so that no wires got crossed. Also, he was able to look straight into players' eyes and gauge if they still had enough to continue or whether they should be replaced. He wasn't breaking any rules and it made perfect sense.

As heartening as our performance was in that game, it was officially just a warm-up and we had only 10 days to prepare for the first Test match proper. That was still enough time for plenty of controversy, with Rassie trying to bait Gatland into another game against South Africa 'A', while Gatland claimed Faf should have been sent off in the South Africa 'A' game and sounded off about the appointment of South African Marius Jonker as TMO (the truth was that the Kiwi official hadn't been able to travel because of Covid and no other TMOs were available).

With Duane Vermeulen still recovering from ankle surgery, Kwagga Smith was selected to start at eighthman, which raised eyebrows in the British and Irish media. Kwagga is only 181 cm and 100 kg, which is small for a modern loose forward (Duane is 12 cm taller and about 24 kg heavier). But Kwagga, which was his brother's nickname for him when they were children (a 'quagga' is an extinct species of zebra), isn't a normal human being.

When Kwagga moved from sevens to 15s in 2014, nobody would have predicted he'd represent the Springboks. But he didn't care that people thought he was too small to be a

Springbok forward, and he's made a lot of people look foolish, winning more than 50 caps at the time of writing.

I honestly believe Kwagga is the best impact player off the bench in world rugby, because every time he enters the fray he makes a difference. But I also knew he could do a good job in big games as a starter. He's not the biggest or strongest but he has so much energy packed into that stocky frame. He's quick, he's agile and he has an excellent pair of hands, which all makes sense when you hear stories about him, some of which include him diving onto various wild animals off the back of moving trucks.

Our 46-man squad for the series included 22 overseas-based players, a significant increase from the 2019 World Cup. Putting aside whether that reflected well on South Africa's domestic rugby, the overseas players brought different perspectives and insider knowledge to the Bok set-up. It was almost as if we had spies in the Lions' ranks because the guys who played in Europe had played with or against pretty much everyone in their squad. They had first-hand experience of how they did things, their strengths and weaknesses, which is very different from watching players on tapes.

We even had an assistant coach, Felix Jones, based in Ireland. Having been appointed as an assistant coach just before the 2019 World Cup, Felix now spent much of his time with the Boks' European contingent, monitoring training sessions, watching matches, liaising with club coaches and sharing feedback with players in places such as Montpellier, Toulouse and Sale, where five of our squad were based.

Felix is one of the best coaches I've worked with and I don't think I've seen anyone graft as hard as he does. I'm told he was up every morning before it got light, analysing training and games on his laptop. He was quite hard on players, could be blunt when pointing out mistakes in training videos, and became upset when anyone didn't meet his high standards. But that's exactly why I loved him.

Unfortunately, we had our first full training session only on the Monday before the first Test match, and some Covid-affected players didn't take part. In addition, while Rassie, Jacques, Felix and Mzwandile Stick had been around for a while, strength and conditioning coach Andy Edwards and forwards coaches Deon Davids and Daan Human were new, which meant they didn't have time to teach us anything fresh and we had no choice but to keep things simple. All we could really do was work on what attacking plays the Lions might use and sort out our defence accordingly, prepare three or four basic moves of our own, and make sure our set piece and kicking game were in decent shape. It wasn't going to be a pretty series.

I hadn't expected to be playing against Alun Wyn Jones in the first Test but the Lions captain had made a remarkable recovery from a dislocated shoulder. Meanwhile, there had been newspaper reports that we didn't rate Jones's lock partner Maro Itoje, which wasn't true.

We knew how good Itoje was – he put scrum halves under pressure, was busy in the loose, disruptive at the breakdown, and clearly knew the laws back to front because he pushed boundaries and got away with it.

The media had been trying to stir up a rivalry between Itoje and me for years, as if we were a couple of boxers. But when you're a lock you don't really have those head-to-head battles that other players engage in (loose head versus tight head, right wing versus left wing, inside centre versus inside centre). You do a bit of contesting in the line-out but you also have flankers jumping, and you seldom find yourself running straight at another lock. It's natural to compare your performance with an opposition lock who comes with a reputation, because you want to be the best in the world in your position.

I've had a couple of scuffles with Argentina's Tomás Lavanini (there's a great photo of the two of us going at each other in the 2015 World Cup bronze medal match) and journalists like to make out that we're mortal enemies. Even my teammates and coaches make a thing of it. Whenever we play Argentina, Siya always says to me in the changing room beforehand, 'Are you and Lavanini going to fight again today?' But we had a nice chat after we last played against each other and he's a really sound guy.

I'd been fantasising for years about playing against the Lions – stadiums half-full with noisy red-shirted fans, thunderous cheers from our supporters every time we made a big tackle or scored points – so to look out at the stands and see not a single person looking back at us was a bit soul-destroying.

Nevertheless, we were up for the fight and dominated the opening exchanges. Handré kicked four penalties to make it 12–3 at half-time, and with the Bomb Squad standing by we seemed in a good place. But Lions hooker Luke Cowan-Dickie scored a try from a maul shortly after the restart, just before the TMO chalked off a Willie le Roux effort for offside. A try from Faf put us ahead again but it was all Lions from that point on. Scottish flanker Hamish Watson was lucky to get away with a tip tackle on Willie, a late try by Damian de Allende was ruled out for a knock-on by Cheslin, we kept giving away penalties, Dan Biggar kept knocking over kicks, and we ended up losing 22–17.

It's the nature of sport that sometimes you have a bad day, and there were obvious reasons for our under-par performance. But when Rassie took over we weren't allowed to have excuses. It didn't matter if we'd been travelling a lot, playing loads of games, training too hard or not training enough, Rassie's attitude was, 'You can't on the one hand say you'd do anything to play for the Boks, that you'd die on the field for your country, and on the other hand say that you didn't feel quite right. That's bullshit.'

Rassie didn't mince his words at Monday's team meeting. He was beyond angry, going at guys like I'd never seen before. He was very personal, accusing players of lying to the South African people by saying they wanted to inspire them and make them proud then failing to deliver on their promises. He called out a few individuals for trading on past glories and thinking they were better than they were, and it made for quite an unpleasant scene.

But Rassie knows his players inside out, which is what makes him so special. Different players have different personalities and react in different ways, and Rassie will take that into consideration before deciding whether to admonish them in front of the group. There's nothing cruel about him, he doesn't give people a hard time for the sake of it. And however much he upsets players, they always end up understanding that it was simply for the good of the team.

Rassie is also a realist, and just as he studies players' performances he will also point out where a referee made a bad call that led to points being scored against us. That needs to happen because you don't want to change your game plan if it was the referee rather than your team that was at fault. And he found a lot of faults in Nic Berry's performance in the first Test match.

The build-up to the second Test was full of controversy, with Mako Vunipola being accused of 'reckless and dangerous' play. There was also a video shared on social media that highlighted several questionable refereeing decisions, and the British and Irish media suspected the account that retweeted it was run by Rassie, which he denied. But that was just the start of it.

Two days before the second Test an hour-long video of Rassie critiquing the officiating in the first Test appeared on Twitter. He'd sent it to Berry, referees manager Joël Jutge, World Rugby's Joe Schmidt and most of the Springbok squad, but someone had leaked it.

It consisted of 38 refereeing incidents, including a late hit by Tom Curry on Faf which was punished with only a penalty, that tip tackle by Watson on Willie, various ruck infringements and what Rassie believed was evidence of disrespect towards Siya in his role as captain. He also said he'd stand down for the rest of the series if they thought he'd overstepped the mark.

I hadn't seen the video before the leak but when I did I thought it was very entertaining. And I agreed with everything he said, as I always do. When the story blew up in the media, Rassie sat us all down, explained what had happened – that he'd meant for only a few people to see it and that it wasn't him who had leaked it – and asked if any of us was responsible. Maybe, he suggested, someone had forwarded it via WhatsApp to someone outside the group and someone else had posted it on Twitter. Nobody owned up and Rassie seemed satisfied. Then we got back to fixing things for the second Test.

The consensus in the media, in South Africa and elsewhere, was that the pressure had got to Rassie, that he'd lost the plot, that the video was a desperate attempt at mind games. But I don't think that was the case at all. Yes, Rassie is good at getting in people's heads, but most of the time he doesn't do it on purpose. He genuinely thought that the officiating in the first Test was unacceptable and he was going to let the relevant people know about it, which seemed fair enough to me. And while he knows that some of the stuff he comes up with is close to the mark, if he believes it will benefit the team in the long-term he'll go ahead and do it, even if it causes him aggravation in the short-term. If I were a coach I'd do the same.

Of course, the fact that Rassie's video was leaked for all the world to see had ramifications for Berry. His reputation was tarnished and he and his family suffered horrible abuse, and there's never any excuse for that, however much you want your team to win.

The players went into the second Test angry: angry about the officiating the previous Saturday, angry that we'd played so badly. But we had to channel that anger properly. If we lost our discipline we'd lose the match and the series, and apart from maybe a couple of youngsters in the squad, we'd never get a chance for revenge.

It took only a couple of minutes for the tension to bubble over, and a scuffle ended with me and Alun Wyn Jones eyeballing each other. However, the first half wasn't much of a spectacle, neither side showing much attacking intent, and we trailed by three penalties to two at half-time.

But our forwards turned the screw after the break, we started winning the aerial battle, and Kiwi referee Ben O'Keeffe ruled with an iron fist, awarding 15 penalties against the Lions and yellow-carding Lions winger Duhan van der Merwe for a deliberate trip on Cheslin. He also showed Cheslin a yellow for a clumsy tackle on Irish scrum half Conor Murray.

Mapimpi gave us the lead with an early second-half try, after a beautifully judged cross-kick by Handré, before the Bomb Squad was introduced. Unlike in the first Test, the Lions weren't able to deal with a fresh set piece and a reinvigorated maul, and when Faf chipped through after a driving maul to within five metres of the Lions' try line, Lukhanyo was quickest to react (some observers thought he wasn't in control of the ball but I thought it was a legitimate try). Handré's conversion made it 18–9 and he twisted the knife with three more penalties in the last 10 minutes.

The game lasted two hours, what with all the stoppages, and in the days after the game, accusations flew from all sides. On social media, South African fans accused Maro Itoje of kneeling on Damian de Allende's neck, full back Stuart Hogg of biting Willie le Roux and prop Kyle Sinckler of biting Franco Mostert (only Sinckler was cited but he was cleared for the third Test because of a lack of evidence).

Meanwhile, Gatland called on World Rugby to punish Rassie for his leaked video (that would happen, but only after the series had ended) and the British and Irish media got more and more wound up about Rassie's water boy role, as well as the rugby played so far, which they thought had been a poor advert for the game. But if they expected us to start chucking the ball around just to keep them happy, they were deluded. They could keep dreaming of bells and whistles but we were going to do what we needed to do to win.

Pieter-Steph injured his shoulder in the second Test, making him unavailable for the decider. From the outside looking in, that was a huge blow to the team. However, we knew that Franco, who started the first two Tests alongside me in the second row, could do a good job in place of Pieter-Steph at flanker.

Franco is a true team man, a warrior, one of the most respected guys in the Bok set-up, and he'd never let us down wherever he played. Also, the No 7 role in the Bok team is equivalent to No 6 in the northern hemisphere and similar to the No 5 role in terms of defence and attack, so Franco's switch really wasn't a big deal. That we had Lood de Jager available to slot in at lock made the reshuffle as smooth as anything.

The Lions were heavily criticised by the British and Irish media for their lack of ambition in the second Test and Gatland made wholesale changes to their backline, though not at fly-half. I think Rassie had a feeling the Lions might start with Scotland's Finn Russell at No 10, instead of the more conservative Dan Biggar, but he couldn't have been surprised when he heard Biggar had been given the nod. He was reliable off the tee and put us in difficult places with his kicking out of hand. Plus, Wales had won four of their last five games against us and come close to beating us in the World Cup semi-finals, and Biggar had been involved in all but one of those encounters.

But having prepared for Biggar, he suffered an injury after just 10 minutes and was replaced by Russell, which completely changed the game's dynamic. Russell is a fly-half who makes things happen, whose first instinct is to run with the ball rather than kick it, and immediately after he was introduced the Lions looked more threatening in attack.

Their forwards were up for it as well, and Russell levelled the scores at 3–3 after a scrum penalty. The Lions then went into the lead when hooker Ken Owens barged over after a driving maul. But they butchered two or three more try-scoring opportunities, and having dominated possession and territory they should have led by more than four points at half-time. The chat in the changing room centred on how

Russell had changed things, with more running and less kicking, and we spent our time working out how to fix it.

Gatland would have been rueing all those missed chances when Cheslin scored a typically miraculous try 15 minutes after the restart, taking a pass from Willie le Roux, stepping inside Liam Williams, spinning out of the clutches of Luke Cowan-Dickie and touching down in the corner. Russell then nudged the Lions ahead with a penalty before Morné Steyn replaced Handré.

When Morné was named in our matchday 23, former England fly-half Andy Goode said on a rugby podcast that it was a sign that the Lions were going to win, presumably because Morné was 37 and hadn't played for the Boks for five years. But Goode should have known that class is permanent.

At breakfast that morning I'd told Morné how excited I was about the game, how I'd been at school when he kicked that winning goal against the Lions in 2009, and how amazing it would be if he did it again. He just laughed, but no sooner had he entered the fray than he'd put us ahead from the tee. Russell responded with a long-range penalty to level the scores at 16–16 before the Lions were penalised for a ruck infringement with a minute to go. Herschel Jantjies had a rush of blood to the head, tapping and going and running straight into trouble, but referee Mathieu Raynal decided he'd taken it from the wrong place, meaning Morné had a chance to make it déjà vu.

It was about 35 m out and bang in front of the poles, and Morné stroked it right through the middle. Just as he'd done at Loftus in only his second Test match 12 years earlier, he'd broken Lions hearts at the death. There can't have been two more dramatic bookends to a Springbok career.

I told Morné at the post-match press conference, 'Remember what I said to you at breakfast?' He was lost for words, probably still trying to process what had happened. From the stadium, we went straight to our hotel and had a massive celebration. My overriding emotion was relief rather than satisfaction. Had we lost the decider I'd never have been able to put it right. But there was also the feeling that winning the series was as big an achievement as winning the World Cup.

We had a lot of faith in our ability but the fact that we were even competitive was amazing, given the restrictions placed on us and the amount of training we were able to do. That we managed to beat the Lions was almost beyond belief. Not that many people outside our camp saw it that way.

The British and Irish media were scathing about the series in general, calling it boring, an eyesore, sleep-inducing, damaging for the game. A couple of reporters even suggested it threatened the future of Lions tours. I'm sure they would have been playing a different tune if the Lions had won. Besides, we couldn't have played an expansive game even if we'd wanted to. That takes time, which we didn't have. And losing beautifully has never appealed to me. It was all about playing to our strengths and winning any way we could.

I'm also sure that the South African media and public only really cared that we won. Covid was killing thousands every week; millions were unemployed; sexual violence against women was out of control; there were violent protests all over the country, ignited by the arrest of former president Jacob Zuma; scores of people had died, hundreds of millions of dollars of damage had been done to property. The Boks beating the Lions wasn't going to solve any of that but it might make some people happy for a day or two.

10

LOVE AND FRESH PERSPECTIVES

I spent a lot of time on my own during that Lions series, and while I'm not into computer games or mindlessly scrolling through social media (I must add, we had a couple of poker tournaments in the team room), I did make first contact with my future wife.

Anlia van Rensburg was a singer and actress who starred in the Afrikaans soap opera *Getroud met Rugby*, which means 'married to rugby'. We followed each other on Instagram and she seemed lovely, so one day I decided to send her a direct message. It wasn't the greatest opening line – something like 'Hey, how you doing?' – and unsurprisingly, she didn't reply.

I'm not one to give up easily but Anlia was proving a tough nut to crack. She did eventually reply, but it was along the lines of, 'I'm good, thanks'. Hardly grounds for optimism. And by the end of the series I was thinking, *I should leave it, she's obviously not interested.*

But in the week of our first Test match against New Zealand in the Rugby Championship (in Townsville, Australia) I decided to give it one last go. This time she was a bit more responsive ('I'm good, thanks, hope you are too') and by the time of the second

Test in Gold Coast we were having fuller conversations. And when I asked if she wanted to exchange numbers, she said yes.

I was almost 30 and thought it was time to start thinking seriously about having a proper relationship. And I had a clear idea of what kind of person Anlia was, namely a nice Afrikaans girl, who seemed very down to earth and appreciated the smaller things in life, which was exactly what I was after.

I remember the first ever photo I sent to Anlia. It was after the Gold Coast game, Andy Edwards and I had gone for McDonald's, and I sent Anlia a snap of the two of us, me with a big cut on my head, having collided with Malcolm Marx. And before flying home to South Africa I told her that I'd be off for about four weeks, including two and a half weeks in Cape Town, and asked if she had any intention of being in Cape Town before I headed to Mauritius for my 30th birthday (I was heading there with my family before meeting up with the Springboks in Europe for end-of-year tour). It just so happened that she was scheduled to be there for a fitting on 12 October, so I invited her out for dinner.

I made it clear that it wasn't going to be a romantic thing, that I didn't have any expectations and that I just wanted to have a nice chat and get to know her. But it couldn't have gone any better (I even limited myself to 20 pieces of sushi instead of the usual 28 so she didn't think I was an animal).

My parents were living in my house while I was in France, and Mom was particularly excited that I was out for dinner with an actress from *Getroud met Rugby*. So I asked Anlia after dinner if she wanted to come for coffee at my place, knowing that my parents would love to meet her – especially my mom. I could tell Mom and Dad were desperate to sit with us in the lounge, but politeness got the better of them and they retreated to their room. And after a coffee I drove Anlia back to her hotel, which was just around the corner. When I returned home, Mom was waiting for me in the hallway. The first thing I said to her was, 'I think I've met my wife.' Mom was delighted because she thought Anlia was great as well.

The following morning, Anlia and I went for a long walk on the beach (where we bumped into my mom, who was walking the dogs, accidentally according to her, although I knew she was on a spying mission). We knew it was slightly complicated, what with me playing for Toulon and her being in South Africa, but we agreed to keep chatting on WhatsApp and see how things panned out. And I spent a lot of my time in Mauritius lying on a sunbed chatting to Anlia on the phone, liking her more and more as the days rolled by.

I'll never forget visiting Bismarck du Plessis and his family in Montpellier, when Handré and his wife Marise were also invited. That evening, Marise told me that one day I'd meet someone and immediately know she was the one. 'Nah, man,' I said, 'it doesn't happen like that.' I'd always thought that the idea of love at first sight was nonsense, but now there was no denying that I was smitten.

When I reunited with the Boks in Wales, the first person I bumped into was my roommate Siya. And the first thing he said to me was, 'What's wrong with you? You look different. You're moving different.' He was probably the only person on the planet who could have sensed that something potentially life-changing had happened to me.

When I told him what I'd told my mom – that I thought I'd met the woman I was going to marry – he freaked out. And he says that the first time he saw me with Anlia, he knew it was a done deal between us because I kept rubbing my feet against each other when I was laying on the bed and talking to her and looked like I had chills!

After our last end-of-year Test match against England, Anlia came to stay with me in Toulon for two weeks so we could get to know each other better. A few days into her visit, I was 100 per cent certain she was the one for me and I really wanted to propose. I managed to rein myself in – that would have been crazy, right? – but before she flew back to South Africa we spent an evening on a beach near my house and I asked her to be my girlfriend. A couple of months later I saw Marise Pollard and said, 'Do you remember what you said to me that night in France?' If I had to pick one highlight from 2021, it wouldn't be winning the Lions series. It would be meeting Anlia.

After Christmas with Anlia in South Africa, she booked to visit me in France the following March. She was due to land in Nice on the afternoon of her birthday and it seemed like the perfect time to pop the question.

The right person will bring out the romance in me – and Anlia was the right person. So before leaving Toulon I set up a treasure hunt with clues starting at the front door, continuing through the house, and including a note on a bottle of champagne that would direct her to the final destination. The plan was to apply the final touches when we returned from Nice that evening.

Unfortunately, Anlia mixed up the boarding and flight times and missed her plane from Frankfurt to Nice, but she was able to get the next one and landed just a couple of hours before our restaurant booking. I thought we'd be out of there by 10 pm but the courses kept coming – it was an unbelievable restaurant called Jan, run by chef Jan Hendrik van der Westhuizen, who cooked South African dishes with a French twist – and we left at about 12.15. We got back to my house in Toulon at about 2 am, and when we reached the front door I handed Anlia the house keys and said, 'Okay, bye.' With that, I headed to the beach to set up the grand finale while Anlia got busy with the treasure hunt. When she opened the fridge, the note on the champagne said, 'Meet me where I asked you to be my girlfriend.'

I was sitting on a blanket on the beach, surrounded by candles, when I saw Anlia's car . . . drive towards me in the far distance. By the time she located me it was about 2.30. We'd known each other for only five months, and while I was confident that she thought as much of me as I thought of her, I couldn't help imagining how awkward it would be if she said no. There were a lot of candles to blow out and it's not as if she could just drive home. Mercifully, she said yes. That was a very special evening, probably one of the best nights of my life. We got home at 3.30 am and I had to get up early again for training the next day.

*   *   *

Remarkably, the 2021 Rugby Championship had started the weekend after the third Test match against the Lions. There had been a bit of a tug of war about where the competition should take place but it was eventually decided that we'd play our first two games against Argentina in South Africa and the rest in Australia, even though it was still in virtual lockdown.

Having beaten the Pumas twice, both squads flew to Australia on the same plane, and I couldn't believe how restrictive things were down under. We were treated like zombies. We were herded off the plane and taken to the hotel before being herded straight to our rooms. There didn't seem to be any staff at the hotel but every morning someone would announce that breakfast was ready, we'd file into the room and the food would be waiting, as if prepared by fairies. We had to dish it up onto paper plates, eat it with wooden knives and forks, then go straight back to our rooms.

We had one gym session and one training session a day, and we had to juggle slots with Argentina. But if someone in our squad tested positive for Covid we'd all be confined to our rooms. Someone would knock on our door three times a day, and when we opened it our breakfast/lunch/supper would be sitting there with a few sheets of toilet roll. If we were lucky, we'd get a glimpse of the person who had delivered it scurrying off down the corridor as if they were fleeing the plague.

Australia beat us in Gold Coast and again in Brisbane, then the All Blacks narrowly beat us in Townsville, Jordie Barrett kicking the winning penalty with 2 minutes remaining. We managed to arrest our losing streak back in Gold Coast, Elton

Jantjies slotting a three-pointer with the last kick of the game, after which we could finally go home.

Rassie missed our games in Australia because he was preparing for his disciplinary hearing with World Rugby, which was scheduled to take place just before our end-of-year tour to Europe. He arrived in the UK a day later than the squad and was involved in our games against Wales and Scotland, both of which we won (that was the first time we'd beaten Wales in Cardiff since 2013, and we won thanks to a late try by Malcolm Marx). But three days before our game against England, World Rugby announced that Rassie had been found guilty of six charges\banned from all rugby activities for two months and suspended from all matchday activities until September 2022.

I thought the verdict and the punishments were unfair. I know it's awful when referees get abused, and for fans to threaten a referee's family members is a terrible look for the game, but I don't believe for 1 minute that Rassie set out to destroy Berry's career. Having said that, coaches are defined by results and if a referee has a bad day it can cost a coach his job. As such, a referee's mistakes should be pointed out in the same way as a coach or player's mistakes are pointed out.

Any criticism should be measured and constructive, but I understand why a coach's frustration might boil over if it seems there are no consequences for a referee blowing badly. And once people on social media get involved it's almost impossible to prevent criticism from curdling into disgusting invective.

There was a lot of talk of revenge in the build-up to the England game, our first encounter with them since the World Cup final. It looked like we were going to beat them again when Mapimpi scored in the corner 10 minutes from the hooter. Unfortunately for us, someone infringed at a ruck right in front of our poles and Marcus Smith duly slotted the winning penalty.

In a strange quirk of fate, that game led indirectly to the end of my career with Toulon. I hadn't played for the club at all that season because of my Bok commitments, but they knew that would be the case when I signed. I was due to start playing for them again that November, but after I got a whack on the head against England, my relationship with the club turned sour.

On my return to France, Toulon's medics confirmed that it was another concussion and because it was my third concussion in a year (the other two had happened while playing for Toulon), Top 14 rules forced me to take three months off. When I spoke about it to Toulon's president, Bernard Lemaître, he seemed sanguine. But a couple of days later, I started getting messages from people saying that they'd heard I might be for sale, which I obviously denied.

I went to see Lemaître, told him I was happy at Toulon and asked why there were rumours that I'd been made available. He said he was happy to have me and didn't know where the rumours had come from. But a few days later he described me in a newspaper interview as a 'handicap' to his club because of the money they were paying me and my international commitments.

I was obviously upset about that. Lemaître knew before he signed me that I'd be spending a lot of time with the Boks, he knew that injuries were a part of rugby, and I'd suffered two of my concussions while putting my body on the line for his team. How could he possibly be angry with me? Besides, if a club president has a problem with a player he should speak to him man to man, not gossip about him behind his back in the media. But when I went to see Lemaître again, all he could say was that it had come out wrong.

After that conversation our once good relationship was broken. I don't like it when someone talks behind my back, and it's even worse if someone can't own up to it when you speak to them man to man. I still had two years left on my contract but everything changed after a seemingly random phone call with Siya. I jokingly told him that he needed to secure me a contract with the Sharks, obviously thinking that nothing would come of it. But Siya called me back the following day, telling me he'd spoken to Sharks' boss Marco Masotti and that he'd like to chat.

Negotiations started almost immediately, and a couple of days after playing my first game of the season for Toulon against Bordeaux Bègles (which we won, despite them being top of the log and us being bottom), I told Toulon I wasn't happy being there, and they clearly weren't happy with me, so maybe we could reach a gentleman's agreement that I finish the current season before heading back to my beloved South Africa.

That was a sad end to my time in France. Toulon looked after me well financially but money isn't the be all and end all. And while I loved the city and the weather and had made some good friends (Cheslin had joined that season, as had Quinn Roux and Cornell du Preez, and I was really good mates with some of the French guys, especially eighthman Raphaël Lakafia, as well as some locals, including butcher Paul, his family and his friend Olivier), my heart belonged in South Africa, as it always will.

I'd barely seen my family for two years, during which my dad was battling cancer, and I knew he didn't have long left (he'd already lost four brothers by then). I also had a lot of old friends and teammates at the Sharks, including Siya, Bongi, Mapimpi, Lukhanyo and Thomas du Toit, and it felt like a club with ambition.

On top of all that, Anlia would have to give up her singing career to be with me in Toulon and family was also important to her. She wouldn't even get to hang out with me every Sunday because I was often playing in the evening, the thing I most disliked about French rugby. So while she always said she mustn't be the reason for me returning to South Africa, it made a lot of sense for her as well.

As for why I didn't rejoin the Stormers, it was simply because the Sharks moved so fast that WP didn't have the chance to swoop. And while it would have been nice to go back home to Cape Town, it would have been unethical to get a nice deal from the Sharks and use that to leverage more money from the Stormers. The Sharks had put the work in, I was happy with what they were offering, and that was the end of it as far as I was concerned.

A few days after my impending departure was reported in

the media, I was dismayed to hear that my old teammate Bakkies Botha had criticised me in an interview with a French rugby newspaper. Bakkies accused me of 'turning my back' on Toulon, reneging on my promise of wanting to win the Top 14 and only 'showing my best face with the Springboks'.

When you play for the Boks, you expect to get grief from the media and fans, but I was upset and angry to be getting *kak* from a former teammate, especially someone with whom I thought I had a good relationship. As well as that, when you become a Bok the coach reads you a code of honour which includes a bit about respecting other guys in the jersey. That's why I'll never say anything negative about a former teammate, even when I'm retired.

I decided to put out a tweet – 'Next time you want to ENFORCE an opinion, you've got my number #exspringbok-teammates #onthoujouerekode ['remember your honour code']' – and Bakkies called me shortly afterwards and said his comments had been taken out of context. It wasn't a bad-tempered conversation, we certainly didn't fall out, and I took Bakkies at his word. Then I got back to training so that I could be at my best for Toulon until the end of the season.

Injuring my calf before our game against Perpignan, which led to another spell on the sidelines, wasn't part of the plan but I was back for the knockout stages of the European Challenge Cup. And after wins over London Irish in the quarter-finals and Saracens in the semis, what had at one point looked like being a disastrous season for Toulon suddenly looked quite bright (a run of wins had also lifted us to mid-table respectability in the Top 14).

Cheslin was back for the final against Lyon in Marseille, having recovered from a broken thumb, but neither he nor tens of thousands of our fans who had made the trip were able to prevent us being blown away in the second half. We made too many simple errors and butchered too many try-scoring chances, while Lyon were far more accurate and good value for their 30–12 victory.

Some might think that two European finals in two years represented a successful stint in France, but that's not how I see it. If you come up short in a final you're just the first of all the losers. And it was only the final of the Challenge Cup.

I went into our series against Wales on 97 caps but I knew Rassie and Jacques wanted to experiment with new players, so I wasn't guaranteed to reach 100 caps in the third Test in Cape Town.

We trailed 18–3 at half-time in the first Test at Loftus, but four of their players were sin-binned (they were down to 12 men at one point in the second half) and we ended up winning a thriller 32–29, Stormers' full back Damian Willemse slotting the winning penalty with the last kick of the game.

Sure enough, our run-out XV showed 14 changes for the second Test in Bloemfontein, and Rassie told everyone I'd kept my place only so I could win my 100th cap in Cape Town. Some Welsh commentators, including legendary scrum half Gareth Edwards, thought our coaches were being disrespectful by fielding what they regarded as a B team, while South African publications wondered why Rassie and

Jacques would risk losing a Test match. But it was all part of their grand plan.

Since taking over in 2018, the coaching duo had been trying to build a squad of more than just 23 match day players. For that to happen they needed 30-odd players who could perform in big games and slot in and out without making any difference to the team's performances. As Jacques put it, 'If the players chosen for the second Test are going to face New Zealand at the World Cup next year, they must perform under pressure. Should we win, the Cape Town Test will become a dead rubber.'

Furthermore, while six uncapped players were selected for the game in Bloemfontein, including two starters in 22-year-old Stormers loose forward Evan Roos and Bulls flyer Kurt-Lee Arendse, who wasn't much bigger than Cheslin but almost as elusive, they weren't exactly lambs to the slaughter.

Roos had recently been voted the United Rugby Championship (URC) player of the season; Harlequins' André Esterhuizen, a beast of a man, was without doubt the most destructive centre in the English Premiership; Marcell Coetzee was returning to the fold after a three-year absence but had never stopped being a world-class flanker; 35-year-old Stormers flanker Deon Fourie hadn't played a Test match but was vastly experienced; and Sharks scrum halves Jaden Hendrikse and Grant Williams were both extremely talented.

Rassie and Jacques genuinely thought those guys were good enough to beat Wales, and the fact that we ended up losing that second Test when we should have put it to bed by half-time was neither here nor there in the grand scheme of things. As Jacques said, 'The answers we got outweighed the risk.'

I didn't want to make a big thing of my 100th cap but I didn't have much choice. The media wanted to talk about it, my teammates wanted to make it a special week, and the coaches were bound to mention it at some point. Not only that, but my family was also going to be at Cape Town Stadium, including my sick dad, who probably wouldn't have been able to make it had we been playing anywhere else.

It was going to be an emotional occasion, for sure, so when I suspected that Anlia was hiding something from me I had to act. I said to her, 'Listen, my love, it's going to be a big week for me so please don't spring any surprises. Just tell me if you're planning anything.' Anlia is terrible at hiding stuff from me and she quickly told me that she was going to sing the national anthem before the game. Thank goodness she cracked because I'd have been in serious shock running out and seeing her on the field.

Anlia had promised SARU that she wouldn't tell me and I fully intended to keep it under my hat. Then came Monday's team announcement. Rassie started by reading out the names as normal – '1, Trevor; 2, Bongi; 3, Frans' – but when he reached me he said, 'Eben, it's your 100th game, congratulations. By the way, your fiancée is going to sing the national anthem. I don't want you to be too emotional. So now you know. 5, Lood; 6, Siya . . .' He wasn't meant to tell me, either, but Rassie, who is one of the most matter-of-fact men, was more concerned about winning the series than any personal milestones.

Frans Malherbe and I were feeling under the weather a day or two before the game and we both thought we might have to pull out if we didn't feel better by Friday morning. As it turned out, we didn't improve much but the doc did what he could and we both made it to the starting line.

It was also Bongi's 50th cap but I had the honour of running out first, and the sight of 'EBEN 100' writ large in fire, accompanied by the colossal roar of the crowd, gave me goose bumps. It was extra special standing next to Frans for the anthem because he'd been beside me – No 3 to my No 4 – since we were teenagers at Craven Week. For me, he's the best tighthead to have ever worn the green and gold, and he's such a respected guy in the Springbok setup. Hopefully, he'll be by my side for many more years after we're done with rugby.

When Anlia started singing I really struggled to hold it together. If you look back at the footage, I manage to sing along for a while but I'm pretty much gone by the end of the second verse. By the time Anlia reaches the end of the fourth and final verse, I can no longer hold back the tears.

Rassie had sent me a voice note the day before, telling me that he knew it would be an emotional day and that I should get it all out during the anthem. That way, he said, I'd be focused on the game when it started. That was wise advice, as always. You get judged on your performances in professional sport, and if we lost the Test match it would be the first time Wales had beaten us in a series. It wouldn't have mattered that it was my 100th cap, or that my fiancée had sung the anthem, or that I hadn't felt great in the build-up, or that my dad had been ill. The record books would simply have said: South Africa 1–2 Wales.

Rassie and Jacques made 10 changes to the matchday squad, with only five of us retaining our run-out spots and eight starters from the 2019 World Cup final brought back into the fold. It wasn't that the other guys had performed badly in Bloemfontein, just that we needed our most battle-hardened players on the field to finish the job. And you'd have to say they got their selections spot on.

We would have been over the hill and far away by half-time had we not missed a host of chances, but the result was never really in doubt after we changed our entire front row 5 minutes into the second half. We were leading 24–14 when Franco Mostert replaced me on the hour, and two late penalties by Handré sealed the deal.

We had a nice function after the game, where I received my 100th cap (my dad was part of the presentation), followed by some beers back at the hotel. Anlia arranged something special at our house on the Sunday, with close family and friends but my achievement only really sank in later that day when I looked at my phone and saw I'd been added to a WhatsApp group called 'Boks Centurions'.

There was my name alongside six bona fide Bok legends: Percy Montgomery, the first to reach the milestone and still South Africa's leading points scorer; John Smit, 83 times a captain and the man who led the Boks to World Cup glory in

2007; Jean de Villiers, one of the classiest centres ever to wear the green and gold; Bryan Habana, South Africa's leading try scorer; Beast, who terrorised opposition front rows all over the world for more than a decade; and Victor Matfield, with a Bok record 127 caps to his name.

I was transported back to joining the Stormers as a 19-year-old, when I was in awe of anyone who had worn the green and gold and looked upon the likes of Montgomery, Smit, De Villiers, Habana, Beast and Matfield as almost mythical beings. And now here I was, part of the same special club as them.

Karen Etzebeth, Eben's mom: When Eben started playing for the Springboks I couldn't quite believe it but I was very, very proud. And it was overwhelming reading all the nice things that people were writing about him. I'd think, Wow, this is my son they're talking about, *and tears would well up in my eyes.*

I will never forget his first Test match for the Springboks on 9 June 2012, a day before my 50th birthday. He flew me, my husband and Ryen down to Durban for the weekend, we watched them beat England, and on the Sunday morning, Eben arranged for a birthday cake to be delivered to our room. It's a memory I'll cherish forever.

I'd pray for him before every game and I'd get upset if he got into fights on the field. If he got involved in some pushing and shoving, Ryen would try to stir the pot – 'Look, Eben is fighting!' – and I was in tears when he played his 50th Test and they ripped his jersey off him.

But I knew he'd never punch anyone and he seemed to become less angry as time went on. He'd have that smile on his face whenever he scuffled with an opponent, and I'd know he had his emotions under control.

Eben has a lot of friends but family is the most important thing to him. If he has a spare weekend he'll always choose to spend it with his family and he loves sharing big milestones with us. He made sure we were in the stadium for his first Test, and almost as soon as the 2019 World Cup semi-final was over he called us to say we had to fly in for the final. He was so thrilled.

That was one of our biggest family highlights, especially when they won. I couldn't wait to get to Eben after the final whistle, and he managed to smuggle us past security. We were then invited back to the team hotel and really made to feel part of the celebrations. They went on long into the night but I couldn't sleep when my head hit the pillow. I was still too excited.

Someone took a photo of me and Eben hugging on the field, which Gavin Varejes got someone to do a painting of and sent to Eben as a present. It's now in my kitchen and I look at it every day and smile. He gave his World Cup final jersey to his brother and it now has pride of place on a wall in Ryen's house.

As well as that painting, I've got his jersey from his 55th Test, which was against France on my birthday. He kept the jersey from his 100th Test but we were lucky enough to be in the stadium that day. My husband Harry was very sick at the time so Eben arranged for us to sit in the VIP suite, where they made him as comfortable as possible. That day couldn't have been more perfect: the game was played in our home city of Cape

Town, the organisers put on such a great show, and the realisa-
tion that my son was now a Springbok legend made me so
emotional.

Eben doesn't show a lot of emotion but his dad's passing was
a very difficult time for him. Eben couldn't fail to feel his dad's
pride, and they'd grown closer towards the end. When Harry
was in hospital he told Eben how sorry he was that he wouldn't
get to meet his granddaughter, and Eben had to leave the room
because he was so overcome. He was heartbroken when the end
came.

Ryen and I were also in the stadium when Eben became the
most-capped Springbok in history, which still sounds crazy. But
he seems to care more about his loved ones the more caps he
wins, and he's a mommy's boy, in a nice way. He calls me every
morning on his way to training.

His faith is very important to him – it's nice to see him praying on his knees before every game – and it's wonderful seeing
what a good husband he is. Anlia is such a good-hearted, down
to earth girl and Eben is so happy with her. I can see it in his
eyes; they're always smiling since he met her.

He's also a very happy father and so involved in raising their
daughter. He's away a lot with his rugby but he bathes, feeds,
changes and plays with his daughter whenever he's at home or
away on a family holiday, rather than going out with his friends
and leaving his wife to do all the work.

We're used to sharing Eben with the rest of the country now,
and it's just about sunk in what an iconic figure he is in South
African rugby. But while Eben is a very proud Springbok and

loves achieving things for his country, rugby isn't everything to him. As long as his family is happy, he's happy.

We started the 2022 Rugby Championship with a bang, beating New Zealand 26–10 in Mbombela. It was our biggest victory over the All Blacks since 1928, the first time we'd won consecutive games against them since 2009 and the first time we'd beaten them at home since 2014. It also meant the All Blacks had lost five of their last six Tests and dropped to fifth in the world rankings, which by their standards was a crisis of unprecedented proportions.

In the previous nine months they'd been beaten by France in Paris and lost three out of four against Ireland. France and Ireland had developed into fine attacking teams full of skilful, mobile forwards, which reflected how the game had changed quite a bit over a short period. Not too long ago, most sides had big, lumbering locks who were mainly prized for their power in the scrum and height in the line-out. But now there were locks such as New Zealand's Scott Barrett, France's Cameron Woki, Ireland's Tadhg Beirne and the Boks' Franco Mostert, guys who were still relatively big but were also supremely fit and athletic, more like extra loose forwards.

Something similar had happened to wingers. England's Jason Robinson was one of my favourite players when I was a kid and he was 173 cm and 80 kg. Wales's Shane Williams was widely viewed as an anachronism (along with Jason), perhaps the last of his kind. People thought modern wingers needed to be at least 100 kg so they could run over the top of defenders. Then Cheslin, who is about the same size as Robinson and Williams were, came along and changed the conversation.

Kurt-Lee Arendse came hot on Cheslin's heels and other countries were also selecting steppers and outright speedsters rather than bulldozers. Argentina had some electrifying smaller wings, including Mateo Carreras, France had Louis Bielle-Biarrey and Gabin Villière, Italy had Ange Capuozzo, Scotland had Darcy Graham. They were what you might call 'X-factor' players, guys who could produce something from nothing when their teammates were struggling to find a way through. And none of them would be on the field if they didn't punch above their weight and do their defensive duties properly.

Our coaching team had come to understand that we couldn't be direct all the time and expect to keep beating the best teams in big games; we had to start being more unpredictable. We'd been able to win a World Cup and a Lions series by being predictable, because we were so good at what we did. But opposition teams were bound to adapt and find ways to counteract our strengths, so we had to evolve.

Instead of going into every game thinking, 'We'll just scrum and maul them to death,' we needed to start thinking, 'Everyone expects us to do that, what if we sometimes do something else?' Perhaps we'd even reach a stage where we caught teams off guard by mauling rather than running the ball!

We hadn't had time to upskill ourselves before the Lions

series but it had always been the plan to add a new dimension to our game in 2022, and Felix Jones was central to this plan. As South Africans, Rassie and Jacques knew what we needed in terms of the set piece and physicality, but Felix, while knowing we were never going to abandon our traditional way of playing, gave us fresh perspectives and a sharper attacking edge.

Having said all that, anyone who thought New Zealand rugby was in terminal decline got a rude awakening when we played the All Blacks at Ellis Park. With the media reporting that head coach Ian Foster's job was on the line, the All Blacks reverted to their old ruthless selves, scoring two tries in the last 7 minutes to take the game away from us. That was them saying they hadn't gone anywhere and remained a formidable outfit.

Another team apparently in a bit of a fix were Australia, who had lost six of their last eight Test matches. Argentina had drubbed them 48–17 in their most recent game, leading their head coach Dave Rennie to make wholesale changes for the game against us in Adelaide. And they worked. Young flanker Fraser McReight went over for their first try after only 2 minutes and they defended like madmen for the rest of the half. Two more tries after the break put them out of sight, and two late tries by Kwagga were mere consolations.

Australia had rarely been a happy hunting ground for the Boks since readmission – we hadn't beaten the Wallabies on their patch since 2013 – but Rassie didn't care about any of that and was really pissed off on the Monday after that game (he was still serving a matchday ban). Rassie is brilliant at that: whenever he thinks we're showing signs of complacency he'll grab us by the throats and shake us out of it. 'Hey,' he'll say, 'don't think you've arrived.' That's what you need if you want to keep winning.

Our coaches could accept a team outsmarting us but they couldn't accept a team outmuscling us and looking like they wanted it more. So they made our next game against the Wallabies very personal and told us to treat it like a World Cup semi-final, which ramped up the pressure and was great preparation for France 2023.

The coaches made eight changes for the Test match at the new Sydney Football Stadium (some injury-enforced, some tactical) and we were a completely different proposition. We battered them up front, our kicking game was spot on, our finishing was clinical and we won 24–8, scoring four tries to one. It was a spiky, belligerent performance, just what the doctor ordered.

Two victories over Argentina, including a bonus point in Buenos Aires, would have been enough to win the competition had something weird not occurred when Australia played the All Blacks in Melbourne: the Wallabies fought back from 18 points down to lead by one with seconds to go, and when Lalakai Foketi secured a turnover penalty in front of his own posts it seemed like the Wallabies had won. But the referee adjudged that Aussie fly-half Bernard Foley had taken too long lining up his kick to touch and awarded a scrum to New Zealand. Inevitably, the All Blacks rumbled forward, spun the ball wide, and Jordie Barrett went over in the corner to win it.

The following weekend, the All Blacks battered Australia in Auckland to pip us to the Championship by a point. It was their third title in a row and their ninth since the competition was expanded to four teams in 2012, compared to our four titles since 1996.

Before our end-of-year tour there was a lot of talk in the European media about a changing of the guard in world rugby.

Only one northern hemisphere side had won the World Cup, England in 2003, while New Zealand or South Africa had won every tournament since then, as well as dominating the world rankings. But France topped the rankings for the first time in 2022 off the back of a big win over the All Blacks in Paris and a Six Nations Grand Slam, before Ireland replaced them as top dogs after their historic series win in New Zealand.

I could understand why European journalists and pundits were getting excited about the possibility of a northern hemisphere World Cup winner, because Ireland and France were very good teams. What they might not have known was that we were loving it because it took some pressure off us.

We were also able to take lots of positives from our defeats by Ireland and France on that tour. The game in Dublin was a thunderous yet tense affair which they won 19–16. But we made a lot of errors, missed try-scoring opportunities, as well as a few kicks at the poles. If they were a better team than us it wasn't by much. And when we played them next, in the pool stage of the World Cup, it would be on neutral ground.

I'd never lost to France in five Test matches before then, and they hadn't beaten the Boks since 2009. We even put 30 points on them three games in a row in 2017, when we were going through one of our worst patches. But having underachieved for so long this French side was very different, full of players who had come through successful junior teams and were now world-class and brimming with confidence. They also had a genuine contender for one of the best players in the world and best scrum half of all time in Antoine Dupont. Some said he couldn't be considered great because he'd barely played in the southern hemisphere, but I didn't understand that argument. Wherever he had played he was usually superb.

But despite all their talent they only just edged a titanic battle 30–26, even though we played with 14 men for 69 minutes and had some questionable calls go against us. Referee Wayne Barnes showed Pieter-Steph a red card (for a clash of heads with Jonathan Danty) and Dupont a red card early in the second half (for taking Cheslin out in the air). But having put in a monumental shift to lead by four points, Deon Fourie was sent to the bin for a maul infringement with 10 minutes to go, and a few minutes later replacement France prop Sipili Falatea forced his way over for the winning try.

Replays suggested it might have been a double movement, and Barnes lost communication with the TMO while they were reviewing it, which sparked social media conspiracy theories. But once the dust had settled our main takeaway was that if we could almost beat France in those circumstances, we had it in us to beat them if we were at full strength, which we'd hopefully be if we played them again at the World Cup.

We were also cheered up by the clip of Cheslin bumping Anthony Jelonch, France's 112 kg flanker, that was doing the rounds on social media. However, the mainstream media preferred to make a big thing of tweets by Rassie.

The tweets drew attention to a handful of marginal refereeing decisions, including Falatea's try, a pass from Willie le Roux that was called forward and a forearm hand-off by France full back Thomas Ramos, and they ignited another storm. Barnes received horrendous abuse on social media, while some vile characters also threatened his wife and children.

Rassie tried to explain himself at a press conference, saying the tweets were only meant for Springbok fans, but World Rugby took a different view, condemning his criticism of match officials and banning him for our games against Italy and England. (We put 60 points on Italy in Genoa, while Kurt-Lee Arendse starred in a pretty comfortable win over England, which made the tour a positive one despite the 50 per cent winning record.)

I can't say everyone always agrees with Rassie's methods but people are mistaken if they think those tweets were the work of an unhinged madman. Everything Rassie does, he does for a reason. He reminds me of Michael Scofield, the main character from *Prison Break*, in that he's constantly hatching elaborate plans. And however crazy they sound, they always come off.

11

THE CIRCLE OF LIFE

Anlia and I wanted to get married in October 2022, but international duty meant I'd miss the start of the season with my new club the Sharks and I couldn't really be swanning off on honeymoon between the end of the Rugby Championship and the start of our European tour. In addition, I didn't want to be one of those guys who got married on a Saturday and was back training on the Monday (I'd seen an awful lot of those during my career).

We were going to do things properly and we booked La Paris Estate in Franschhoek, a beautiful old town in the Western Cape, for the following February. However, in September the doctor told my mom that Dad was unlikely to make it past December, and Anlia suggested we move the wedding forward to October and make it a smaller affair. Most women dream of having a big fairy-tale wedding and I was in awe that Anlia was suggesting something else, so that Dad could be there. I really was marrying my soulmate.

Nevertheless, I decided to stick with February because I was confident Dad would make it. He never wanted to miss out on anything and was a stubborn so and so. We did have a small engagement party at our house in October, but Dad would have seen it as just another goal achieved before looking forward to the next one.

We wanted to keep the wedding smallish, but that's not easy when one of you is in the TV/music industry and the other is a rugby player. Luckily for us – and I mean that in a nice way! – a lot of my teammates, current and former, were playing in Europe or Japan, all of them had games that weekend, and only six or seven of my Sharks teammates (those who were on a rest period with the Boks) had the weekend off. The rest were playing against the Stormers! Plus, my good mate Frans Malherbe was getting married on the same day (men tend not to compare notes on that kind of thing), so I lost a few friends to his wedding and he lost a few to mine.

My brother was my best man, naturally, while Siya was a groomsman alongside my brother-in-law, my cousin and an old schoolfriend. I'd asked a guy called Paul, who looked after me when I was in Toulon, to bring over a small bucket of sand from Plage de l'Almanarre, where I asked Anlia to be my girl-friend and my wife, and we poured that into a big shell and placed our rings on top. When the time came, Dad brought the shell up to the altar, which was just one special moment on a very special day.

The reception took place in a big marquee, and because it was such a beautiful evening –warm with no wind – we opened the sides so we could move seamlessly between inside and out. Just before I had to go up for my speech, Anlia stood up, took the microphone and said she had a surprise for me – it wasn't going to be a speech. She'd written a song for me, with the words describing our lives together since we'd met. I got very emotional when she sang it, and I couldn't really fight back the tears.

Later that night, we went for a stroll and looked back at the marquee. It was such a special moment: the most precious people in our lives celebrating our union. My life had been full of highlights, on and off the field, but I was sure nothing would ever top marrying Anlia.

Our honeymoon in the Maldives and Dubai was awesome, two weeks of total relaxation with the woman I love – and not thinking about anything. However, a couple of days after returning home I was in a Springbok training camp, the first of a World Cup year. Strength and conditioning coach Andy Edwards had been at my wedding, and something must have pissed him off that night because it was one of the worst sessions ever, it felt like he was trying to kill us. Sometimes we're asked to rate a session out of 10, eight being really tough and nine being ridiculously tough. That first day back training was a 10, as in I felt like I was going to die.

Moving to the Sharks meant playing in the URC, which had started out as the Celtic League (Welsh, Scottish and Irish teams) before the addition of Italian then South African sides.

Before joining the Sharks I kind of understood why South African teams had swapped Super Rugby for the URC, but after playing in it for a few months I sensed that some players really missed Super Rugby. Initially, the guys thought the travel would be easier because Europe was in roughly the same time zone as South Africa. But we didn't take into consideration that the flights wouldn't be direct and we wouldn't be travelling business class, as we were used to in Super Rugby.

In Super Rugby, South African teams would have one tour down under in the regular season, then maybe another if we reached the play-off stages. But the Sharks had three regular season tours to Europe in my first URC season, plus another for our quarter-final against Leinster. On top of that, we had two trips to Europe in the pool stage of the Champions Cup, and while we secured a home draw for the round of 16, we were back in Europe for our quarter-final against Toulouse.

I could also see why the European teams were annoyed, because they'd had a nice local thing going on before South African teams turned up. The furthest they'd had to travel for a game was a few hours on a plane, and now they were having to fly 11+ hours to South Africa.

Sometimes it's tough to see our guys travel economy class for such long flights, especially the bigger ones, and then have to perform for 80 minutes a couple of days later.

It's not the most professional preparation, but while some guys complain about it they're the cards we've been dealt, and they should never lose sight of the fact that they're lucky to do what they do for a living (and we've been assured that travelling will only become easier).

Springbok players were also used to being off from the end of November to January, but that was out of the window. Suddenly, we were playing rugby over Christmas and New

Year, which is traditionally when South African players recharge their batteries and spend precious time with their families.

Twelve or 13 Test matches a season is a gruelling schedule but we were okay with it when South African franchises were playing in the southern hemisphere. However, now that Springboks were playing their club rugby to a northern hemisphere schedule and their international rugby to a southern hemisphere schedule, we almost never got a break.

Moreover, South African franchises were forced to play the start of the URC without their Boks, who were playing in the Rugby Championship. And once the Champions Cup kicked in, coaches had to prioritise certain games to protect their players, compromising the integrity of competitions.

I also felt a bit sorry for South African rugby fans, because they loved Super Rugby. When I played for the Stormers, whenever a New Zealand team came to Cape Town the locals would gather outside their hotel in the hope of getting a selfie or an autograph, or even just a glimpse of a Ma'a Nonu or Julian Savea, and they were almost as enthusiastic about superstar Wallabies such as Quade Cooper and Will Genia.

Those guys were household names in South Africa, and I'm not sure some of the URC teams hold the same appeal for South African fans as the Crusaders, the Hurricanes or the Highlanders. Beyond that, franchises involved in the URC are unable to make top players available for the Currie Cup, further devaluing that proud old competition.

But while I'd choose Super Rugby over playing in Europe,

the move to the Sharks was the best I ever made, and I thought we might have a chance of winning some silverware. That said, I certainly didn't expect us to rock up in Europe and blow teams away. The URC wasn't as tough as Super Rugby and we were very competitive when we had all our Boks. But, as I already knew from my time in Toulon, the Champions Cup was the toughest club competition out there, especially when we played against French sides.

Because the Top 14 salary cap is much higher than in other leagues, teams can assemble sides full of stars, homegrown and foreign, plus lots of decent back-up players. In contrast, South African teams generally have a very good starting XV, some good reserves and lots of younger works in progress.

While the URC could be quite fast and expansive (unless weather conditions made running rugby almost impossible, which would often be the case in the UK and Ireland), some Champions Cup games felt more like Test matches. Not quite as intense, but close. If we played Leinster in the Champions Cup, their line-up would be most of the Ireland team, while the top French sides were packed with internationals from all over the world. And when we played teams like Toulouse, La Rochelle or Clermont on their patch, their grounds would be packed and the fans would be noisy and hostile, more like a football crowd, which would give the games a real edge.

I made my Sharks debut against The Glasgow Warriors in Durban, a URC game we won quite easily. But we got a taste of how difficult life in Europe would be when we got beaten 35–0 at home by Cardiff (The Springboks were away on end-of-year tour). Head coach Neil Powell then decided to rest a few players for a URC game against Ospreys, with a Champions Cup home game against Harlequins followed by an away fixture against Bordeaux Bègles in mind. That was the problem in a nutshell: by prioritising the Champions Cup we had to sacrifice some results in the URC, while also trying to do well enough to qualify for the Champions Cup the following season. And while some accused us of disrespecting the URC, we were just trying to manage our resources the best we could.

We pulled out a great performance to beat Munster 50–35 in the Champions Cup round of 16, but I dislocated my shoulder in the first half, making for a particularly unfunny April Fool's Day. It served me right for thinking I was a fetcher, sticking my head into a ruck and getting cleaned out.

I hoped it wasn't something that was going to keep me out for six months because that would have jeopardised my World Cup chances. As it turned out, my surgery went well, I was given a recovery time of 12–16 weeks, and the medical people at the Boks and the Sharks came up with a rehab plan so that I might be ready for the start of the Rugby Championship in July.

While I was out injured, the Sharks had the misfortune of playing Toulouse at their place in the Champions Cup quarter-finals. They beat us, scoring seven tries to two, though it meant we could focus on qualifying for the URC play-offs. But having just managed to scrape eighth place on the log, Leinster beat us with not much fuss in the last eight.

Instead of playing in the Champions Cup the following season we'd be playing in the second-tier Challenge Cup, which wasn't what the Sharks' owners, who had pumped lots of money into the team, had planned. Still, it was the best rugby environment I'd ever been in at club level, in terms of the way they treated me and my family, and I was sure silverware would come.

After our wedding, Dad's next goal was to make Mom's birthday on 10 June. I'd booked for both our families to stay in Montagu, Avalon Springs, a place we'd been visiting since we were little (our parents had a timeshare there back in the day). And because it had hot springs it was the perfect place for a chilly South African winter.

A week before we were due to go, Dad had a big setback and was in and out of hospital, so we wondered if we should cancel. But when we raised the subject with him he was matter-of-fact: 'I'm coming with you.'

Then, a few days before we left for Montagu, Anlia told me something that would make our trip a double celebration: she was pregnant. Wow, what a moment.

We wouldn't normally have told anyone that early, but with both sets of parents there it seemed like the perfect opportunity. We revealed our wonderful news on the evening of Mom's birthday party, and it triggered lots of tears and popping of champagne corks. Afterwards, Dad told Anlia's father, 'Okay, now I've got another reason to keep living.'

Dad soldiered on into July, but when I visited him before leaving for our Rugby Championship game in New Zealand I had a feeling it might be our last goodbye. Even so, there was never any thought of staying home. Had I suggested that to Dad he would have said, 'Have you lost your mind?'

It was Tuesday and I'd just boarded the team bus when I got the text from Ryen: 'Can I phone you quickly?' I knew immediately what he was going to tell me. Sure enough, Dad had passed away. I walked down the front to tell Rassie and Jacques that I wouldn't be able to train, and they knew what had happened just by the look on my face.

When the guys got back to the hotel after training, Rassie and Jacques asked if I wanted to go home. I was meant to be captain in Siya's absence and they were probably worried that I wasn't in the right frame of mind to lead the team. But there was no part of me that wanted to miss that game.

Some probably thought I should have been with my family, but they didn't know my dad. I suspect he would have said, 'What for? I'm dead now, there's nothing you can do. And your brother is with your mom. They'll be fine and you've got an important job to do, playing for your country.'

Dad loved rugby, especially the Springboks. When I was named Springbok captain first time around, he almost couldn't handle the pride. When we went out for dinner, Dad would go to the bathroom, return to our table with a handful of random people and say, 'This is my son, you probably know him.'

I'd have to chat to these people and have my photo taken with them, and when it was finally over Dad would sit down looking sheepish, like a naughty child. 'Dad,' I'd say, 'why are you bringing people to the table? How did they know I was even here?' 'I don't know,' he'd reply, 'they probably saw you walking in.' That obviously wasn't true – he was asking those people in the bathroom, 'Do you know who my son is? Would you like to meet him?'

He would have been mad if I had turned down the chance of leading the Boks in a Test match against the All Blacks. And I truly believe he was watching, just as he's watched everything I've done since he physically departed. That's why I'll never stop making him proud in green and gold, but also by being a good son, a good brother, a good husband and a good father.

That was an emotional week for me and the team didn't play well at the end of it, losing 35–20 in Auckland. We pipped Argentina by a point two weeks later but still finished second on the log behind New Zealand, who hammered Australia in Melbourne. Our last game before flying to Europe was against the Pumas in Buenos Aires, and we won more comfortably, although I missed it because of my knee, which had been bothering me all year. Then we all had to sit tight for a couple of days until our World Cup squad was announced.

An injection in my knee was set to put me out of action for 10 days or so, meaning I'd also miss the warm-up game against Wales (in Cardiff). But others weren't so lucky.

My old lock partner Lood de Jager was ruled out of the tournament through illness, while another big loss was Handré, who had been struggling with a calf injury all year. We had a braai and a couple of drinks after the squad was announced, and I felt bad for the guys who hadn't been selected, especially Handré, who seemed to be in a bad place. He thought he could have been ready in time but Rassie and Jacques wanted to treat those warm-up games as if they were part of the tournament, so they didn't want to take too many players who couldn't play in them.

After the function I went to Handré and told him, 'Listen, I know this is tough for you but I've got a funny feeling you'll somehow get called up and win the World Cup for us.' He probably thought I was just saying that to make him feel better, but I really believed it.

One guy who would be on the plane was Siya, despite not playing a Test match all year. He'd busted his knee playing for the Sharks against Munster in April and had two or three medical opinions before undergoing surgery.

He went through some dark times over the next four months and wasn't always convinced he'd recover in time. But having fought back from a couple of bad injuries myself, I was able to empathise. I'd say to him, 'Just take it day by day and make sure you've got the right people around you.' I knew how much the Boks meant to him and how desperate he was to lead them at the World Cup, so I never had any doubts that he'd be ready.

The morning after the Boks put 50 points on an experimental Wales side, I went for a gym session in the hotel. On my way into the gym, I saw Rassie drinking a coffee on his own. He called me over and asked if I'd be fit for the All Blacks at Twickenham, and I told him I'd be ready. He replied, 'Okay, great. But don't worry, you might only play 45 minutes anyway, we're thinking of putting seven forwards on the bench. Don't tell anybody else.' I loved the idea, as you might expect, though I can't say it didn't take me by surprise. I walked off shaking my head and thinking, *This guy is on another level.*

Some people thought a 7–1 bench split was against the spirit of the game but I had no time for that argument. First, we were playing by the rules and any team could do the same. And while rugby involves lots of different skill sets – speed, coordination, agility, fitness – it's ultimately a collision sport and teams must do whatever they can to win the confrontational battle.

It's about playing to your strengths, so while other teams were happy to continue with three backs on the bench, guys who could open up defences when things became a bit more broken, we had two packs of forwards that were equally capable in the set piece. That's why having seven forwards on the bench and introducing them with 35 minutes to go made total sense to us.

Obviously, having only one back on the bench was a risk. It meant the coaches would have to delay introducing him until absolutely necessary, because he was covering all positions from No 9 to No 15, and if two or more starting backs got injured we'd have to replace them with one or more forwards. But being the genius that he is, Rassie considered all eventualities – *What if the scrum half gets injured? What if a centre has to go off?* – which is why Kwagga and Pieter-Steph trained to slot into the backline if needed.

The backline might have to be rejigged (you're never going to see Kwagga or Pieter-Steph playing at 10) and you'd put them in positions in defence and attack where they wouldn't have to think too much. But they certainly wouldn't be panicking, and neither would their teammates, because we'd have seen them playing there in training and coping perfectly well.

There was so much excitement that week, at least among the forwards (I didn't ask any backs what they thought about the 7–1 split because I didn't really care!), and the game couldn't have gone much better. We were 14–0 up when All Black lock Scott Barrett was shown a red card just before half-time, and all seven of our replacement forwards entered the fray in the 48th minute.

I'll never forget the ref saying, 'Okay – 1, 2, 3, 4, 5, 6 and 8, you're all off', and it was only our No 7, Pieter-Steph, who stayed on. Us seven big guys being replaced by seven more big guys must have been an arresting sight, and I was almost giggling by the time I reached the bench. I honestly hope Rassie goes 8–0 one day, just to see the reaction!

We ended up beating New Zealand 35–7, their biggest defeat. But while it was one of the most enjoyable games I'd played in, it worried me slightly. I said to a teammate that night, 'I hope we don't play them again at the World Cup because I'm scared that some guys will think, *We hammered them a couple of months ago, of course we'll do it again*.'

I knew how New Zealand could turn things on when they wanted to, so I hoped everyone in the Bok set-up would forget about that admittedly great day at Twickenham as soon as possible.

12

THAT'S TRANSFORMATION

The draw for the World Cup was made at the end of 2020, and a lot had happened in rugby since then. By the time the tournament started it looked likely that only two of the top five teams in the rankings would reach the last four, and three of the top five were in Pool B: South Africa, Ireland and Scotland.

But there was no point dwelling on our bad luck; we'd just have to beat Scotland in our opening game and take it from there. If we did beat them it would give us breathing space; if we didn't we'd have a knife against our neck when we played Ireland. Lose that one as well and we'd be dead men walking.

We had a good training camp in Corsica, where it was hotter than the sun. As ever, our big rocks would be the set piece and defence, but Rassie had concluded that scrums and mauls had become so difficult to officiate that we needed more clear-cut ways of scoring points. As such, there was more emphasis on improving skill sets – basic but important stuff like passing properly – especially for the forwards. Opposition teams knew we were going to scrum for a penalty here and maul for a penalty there, but we introduced some quick tap moves and special plays. And everyone in our squad needed to have the necessary skills to pull off the unpredictable.

Scotland were one of my favourite European teams. Not only did I love the passion and atmosphere the Scottish fans brought to Murrayfield (my favourite stadium outside South Africa) but I also loved the obvious pride of their players.

They had some very good backs in 2023, quick, powerful guys such as Duhan van der Merwe and Sione Tuipulotu. And while their forwards weren't the biggest, they could really get themselves up for a game and match any pack in world rugby. Then, of course, they had a puppet master in Finn Russell at No 10, a guy some might call a magician. They'd proven they were a proper team by beating England three games in a row, as well as thumping Argentina and Wales in the last 12 months, so we knew we'd have to be switched on to see them off.

Maybe some people found it a bit odd that Scotland had so many imports in their team, including three South Africans, but no one was bitter about it. Before joining Edinburgh, loose head Pierre Schoeman and winger Van der Merwe had been at the Bulls with Lood de Jager, Jesse Kriel, Trevor Nyakane and a few others, and while they would have been desperate to put one over on their old teammates, our guys would have felt much the same.

As expected, Scotland's forwards came at us hard in the first half in Marseille and we led only 6–3 at the break. But Pieter-Steph barged through the Scottish defence for our first try then fly-half Manie Libbok produced a moment of genius, a no-look kick-pass that fell straight into the arms of Kurt-Lee Arendse, who scampered over unopposed.

Not that Manie's kick had anything to do with pre-tournament upskilling, it was just a moment of individual brilliance from a special player who did things like that for the Stormers whenever his forwards gave him front-foot ball. In contrast, Russell didn't have the time to create much magic in that game, because we limited his space as much as possible, and we won 18–3.

A few days later, Malcolm Marx suffered a cruciate ligament injury in training. There was a mistake at a breakdown – unfortunately these things sometimes happen in training – and I knew it was bad as soon as it happened. Malcolm is one of the toughest players I've shared a rugby field with and hearing him scream, I immediately knew that something bad had happened.

That caused a bit of a stir in the camp because we'd brought only two specialist hookers, Malcolm and Bongi. Deon Fourie had played quite a lot at hooker, but not for a while, and he'd really been selected as a loose forward; meanwhile, Bulls flanker Marco van Staden had occasionally been practising as a hooker, though I don't think he'd ever played there.

I was hoping we'd be calling up Handré as a replacement for Malcolm, because we only had Damian Willemse as a back-up to Manie and he wasn't a specialist No 10 (Willie le Roux and Faf could also do a job at fly-half but it would be a big ask to play there in a knockout game). But when it was announced that Handré would indeed be replacing Malcolm, on the

Monday after our 76–0 victory over Romania, there was a media frenzy.

Reporters and pundits thought Jacques and Rassie had gone mad – again! – but it made perfect sense to me. Deon was perfectly capable at hooker, while Handré had recently played for his club side Leicester, so he wasn't coming in cold. He wouldn't be playing against Ireland anyway so he would have a couple of weeks to sharpen up his fitness. But more than any of that he was undoubtedly the world's best off the tee under pressure. Even if Manie kept his starting spot, who better than Handré to come on in the dying seconds of a close knockout game and kick a penalty to win it? Nobody, that's who.

Throughout the build-up to the World Cup, Rassie had been sharing criticism of South African rugby by foreign media, to create an extra bit of spice. I screenshotted one journalist's article, the gist of which was that it would be a minor miracle if a southern hemisphere side made the final. As good as Ireland and France were, I still didn't see them as superior to New Zealand.

Having said all that, Ireland were ranked number one in the world for a reason. We hadn't beaten them since 2016, they'd won 28 of their last 30 Test matches, including their last 15, they had outstanding individual players all over the field, and they had real depth in their squad. Their attention to detail in terms of the breakdown and running lines was meticulous, and they were very technical, which enabled them to neutralise teams in certain areas. In addition, they planned further ahead than other teams, like chess grandmasters: a specific player would clean out a ruck after five or six phases and the right men would be in exactly the right place to run the play. All in all, Ireland were a very well-oiled machine.

They'd also developed a real edge, exemplified by veteran fly-half Johnny Sexton. After the Sharks played Leinster earlier that year, some of the guys complained about Sexton's constant verbals. But I try not to get distracted by players' chat on the field, and I thought Sexton's outbursts were simply a sign of his ultra-competitiveness. He hated losing – which had clearly rubbed off on his teammates – and I had to respect him for that.

It was an intense occasion at the Stade de France, and often brutal. Ireland wing Mack Hansen scored the only try of the first half after a great run by centre Bundee Aki; and after the break, they were able to shrug off a Cheslin try, withstand the detonation of the Bomb Squad and hold on for the win.

It was an impressive performance by Ireland, they beat us 13–8 and we missed a couple of points off the tee, which gave us some perspective. There was obviously a lot of work to be done, but we weren't far off. As such, I was a bit taken aback when a couple of players shook my hand and said, 'See you in the final.' It turned out they'd said it to quite a few of our guys, which I found a bit weird when they were most likely to play the All Blacks in the quarter-finals. Maybe it was just their way of speaking and I took it completely out of context, and if that was the case, fair play.

Walking off the pitch, I thought, *Flip, you can't be looking past New Zealand. That's a very dangerous thing to do.* It's good to be confident, and we obviously thought we could win the tournament, but I'd never have said 'see you in the final' to anyone. We'd probably be playing France in the last eight and we certainly weren't looking past them.

Of course we wanted to beat Ireland but I didn't think losing was the end of the world. We'd always said the Scotland game was the most crucial in the pool, and we'd almost certainly qualify for the quarter-finals if we beat Tonga. However, Rassie was madder than I'd ever seen him.

There were a few reasons for that. Tens of thousands of Ireland fans singing their anthem, The Cranberries song 'Zombie', after the final whistle – 'In your head, in your head' – hurt. We'd also found out that after the game, some Irish fans had been quite mean to our wives and girlfriends, which pissed me off. But mostly Rassie was angry with his players.

When I arrived for Monday's team meeting Rassie was quieter than normal and looked agitated, so I could tell something was brewing. Then he exploded. He felt we didn't care enough about losing to Ireland, that our attitude seemed to be, 'Ah well, we only lost by a few points, and we missed a few kicks, and we're probably through to the knockout stages anyway.' He said there wasn't enough pain and regret on our faces and that our egos had grown too big. He said we were liars, because while we made big claims about being willing to die for our country, we hadn't played like that.

The guys always say that even when Rassie is shitting on the whole group, it feels like he's just talking to you and there's no one else in the room. And even though you know you've done nothing wrong, you doubt yourself. But some of Rassie's criticism in that meeting was clearly designed to wound on a personal level.

He said he could sense some tension among me, Siya and Duane and that Siya, being my best friend, was taking my side. He called us a 'virus', said we weren't contributing properly to the team. Then he dropped the bombshell that Duane, Siya and I wouldn't be playing in the quarter-final, and that we'd play the final pool game against Tonga instead. 'Bongi, you're the captain for the France game,' he said, 'make sure you focus on them.'

Straight after the meeting, Rassie pulled Duane, Siya and I outside, sat us down and asked if there was a problem between the three of us. We looked at each other, and said no. Rassie added that he didn't want younger members of the squad to think two of his most senior players weren't getting along, and that the most important thing was winning the World Cup. I thought it best to say that Duane and I sometimes didn't agree on rugby stuff, and that if it came across as if we were at loggerheads we'd do something about it. Rassie then left us to sort things out ourselves.

Duane and I had played a lot of Test matches for the Boks so it was natural that we had opinions and sometimes those opinions weren't the same. But one of the beauties of Rassie's coaching environment was that nobody was bigger than the team, and Rassie obviously felt our pride was showing through, which wasn't great for team unity.

I thought it normal that within any group there would be people who had different opinions on things, and it was never the case that we argued in front of other guys, we normally reached common grounds. Rassie just felt that younger guys could sometimes feel some tension, which he didn't want. As for Siya, he'd been dragged into the situation almost by default, because me and him were just always together. Nevertheless, Duane and I soon agreed that we wouldn't have different opinions in front of the team, and if there really was an issue that needed addressing we'd speak about it afterwards, one on one.

Anlia was waiting for me in my hotel room and she knew as soon as I walked in that something was wrong. I was normally able to shelve my work stresses and strains until I returned to the office, when I put my game face back on, but I couldn't do that this time. And instead of trying to make me feel better with kind words, as she usually did, Anlia knew not to say much. That said, she was there to hold for a couple of seconds.

She'd never seen me like that before and she hasn't since. It wasn't fair on her, I realised that, but I played rugby to be a Springbok and I honestly thought the Tonga game might be my last contribution in the tournament.

I didn't complain to Rassie. Nobody ever complained to Rassie. All I could do was keep my mouth shut, play as well as possible against Tonga and hope to change his mind. But even as I simmered I came to see Rassie's intervention as more proof of his genius.

While Duane and I didn't think our occasional disagreements were much of an issue, Rassie could see a problem before it had become a problem. He was like a mechanic with an engine, and he'd worked out that Duane and I were two cogs that weren't quite meshing. And if our teeth weren't filed down soon, we'd risk crashing the whole machine. Maybe not in the next game but somewhere down the line.

I now believe that if that meeting hadn't happened, maybe we wouldn't have gone all the way. Who knows, but he certainly grabbed the guys by the throats and got everyone back on task, which was to sort out any personal differences and give everything for the team for the next couple of weeks. Having spoken to Siya about it, I know he thinks the same. As it was, Rassie's harsh words made us angry and more desperate. They made us think, *Shit, we do talk a lot about giving everything for South Africa, but maybe Rassie is right: we're not living up to our promise, we've been lying all along.*

Duane and I were a picture of harmony in the lead-up to the Tonga game, and our 49–18 victory in Marseille, combined with Ireland's comfortable victory over Scotland, secured our place in the quarter-finals. Rassie didn't do corridor chats or one-on-ones in his office, so I had to wait until the team announcement to find out if I'd play against France. I knew it could have gone either way because the competition for places was so fierce, and when I saw my name on the team sheet, alongside Siya's and Duane's, I breathed a huge sigh of relief.

It didn't get much bigger than playing a World Cup knock-out game against France in Paris, especially after what had happened to me in Toulon. I never felt any animosity towards my Toulon teammates because they were all great, but I did still have some bad memories of some critics, local journalists and senior management. They hadn't treated me well, which made that quarter-final just that extra bit personal. I knew they'd all be watching and I wanted this Springbok team of ours to knock their French team out of their own World Cup so badly.

France had been in fine form all year, including putting 50 points on England at Twickenham in the Six Nations and 40 points on Australia in their final warm-up game. They'd also outclassed the All Blacks in their World Cup opener, which hardly ever happens. They were solid all over the field and we needed to be extra aware of the threat posed by Antoine Dupont, even though he hadn't played since breaking his cheekbone in France's third game of the tournament against Namibia. Then there was the home crowd to consider.

The atmosphere when we'd played France in Marseille in 2022 was extremely hostile. We felt like gladiators in the Colosseum, surrounded by people baying for our blood, and it was so loud that we struggled to hear each other. Rassie came up with the idea of playing 'La Marseillaise' through a big speaker while we trained, so that we'd be prepared for the noise on matchday.

This speaker was right next to the pitch during line-out practice, so we were barely able to hear the calls; and when we played 15 against 15, Rassie would be running from ruck to ruck with the speaker, like a little kid loving the fact that he was irritating the hell out of us.

Rassie didn't know whether we'd be spied on or not, but he wasn't taking any chances. We were super careful about what we showed in training, and we rehearsed any special plays on an indoor basketball court. There was a CCTV camera in there but we covered it with a Springbok jacket.

I must have heard 'La Marseillaise' 20 times before the evening of the game, and while I think it helped, I don't think anything can fully prepare you for almost 80,000 French fans singing it in the flesh. And the French players were obviously inspired by it because the opening exchanges of the game felt like being in a washing machine. France's intensity was frightening, and there were a fair few Springbok players with eyes like saucers, wishing the spinning would stop.

Prop Cyril Baille went over in the corner after 4 minutes, off the back of an attacking line-out, and we could have been 14–0 down a few minutes later. France were pummelling away at our line and I saw that they had an overlap on the blind side. And when Damian Penaud threw a pass to the unmarked Thomas Ramos outside him, I instinctively stuck out an arm.

I honestly didn't know if the ball had gone forwards or backwards, so I was mightily relieved when I heard the referee say it had gone straight down. A couple of centimetres forward and I'd have been in the sin-bin, France probably would have been awarded a penalty try.

A couple of minutes later, Cobus Reinach put up a bomb, the ball ricocheted off a French defender and Kurt-Lee did the rest. Boos had never sounded so beautiful, and having gained a foothold we found ourselves ahead 10 minutes later, courtesy of one of our special moves. Manie kicked high to the right, where we'd stationed Franco Mostert, Pieter-Steph and

Damian de Allende. Cameron Woki juggled the ball, which ended up in the hands of De Allende, who was brought down just short of France's line before scoring from the next phase. We'd only practised that move on a basketball court, where Manie threw the ball instead of kicking it because the roof was too low.

That was classic De Allende, someone who is criminally underrated. Some people think he's just a hard carrier but he's actually one of the best passers in the game. He almost never plays badly and always comes up with big moments in big games, such as his brilliant try against Wales in the 2019 semi-final. I honestly think he's one of the best 12s to have played rugby or at least in the generation I played in.

Four minutes later, France were ahead again, hooker Peato Mauvaka scoring in the corner after a quick tap by Dupont. But that try, good as it was, will always be remembered for what came immediately afterwards.

Ramos doesn't really miss, so most of us were standing behind the poles thinking he was going to knock the conversion over. But not Cheslin. He saw that Ramos had made a small movement towards the ball, ran hell for leather and charged down the kick. I'd never seen anyone do that before, not even at school. They should think about making Cheslin the patron saint of lost causes. A few minutes later, France coughed up the ball, Jesse Kriel kicked it through with pinpoint accuracy, and Cheslin raced onto it and scored.

Baille soon went over for his second try of the game, and this time Ramos popped his kick over to level things at 19–19.

Then, a few minutes before half-time, Louis Bielle-Biarrey kicked long, Damian Willemse caught the ball inside our 22, called for a mark – despite there being no French players anywhere near him – and signalled for a scrum. That hardly ever happens, and some people watching probably wondered if it was even allowed. But our coaches identified that potential situation in the lead up to the game and told our back three that if there's an opportunity to do it, they must.

Damian did it because while France's forwards were a powerful bunch and excellent in the set piece, and their half-backs did a good job of making sure they didn't work too hard and blow themselves out, we thought that if we made them run more than usual, they might flag.

If Damian had booted the ball back downfield, as normally happens, their forwards wouldn't have had to move – they'd have watched it fly over their heads and waited for the catcher to boot it back again. As it was, they had to jog 35–40 m to the mark. And when we won a penalty from the scrum, we kicked downfield, they had to run back again, we won the line-out ball and suddenly they were defending. It wasn't macho posturing, as some journalists suggested, it was a clever way of sapping their energy.

On the stroke of half-time, French prop Uini Atonio stepped inside me – not really what you expect from a guy who's 196 cm and 150 kg – and I wasn't able to adjust in time. We clashed heads, I was yellow-carded, and I spent an uncomfortable 15 minutes in the changing room, wondering if it would be upgraded to a red. It was more of a muffling tackle than a hit but you never know for sure which way TMOs will go. Thankfully, I was back on the field 10 minutes into the second half and we conceded only three points while I was in the sin-bin.

Watching a game as intense and frenetic as that, involving two teams who want to win so badly, you wonder how anyone on the field can feel in control. How can players execute what they've been practising in training in that kind of atmosphere? How can they not make mistake after mistake? But when you're out there you feel like you can influence proceedings. Whenever they went ahead I thought, *We need to score next*, because going two scores behind would be hard to remedy. But I never thought we might not win.

Seven of our replacements were on the field after 51 minutes, and Vincent Koch made it eight with 17 minutes left. And not long after that we were five metres from the French line, we opted for a training ground penalty move: RG Snyman took the tap, offloaded to Duane, and the next ruck was me, Kwagga and Bongi, who was stopped just short; Kwagga then picked and went for the line, which wasn't part of the plan, but when the ball went right again I drifted round from the blind side and Faf played me in. French fly-half Matthieu Jalibert was the defender directly in front of me. I knew he tended to tackle quite high, so I ran straight at him, everything worked out in my favour and I scored next to the poles.

It was such a satisfying moment and remember RG being first on the scene, going so crazy that we basically head-butted each other. But we quickly had to calm ourselves down, because we still had a job to do.

A couple of minutes later Handré had a penalty from just inside our half, and as he was putting the ball on the tee Bongi said to him, 'Do it for South Africa!' Talk about piling on the pressure, but that never seemed to bother Handré, who struck it straight between the poles to give us a four-point lead.

When the French were awarded a penalty with 9 minutes to go I expected them to kick for touch. I was surprised – almost relieved – when Ramos went for the poles instead. I'd rather have been one point ahead and deep in their half than four points ahead and defending our try line. They did manage a late foray into our half but we snuffed out the threat on our 10 m line and the crowd fell almost silent, which was a wonderful sound. France strung a few phases together with the clock in the red but Faf, terrier that he is, managed to rip the ball from replacement prop Reda Wardi, then Cheslin scooped it up, swivelled and booted it into the crowd.

That was the kind of game every rugby player wants to be involved in when they're just starting out in the sport. It was the absolute pinnacle: a World Cup quarter-final against the host nation with almost the whole stadium against us, almost every neutral watching on TV wanting us to lose and almost every journalist and pundit predicting we'd do so. It's difficult to think of a bigger challenge and I loved every minute of it.

Former All Black fly-half Stephen Donald did an interview before that game that I loved. He talked about everything being against us – the French being in fine form and playing at home, 80,000 fans willing us to lose, most people thinking we didn't stand a chance – before adding that if there was one group of individuals who wouldn't care about any of that, it was the Boks. He described us as a 'special breed' in terms of our single-mindedness and correctly identified Rassie as a genius. And we proved him to be exactly right.

I didn't see any of Dupont's criticisms of the refereeing because I was too busy savouring our win. But we didn't celebrate for long and there was no alcohol involved. We had a six-day turnaround before our semi-final and we decided as a group that we would leave the celebrations for 13 days if it meant possibly winning the tournament and changing our lives forever.

Ireland had also failed to reach the last four, having lost 28–24 to New Zealand in the quarter-finals. (We'd all watched the game together and were backing our old southern hemisphere rivals – some of us had been playing against the New Zealand guys for the best part of a decade, in the Rugby Championship and Super Rugby, we knew them pretty well, and some of us were good friends with them.) And after all the pre-tournament talk of northern hemisphere dominance, the only European side to reach the semi-finals were our opponents England.

Given their patchy form over the previous couple of years, some people found that surprising. Since Steve Borthwick had taken over as head coach, England had shipped a record 50 points against France at Twickenham and lost to Fiji for the first time. But they tended to do well in World Cups, where the rugby is generally less expansive.

They'd eased past Argentina in their World Cup opener, despite playing with 14 men for 77 minutes, and made short work of Japan before scraping past Samoa to top their pool. Then they'd survived a late scare by Fiji, who had caused a stir by beating Australia in their pool, and while almost nobody was giving them a chance against us, we knew they'd be dangerous for exactly that reason. England had nothing to lose and everything to gain.

Furthermore, while England had played only two top-10 sides on their way to the semi-finals (seventh-ranked Argentina and sixth-ranked Fiji), we'd played fifth-ranked Scotland, third-ranked France, who were also the hosts, and top-ranked Ireland.

South Africa media and fans assumed we'd breeze past England. Nobody really rated them and some expected us to beat them by 20–30 points. Even players' friends and families were already talking about watching us in another World Cup final. The players weren't thinking like that – if only rugby were as simple as the higher-ranked team winning every time – but we didn't appreciate just how much the France game had sapped us, mentally and physically, while the build-up to the semi-final was very full on.

Rassie kept showing us clips from recent games against England, as well as negative comments about South African rugby from the English media. A few of our guys played along-side England guys at club level (Handré was at Leicester, so he knew Dan Cole, George Martin and Freddie Steward, while Faf had played with the likes of Tom Curry and Manu Tuilagi at Sale), but Rassie understood that there was always a bit of edge when we played England and he was only too happy to sharpen it. And Rassie reminding us of all that stuff was a good way of getting us emotional, though you have to be able to handle your emotions when you cross the white line.

We'd prevented England from winning the biggest prize in rugby four years earlier, so we knew they'd be bent on revenge and expected them to start fast. And that's exactly what happened. They immediately fell into a groove and their energy in the opening exchanges was unreal. And unlike in the France game, when we were able to wrest back the momentum, we continued to be half a second slower than England throughout the first half.

England had obviously done their research and discovered that the more you kicked in World Cup play-off games, the more chance you had of winning. So instead of playing with the ball (which wouldn't have made much sense in the wind and rain anyway) they bombarded our back three with high kicks, chased hard, let us make mistakes and lived off those. It was a simple game plan but they had complete confidence in it, and we struggled to cope. And while I'm sure some people found it boring to watch, those in the Stade de France bellowing 'Swing Low, Sweet Chariot' certainly didn't.

England were 9–3 ahead after half an hour, at which point Handré replaced Manie Libbok at fly-half. That wasn't the first time Rassie had hooked a player before the break – he always said that if someone wasn't having the necessary impact or he felt that the game is not going as planned and a guy on the bench might be a better fit, he'd take him off and give someone else a go, even after 10 minutes – and while Manie was a special player who could do things with the ball that no one else could, Handré had seen us through similar situations in the past. Maybe we'd have won if Manie had stayed on but I doubt any South African was disappointed to see Handré take the stage.

Not that Handré's introduction had much effect in the short term. We trailed 12–6 at half-time, deservedly so, because they'd been better than us in almost every facet of the game. The first 90 seconds or so in the changing room are always quiet – a time to clear the head after the madness of the previous 40 minutes – but this wasn't a confident quietness, it was an uneasy quietness. Nobody seemed to know what had just happened or what we needed to do to turn things around.

Once Rassie had hit us with a few home truths – he said we looked like we didn't want to be there and called us liars again – we returned to silence, at which point Pieter-Steph got to his feet. Pieter-Steph almost never spoke – before, during or after a game – so his decision to take centre stage really meant something. He implored us to liven up and said that if anyone was scared they should say so, so that someone more up for it could play instead.

Pieter-Steph's unexpected rallying cry didn't do the trick, at least not immediately. I was replaced by RG Snyman after only

6 minutes of the second half, and Siya and Duane came off a few minutes later.

We all know that Rassie is the biggest brain in rugby and it's never nice to go off so early in the game, especially not a World Cup semi final, but we all believed in the plan and also in the guys on the bench. But when an Owen Farrell drop goal made it 15–6 to England after 53 minutes, it was clear that their focus wasn't wavering. I also noticed that they weren't cele-brating knock-ons, turnovers and scrum penalties as much as normal. They didn't have time for any of that bullshit, which they usually thought would get under our skin. They were only thinking about winning.

Rassie had taken the replacement forwards aside at half-time and asked them how they planned to influence the game and reverse our fortunes – 'You call yourself the Bomb Squad, now's the time to show why' – but when Kurt-Lee fumbled a kick just before the hour, giving England a scrum about seven metres from our try line, doubts turned to acceptance. I could tell you a nice story about how I always believed we were going to win, but watching from the sidelines I was thinking, *It's over. Our next game will be the bronze medal match.* People watching in South Africa felt the same. Afterwards, my brother told me he'd stormed out of his lounge because he couldn't see us winning.

'Swing Low, Sweet Chariot' was being sung with gusto while the guys were setting themselves for that scrum, but the Bomb Squad is very effective at exploding the joy of opposition fans. Ox and Vincent Koch hadn't been on the field long, and the penalty Ox forced from England tight head Kyle Sinckler felt like a huge energy swing.

Handré banged the ball downfield, we soon won another penalty scrum, and it was obvious that the guys who'd come on were better than the guys who'd started. It wasn't really a case of England's pack wilting – like us, they had five forwards on the bench – it was more that our replacements had seen that the starters' energy wasn't great and they weren't hitting England in the right places.

Yet another penalty scrum allowed Handré to kick for the corner, and this time RG took a clean catch, our line-out having malfunctioned all evening before then. England's forwards piled into the resulting maul and we surprised them with a breakout move which RG finished off with a try. When Handré kicked the extras there was only one score in it. And it didn't matter that England had dominated us for most of the game, as long as we won the last 10 minutes by three points.

When England full back Freddie Steward opted for an up and under in his own half rather than a long kick downfield, we had our chance. It took an age to set the scrum, but when it finally happened our guys made England crack. When referee Ben O'Keeffe blew his whistle and raised his arm, Frans Malherbe turned to me and said, 'Flip, how did we win that penalty?' It was only when we watched the game afterwards that we noticed that Ellis Genge's knee had gone down just after engagement.

The penalty was 49 m out but there was never any doubt that Handré would have a pop rather than kicking for the corner.

And I was confident he'd land it. He'd been rehearsing for such moments for decades – when he was a kid, whenever he was lining up a kick at goal he'd say to himself, 'This is to win the World Cup' – and, perversely, it was too difficult for him to miss, which is something you could probably only say about Handré.

Just thinking about that kick gives me goose bumps. He struck it so sweetly – afterwards, he said it was probably his best strike ever – the ball went straight through the middle of the poles and suddenly, with only 2 minutes left on the clock, we were leading for the first time in the match.

Our final job was to keep England beyond drop goal range without conceding a penalty, and our commitment and discipline in those final stages were off the scale. England strung together lots of phases but kept going backwards, and when the clock turned red they were marooned on the halfway line, further back than where they started. When an England player finally knocked the ball on, the referee blew his whistle and we'd completed one point game of the greatest comebacks in World Cup history.

Unlike the game against France, this time the feeling in the changing room was that we'd got away with it. England had handled their emotions better than us and they'd been the better side overall. But while it hadn't been pretty and we'd put our fans through the wringer again, maybe we'd got our *kak* performance out of the way. We certainly weren't planning on having another one point game in the final.

New Zealand had blown away Argentina in their semi-final the evening before, scoring seven tries to none. And since losing to France in their tournament opener, they'd also put 90 points on Italy, 70 points on Namibia and Uruguay, and knocked out favourites Ireland. Heading into the final, our record win at Twickenham just two months earlier felt totally irrelevant.

Just as before the England game, fans, friends and family expected us to beat the All Blacks, but I knew they'd be completely different animals this time around. They had so much pride in the jersey, they took any defeat personally, they'd hate the idea of losing to us twice in a row – and this wasn't just another Test match, it was a World Cup final. Any rational person knew it was bound to be a nerve-shredder, as most World Cup finals are.

We'd largely managed to avoid politics in the context of racism until then, but England flanker Tom Curry had accused Bongi of calling him a 'white c*nt' in our semi-final, something the media got very excited about. I wasn't nearby when the incident apparently happened, so I couldn't say if Bongi said it or not (I doubt he did, by the way), but I found the whole situation ridiculous regardless. It was a World Cup semi-final, we were all trying to rip each other's heads off, and Curry's complaints seemed more suited to an inter-house school game. It felt childish, like running to the teacher because someone has called you a name.

Inevitably, Bongi and Curry received loads of online abuse, while World Rugby had to go off and review video and audio footage, plus written submissions from both teams. Bongi vehemently denied Curry's accusation and eventually he was cleared to play in the final. That was a relief because he was the only full-time hooker we had left and the keystone of our pack.

I was quite taken aback when Rassie announced we were going with a 7–1 split, but I also loved the idea. I'd been surprised when we went 5–3 against France and England, while having faith that our coaches knew what was right for each game but having only one back (Willie le Roux) on the bench in a World Cup final was high wire stuff.

We had Pieter-Steph and Kwagga ready to slot in behind the pack if needed, Willie could play every back position apart from scrum half, and Cheslin had assured the coaches he could do a job at No 9. But if the starting No 9 and Cheslin both had to go off early, Rassie would have to do a lot of juggling.

As much as I love a forward-heavy bench, I understood the disappointment of some of the backs at the team announcement. Cobus Reinach had started against France and England but he wasn't in the 23, with Faf starting ahead of him. And having started every game at the tournament before then, Manie Libbok was also out of the squad. As good as he was, I understood that decision because Handré was tailor-made for World Cup finals, which so often went down to the wire.

But there was no sympathy for any lingering negativity because we all knew the score. Everyone wanted to play in every game but it was ultimately about the team and winning. As such, those who missed out on the final were allowed to look glum for half an hour or so but they needed to be ready at training to give us the type of pictures we'd face on the weekend. And if we became world champions again, they'd get a gold medal with everyone else.

During the tournament I'd seen lots of videos from back home – shopping malls stuffed to the gills with fans watching our games on big screens, crazy celebrations in townships – which was tremendously gratifying. And after the France game a clip of a little black kid jumping up and down in his lounge and screaming, 'Elizabedi! Elizabedi!' went viral. (I'd just scored my try and presumably he thought that was how to pronounce my name!)

It warmed my heart that we were making people of different backgrounds proud to be South African (and I've certainly become much better known in the black community since that video, and many people call me Elizabedi when they see me on the street). However, Rassie and Jacques spent the week leading up to the final driving home the message that no one outside South Africa wanted us to beat New Zealand. They told us that no one liked us, for a variety of reasons: we'd dashed northern hemisphere hopes, including 'spoiling' the tournament by knocking out the hosts in the quarter-finals; we'd been lucky against England; we kept stacking our bench with forwards, which was not the 'done' thing; we didn't play the game beautifully enough.

Not that I cared about any of that stuff. After we won the World Cup in 2019, I said to Siya, 'Only people who have achieved less than you will ever be jealous of your achievements.' That struck a chord with him and he still reminds me of the comment.

People willing you to fail is a sure sign of success. Playing a hard, honest game and not coming across as arrogant is important to me, but being respected trumps being loved every day of the week. And I knew that no one would be able to disrespect us if we won back-to-back World Cups. Nevertheless, Rassie and Jacques's words created something of a siege mentality in the squad. It felt like it was us, our families and the rest of the South African people against the world.

Jacques laid it on thick at the hotel before we drove to the game – 'This is not how people wanted the story to be, nobody outside of South Africa wanted you to be here' – and he was proved right when we took to the field. Our fans were outnumbered by New Zealand's and most of the neutrals seemed to be pulling for them. They certainly got a lot more cheers than we did.

The All Blacks performed their *Kapa o Pango* haka, with Aaron Smith holding the paddle, and the noise when it ended was deafening. Most of our guys had seen plenty of hakas by that point, and we always enjoyed the challenge and had the utmost respect for it.

The game started out like two heavyweight boxers feeling each other out in the early rounds, but Bongi was an early casualty, having been neck-rolled by All Black blind side Shannon Frizell.

Frizell was sent to the sin-bin and was lucky not to have his yellow upgraded to a red, but Bongi was out for the rest of the match. He was such a big weapon for us and now we wouldn't be able to put on a fresh hooker after 50 minutes. Plus, Bongi's replacement Deon Fourie hadn't really played at hooker a lot recently.

Deon had returned from France a couple of years earlier to rejoin the Stormers (he was my captain when WP won the Currie Cup in 2012), and he probably expected to play a couple of games while helping the young guys. But after years of being overlooked by South Africa's selectors, he became the oldest Springbok debutant when he came off the bench against Wales in Bloemfontein in 2022 (at the age of 60, or something like that), before being picked for the World Cup, primarily as a loose forward.

On the face of it, Deon having to play 78 minutes of a World Cup final against the All Blacks in a position he'd barely played for a couple of years wasn't ideal. Had I been in his boots, I'd have been seriously stressing. But when Rassie spoke about Springboks being a special breed of warrior, Deon was the kind of guy he had in mind. He wasn't the biggest but he was like a Staffy: as game as they came. He'd stay in a fight, however ferocious the foe and desperate the situation, and none of his teammates was worried when he entered the fray.

Handré kicked us into a six-point lead while Frizell was in the bin, and we were 9–3 ahead when referee Wayne Barnes stopped play and started chatting to his TMO. I'm not sure anyone knew what had happened – there hadn't been any groans or boos from the crowd, the kind of noises you usually get when there's been some obvious foul play – but the replays showed that New Zealand skipper Sam Cane had tackled Jesse Kriel high and slammed his shoulder into Jesse's head. Cane was duly sent to the bin and Handré stretched our lead to nine points. And a few minutes later, news reached Barnes from the bunker that Cane's yellow card had been upgraded to a red.

People watching probably thought the game was over as a contest but I was thinking, *I hope the guys don't think this is going to be easy now*. Yes, they were down to 14 men, and we still had 53 minutes to go, but this was New Zealand, playing against their biggest rivals in a World Cup final. I knew they'd lift themselves and fight harder than they'd ever done, and if we didn't do the same it wouldn't feel like we were playing with an extra man. And that's exactly as it panned out.

Mo'unga reduced our lead to six points just before half-time, then Kurt-Lee pulled off a great tackle on Rieko Ioane, preventing him from notching a try he'd score 9 times out of 10 (with our two Power Rangers on either wing, anything seemed possible). Shortly after the restart, Beauden Barrett dropped a high ball and Siya was snagged just short of their line, before Siya was sent to the sin-bin for a high tackle on Ardie Savea. I didn't think it deserved an upgrade to red. Either way, it was a real shot in the arm for the All Blacks.

While Siya was off the field New Zealand had an Aaron Smith try disallowed for a knock-on at a line-out, and just after Siya re-entered the fray Jordie Barrett slung a long pass to Mark Tele'a, the winger stepped a couple of defenders, dropped the ball backwards, and Beauden Barrett slid over in the corner (that was the first try South Africa had conceded in a World Cup final). Mo'unga missed the conversion but now they trailed by only one.

Someone had said to me that week, 'Please let it not be another one-pointer, I don't think our hearts and minds could take it.' I replied that it surely wasn't possible for any team to have three one-point knockout games in a row, but as I made my way to the bench, having been replaced by Munster lock Jean Kleyn, I couldn't help thinking, *This feels a lot like déjà vu.*

With only 7 minutes remaining, Cheslin was yellow-carded for a deliberate knock-on, meaning his game was over. It was his 30th birthday and watching him sitting on the naughty chair, his head buried in his hands, I really felt for him. If we lost, he'd blame himself and no doubt get terrible abuse on social media. I was struggling to hold things together but those 7 minutes must have felt like a couple of weeks in Cheslin's frazzled head.

Jordie Barrett's subsequent penalty attempt was the most nerve-shredding moment of my rugby career. It was quite a way out, at a tricky angle, and while he was sizing it up I hoped and prayed he'd miss. Sorry, Jordie, but you'd do the same! Luckily he did, his attempt drifting just left of the poles.

I expected them to carve out at least one more chance but it never happened. We kept them pinned in their own half for most of the rest of the game, and when Kwagga stole the ball at a breakdown with a minute left – his third turnover since being introduced midway through the half – I could finally breathe. The All Blacks did have one last dart but Anton

Lienert-Brown knocked on and Cheslin felt able to show his face again.

That last scrum was a moment the Bomb Squad were made for, though it wasn't the most clinical of endings. After one false start, when the All Blacks thought they might have forced a penalty, the clock went red. Second time around, Faf was collared trying to get the ball into touch. For a horrible moment it looked like New Zealand might steal it, but with both teams scrabbling for the ball as if their lives depended on it, Wayne Barnes blew his whistle to signal the end of the game.

It's difficult to explain how it feels to win the World Cup. Such was the euphoria, I felt like I'd been catapulted into a different world, where normal emotions don't apply. And that second World Cup victory felt even sweeter.

In 2019, we received a lot of criticism for our style of play and the calibre of our opposition, but no one could say we'd had it easy this time. We'd played five of the top 10 teams in the world, including numbers one, three, four and five. We'd seen off the hosts and the All Blacks and edged three one-pointers in a row. If any team has a tougher route to the title in the future, they'll be unfathomably tired in body and mind.

As always, the All Blacks were gracious in defeat, shaking our hands and congratulating us, which must have been tough to do. But I was so happy for myself, the team and my country. We'd delivered, as our countrymen and women always expected us to, and people all over South Africa would be chucking another slab of meat on the braai, cracking open another beer, turning up the music and taking their partying to the highest levels.

Four years earlier I'd looked straight at my family after receiving my medal, but this time my mom and Ryen were back in South Africa and my dad was no longer with us. I got a bit choked up about that, but when Anlia came onto the pitch with our unborn child in her tummy, I broke into a huge smile. I knew Dad would be looking down on us, bursting with pride at my achievement and the fact that there was a new Etzebeth on the way.

Professional sport is all about fine margins, and to win three World Cup knockout games by a point you need a bit of luck. But so many of our players had been through tough times in their lives – growing up without shoes and too poor to eat, surrounded by people who were tempted into crime and wound up in jail, stuff that players in other top teams couldn't even imagine – and that surely enabled them to dig deeper at clutch moments in big games.

That night I told Handré, 'Remember what I said to you after the squad announcement, when you hadn't been selected and you were down and out?' He laughed, just as Morné Steyn had laughed when I reminded him what I'd said before our deciding Test match against the Lions.

Back at our hotel we combined the consumption of a ludicrous amount of alcohol with quality time spent with each other and our loved ones, while we were all aware of the scenes back home. If only for a day or two, a struggling country was united in joy and the term 'Rainbow Nation' felt apt. Someday,

I'll show those videos to my kids and grandchildren, and hopefully by then the Springboks won't be the only thing that can unite the country.

At about 4 am – four hours into my 32nd birthday – I was reminded of a promise I made before the tournament. We were on a bus to training, talking about haircuts, and I said to RG, 'If we win the World Cup You can cut my hair like yours.' RG was sporting a Mohican, radically different from my unruly mop, but a promise is a promise.

Someone produced a set of clippers and I took a seat and told RG, 'I'm your customer now.' I only trusted RG to do it because I thought he cut his own hair and presumably knew what he was up to. And after I was done, two or three other guys did the same. I thought Anlia would be horrified when she saw me, but she quite liked it, and for weeks afterwards moms and dads were sending me pictures of their kids sporting the same style, for which I take full responsibility.

I stopped drinking at about 8 am, and after an hour's nap I carried on again. Unsurprisingly, I was feeling a bit the worse for wear when we landed back in South Africa. As in 2019, we paraded the trophy all over the country, including some of the poorest townships. And everywhere we were greeted by pure glee, proof that you only really change things by winning.

At one point I was standing between Felix Jones and Andy Edwards on the bus and I asked them what they were thinking. They both said that if Ireland or England had won the World Cup it would have been nothing like that. They couldn't believe what they were seeing and were so emotional at being a part of it.

In Soweto, it took us about an hour to travel a kilometer because the roads were so thick with people wanting to get a glimpse of their heroes. In some places people were chasing the bus on crutches and in wheelchairs.

Siya, Bongi or Lukhanyo would only have to make eye contact with a little kid to make him or her burst into tears. When we drove through Khayelitsha, a sprawling township not far from Cape Town airport, lots of little black kids were running behind the bus shouting, 'Siya! Siya!' But suddenly I heard them shouting, 'Elizabedi! Elizabedi!' I turned to Siya and said, 'You know what, my brother, people think having a certain amount of players of colour in a team is transformation, but this right here is transformation.' My name being chanted in a black neighbourhood.

13

STILL HUNGRY

I'm a big one for celebrating achievements, sporting or otherwise, but there's only so much partying you can do, even if you've won a second World Cup in a row. I remained hungry for more success and I knew that if I eased off even a little bit, younger players would go past me. So after a few weeks spent on cloud nine, I voluntarily crash-landed back down to earth.

While the Boks had been in France the Sharks had made a terrible start to the URC, losing their first five games, including one against Italian side Zebre Parma, who hadn't won for 18 months. Things didn't get much better when the Bok guys returned to action, and we ended up losing 14 of our 18 regular season matches and finishing 14th in the table of 16.

We had a good team on paper, with some great individuals, but we just couldn't make things click. We deserved the criticism we received because some of our performances were awful. We couldn't really blame the fact that we were missing international players for some games, or the schedule, because the Stormers, who won the title in 2021–22, and the Bulls, runners-up twice in their first three seasons, were doing okay.

Mercifully, we managed to salvage something from the season with a run to the final of the Challenge Cup. In our semi-final against Clermont, a team full of gifted strike runners and forwards, we showed great fight to come back from 10 points down at half-time and win 32–31. (Despite being the home side on paper, the game was played at Harlequins' Stoop ground in London, which is far closer to Clermont than Durban! No semis could be played in South Africa, which was just one of the competition rules.)

The final was played at Tottenham Hotspur Stadium, an incredible place with a pitch like a carpet, and we overpowered Gloucester to become the first South African side to win a European trophy. That was only my second piece of silverware at club level, after my Currie Cup win in 2012, so it meant a lot.

People say that the winners of the Challenge Cup can only claim to be the 17th best side in Europe, after the 16 that qualified for the Champions Cup. I can't really argue with that, but coming at the end of a torrid season it represented a big mental victory for our players.

That final, played in front of 35,000 fans, also gave some of our younger players a taste of what it's like to play international rugby, and winning it meant we automatically qualified for next season's Champions Cup, which is the competition every team in Europe most wants to win.

Unfortunately, I didn't play much part in the Sharks' 2024–25 season, first because of the concussion protocol and then, just as I was on the verge of returning to action, a hamstring strain. The sport isn't getting any less physical, that's for sure. Sadly, we didn't manage to add more silverware, bombing out in the pool stages of the Champions Cup, the quarter-finals of the Challenge Cup and the semi-finals of the URC.

The level of brutality differs from game to game, depending on which team I'm playing against and how many contact situations I find myself in, but sometimes I'll play a Test match and wake up on the Monday morning feeling like I've been hit by a truck. The idea of playing another Test in five days' time will seem unfathomable, and only by Wednesday will I feel normal.

Had I not spent so much time on the sidelines, maybe I'd be retired by now because of playing too many games. Having said that, there has been a major mind shift in rugby over the last decade.

When I broke into the Springbok squad, guys still playing professional rugby in their mid-30s were considered ancient. (Before the 2015 World Cup, I remember people saying Jean de Villiers was way too old to be playing for South Africa, despite the fact he was performing week in, week out at the age of 34.) But a 42-year-old Ma'a Nonu recently re-signed for Toulon and more and more guys are playing international rugby into their late 30s. (Wales's Alun Wyn Jones recently retired at 37, Ireland's Johnny Sexton at 38, while Dan Cole, also 38, is still playing in the front row for England, at least at the time of writing.) Tellingly, when Steven Kitshoff sadly announced his retirement at the age of 33, after suffering a serious neck injury in late 2024, people were saying he'd been cut off in his prime.

Quite a few Boks who won the World Cup in 2023 were in their 30s, but only Duane Vermeulen called it quits afterwards. How many of those guys will be at the 2027 tournament in Australia remains to be seen, but I can guarantee you that if they don't make it, it won't be for want of trying. I'll be turning 36 during the tournament but I'm confident my body will hold up. I certainly want to still be involved in as many Test matches as possible, and if I keep playing well, hopefully I'll be in a good position to be selected.

Encouraging news for fans of the Springboks is that 2024 was another good year for us. We won 11 of our 13 Test matches and lost twice by one point (those tight games couldn't keep going our way forever). We beat Ireland for the first time in eight years, which as far as the South African media and fans were concerned was a monkey off our back, especially after losing to them at the World Cup. We also won the Rugby Championship, including beating the All Blacks twice at home, before going unbeaten on our end-of-year tour for the first time since 2013.

Rassie, head coach again after Jacques's departure for Leinster, selected 50 players over the season, and the fact that it was so successful suggested South African rugby was in ruder health than ever. It's mad to think that only seven years earlier sponsors were abandoning what they thought was a sinking ship and pundits were predicting that we'd soon become a Tier 2 team.

(You won't be surprised to learn that Rassie showed us quite a lot of those clips after taking over in 2018.)

Those doomsday predictions never made much sense. There were so many South Africans playing professional rugby all over the world at the time, every kid still wanted to be a Springbok, school rugby programmes were more professional than ever, with top-notch and coaching, and competition between the top schools remained fierce. But more important than any of that was that rugby wasn't only in the blood of white South Africans. It was in the blood of South Africans of colour, too. And more and more players of colour were entering the system and rising to the top.

Then there's Rassie, who changed the whole mindset of the team, tackled transformation head on and redefined what it meant. Without a shadow of a doubt, he is the cleverest rugby coach on the planet.

Rassie's experimentation isn't over, I can guarantee you that. But I reckon that by mid-2026 he'll have identified a big group of players good enough to be selected for the World Cup. Not necessarily the most gifted players but definitely guys Rassie thinks will die for the Boks. Fitting the right people in the right places, on and off the field, is one of Rassie's great talents.

At the start of 2024, Irishman Jerry Flannery and New Zealander Tony Brown took over as defence and attack coach respectively. Jerry, who worked with Rassie and Jacques at Munster, and Tony, who played for the Sharks and the Stormers and did great things as a coach with the Highlanders and

Japan, understood South African rugby culture while providing new perspectives.

Tony, a fly-half who won 18 caps for the All Blacks, comes from a culture that loves attacking rugby, and it was the attacking part of our game that Rassie particularly wanted to improve. As he put it, 'If we don't adapt, we'll die a slow death,' and he was acutely aware that the blueprint for winning the World Cup in 2023 wouldn't win it again in 2027.

Felix Jones had laid the foundations, making sure our players had the necessary ball-handling skills to do more than just bash it up, and Tony took over from where Felix left off. Get your defence and kicking right in international rugby and you'll win more games than you lose, and I'll never waver from my belief that whatever brand of rugby gives you victory is the correct brand of rugby, whether that's kicking and chasing the whole game or weaving beautiful attacking patterns. But I must admit that given the choice of winning one way or the other, I'd always choose the latter.

With Tony pulling the strings, we were suddenly being talked about as one of the most exciting teams in world rugby, even while some journalists and pundits were still grumbling about our 7–1 bench splits. We scored 24 tries in winning the 2024 Rugby Championship, plus another 15 in our three end-of-year Test matches. And we were doing things that no other teams were doing.

Against Australia in Brisbane, Cheslin fed the ball into a scrum (which I found out about only after the game!) and threw the ball into a line-out. We also unveiled a new line-out move that went viral on social media: flanker Ben-Jason Dixon caught the ball in the middle while I was being lifted, he basketball passed it back to me, I set the ball up and Siya rumbled over for a try.

Rugby tends to be very process driven, with teams doing the same things over and over, so fans love it when we're innovative and interesting. If something doesn't work, no problem, we'll give it another shot later in the game. And with Felix recently returning to the fold after a short stint with England, the coaching group has become even more diverse and creative.

Rival countries will also be evolving over the next couple of years, even if their innovations aren't as different as Rassie's. After suffering a bit of a post-World Cup hangover, France looked pretty special in the 2025 Six Nations and England showed signs that they were heading in the right direction. Argentina reached new heights in the 2024 Rugby Championship, putting 38 points on New Zealand in Wellington, 67 on Australia in Santa Fe, and beating us in Santiago del Estero.

Sections of the media seem to have decided that the age of All Black dominance is over, perhaps for good, but I'll never see it that way. It took a late try to beat them at Ellis Park in the 2024 Rugby Championship, and they very nearly beat us with 14 men in the last World Cup final.

While it's nice to have beaten them four times in a row, given how many Test matches I've lost against them, I'd be mad to think we've got a psychological hold over them, and very stupid to crow about it. They can still beat any team in the world on any given day, they'll always be desperate to beat the Boks, and I don't want to give them any extra motivation. Disrespect the All Blacks and they'll put 40 points on you the next time you play them.

How good are the current Springboks? Well, it's difficult answering that question, because I'm part of the current team, but I reckon our toughest competition is the team that came after the 2007 World Cup, peaking in 2009 when they won the Tri-Nations and beat the Lions (the era of Smit, Beast, Matfield, Bakkies, Du Preez, Habana, De Villiers et al.).

We've got two or three world-class players in every position, sometimes more. At fly-half we've got Handré, Manie Libbok and Sacha Feinberg-Mngomezulu, who made a big splash in 2024. And consider our riches at scrum half, with Faf, Cobus Reinach, Grant Williams, Jaden Hendrikse, Herschel Jantjies and Morné van den Berg all vying for the starting spot.

Inevitably, people will make comparisons between us and the great All Black side of 2011–2015, and while it's a fun pub conversation it's a little bit pointless. Every guy who played in their two World Cup wins will say they could have beaten us, every guy who played in our two World Cup wins will say we could have beaten them, and if we played each other 10 times we'd maybe win five games each. I prefer to keep a lid on that kind of stuff anyway, because if we don't stay humble, remain focused and keep working our backsides off, we certainly won't win another World Cup in 2027.

Anlia Etzebeth, Eben's wife: *Some things in life are too perfectly timed to be coincidence. Ours was one of them. As cheesy as it may sound, it was love at first sight – no doubt. If we hadn't both been in Cape Town on that exact day, I don't know if we ever would have met. I lived over 14,000 kilometers away, and Eben was living in France at the time. Looking back, it feels like the universe conspired just to bring us to that moment.*

When Eben first contacted me, I was at a stage in my life where I decided I was going to focus on my music career and was quite stubborn about not getting involved in a relationship, but thankfully, God had other plans! It is probably why I didn't seem too enthusiastic, although not as offhand as Eben always likes to tell people!

Before we started speaking on the phone, I didn't really know what to expect. I didn't watch much rugby, but I knew he had a reputation as a hard rugby player. However, as we got talking, I quickly realized that he was actually a true gentle giant and such a humble family guy.

When we finally met in person, everything felt right and we just clicked. We were at the perfect age, in that we both knew exactly what we wanted from a relationship and we were very honest with each other from the get go. I even met his mom and dad on our first date – which doesn't normally happen! – but it felt so normal and familiar.

After our first meeting, we spoke on the phone for hours at a time. Before I went to go visit him in Toulon for the first time, he sent me a love letter and flowers and has never stopped the romantic gestures. We have a show-cupboard in our home devoted to special memories throughout our relationship, including a special shell his dad delivered our wedding rings in.

Believe it or not, he is not only romantic but also very goofy! I remember coming home one day and him pretending to be the wife and me the rugby player. When I walked into the kitchen, he was cooking for me while wearing one of my aprons and red lipstick, and then went on to ask if he could fix me a beer! Oops! Maybe I shouldn't have said that – opposition players are meant to be scared of him!

I visited Eben a couple of times in France and only five months into our relationship, we got engaged. I flew to France and arrived the evening just before my birthday. I had no idea what a wonderful surprise was in store for me. Eben had made a restaurant reservation in Nice, but he really wanted us to be in Toulon by the time it turned midnight, for some reason not yet known to me.

We were having such a great night and didn't notice that it had gone past midnight! So as a fix, I suggested we turn our watches back two hours and pretend it wasn't my birthday yet. We arrived in Toulon just before our watches showed 12, and I remember him dropping me at his house and saying "See you later!" before driving off. As I entered the house, I was taken on an exciting treasure hunt and thought, Okay, something big is happening here . . .

The last clue was a set of car keys and a note that read, "Meet me at the spot where I asked you to be my girlfriend." I immediately knew it was a specific beach close by called Plage de *l'Almanarre, and when I parked up the car, I heard one of our favorite songs drifting up from the beach ('Wish for the World' by country singer Ryan Hurd, which contains the lyric, "I wish everyone could find someone to love like I love you"). It was a beautiful spring evening, with not a breath of wind, a sky sprinkled with stars and a full moon illuminating the scene. And as I walked closer, there he was, standing next to a blanket surrounded by candles.*

I noticed that he was holding a little box. As I finally reached him, he went down on one knee and I just burst into tears. When he asked me to be his wife, I obviously said yes! We popped some champagne and spent a special couple of hours talking and soaking up the fairytale moment, and when we finally turned our watches forward to the correct time, we realized that Eben only had two hours left of sleep before training started!

It was such a blessing to spend that time in France at the start of our relationship – we were in our own little world and could really get to know each other without any distractions. I wouldn't say I was relieved when Eben said he wanted to return to South Africa, because it was such a special chapter in our lives, but it meant that we could both be closer to family, I could carry on with my career and Eben could be closer to his dad.

Eben's rugby wasn't too hectic at the beginning of our relationship, which was when he was playing and lived in Toulon. It was only when he joined up with the Boks for the first time where I thought, Okay, now I've been sucked into the crazy world of professional rugby...

Playing for the Boks brings lots of rewards, on and off the field, but it's also very demanding and requires a lot of sacrifice, not to mention the physical dangers involved. We wouldn't see each other for long periods of time, and when I did tag along, he'd be busy almost the entire day. But while my career was different in a lot of ways, I understood what it was like to have a big dream, and that you really need to give it your all to make that dream come true. That's a big part of what I admire about him, that he puts a lot of extra time in and always strives to be better and better. His commitment is next level, in his professional and personal life.

Eben was already a well-established Springbok when we started dating, having won the 2019 World Cup, but he didn't get a crazy amount of attention in Toulon. South Africa, however, was very different. Whenever we went out to eat, people would ask for autographs and photos. Some people say that must be difficult, but I was so proud of him and grateful when I saw people being good to him. And because I'd started dating him while he was playing in France, I already knew the real Eben, and not just the rugby player.

Another highlight we shared back in South Africa was when I sang the national anthem before Eben's 100th cap for the Springboks. I was doing something I loved, and it soon dawned on me that I wasn't just singing for the 55,000 people in the stadium, but I was also singing with them – and their singing was incredibly loud and proud. Meanwhile, standing just a few yards away was my fiancé, about to reach this amazing milestone he had worked so hard for. It was a very special moment, and one we can show our children, thanks to YouTube!

We got married 4 February 2023, in the winelands of Franschhoek. And it was magical! I remember the two of us walking away from the wedding venue and just sitting on the grass under the stars with a glass of champagne, looking at all the people we love and soaking up all the blessings in that moment. I also wrote a song for him which I sang that evening. Soon after, I fell pregnant with our first child.

The love a parent has for a child is unconditional, and parenthood completely changes your perspective on life. Eben has become an even better man since the birth of our daughter, and while Liv and I spend a lot of time at home without Eben, we never feel abandoned. He always puts our little family first and we know that coming home to us is the highlight of his day.

Eben almost never brings his work home with him. The only time he was unable to keep a lid on his emotions was after Rassie told him he wouldn't be playing in the World Cup quarter-final against France. When he walked through the door, I immediately saw something was wrong. He loves the Springboks to his core and wants to play every single game. That was certainly one he did not want to miss!

I was in France for most of the 2023 World Cup, which helped me better understand the pressure Eben was under. Eben was so focused on the task in hand, it was almost as if he was operating on some higher plane. Those knockout games were hectic for me (it didn't help that I was heavily pregnant at the time!), but luckily my Mother, Karien, and brother, Gerrit, were with me. Together, we spent a lot of time praying in the stands! I knew how much he hated losing – with a passion! – and how *important it was for him to win the tournament. And I developed an even greater admiration and respect for his mental strength and determination.*

Eben has lost none of his motivation to play for the Boks, and he never will until the day he retires. He does sometimes talk about life after rugby, and when he does finally slip into retirement, I think he'll embrace it. And it will be nice to have him at home more. Our children will certainly love having him around, and who knows how many we'll have by then!

While most of the world will continue to define Eben by his many achievements on the rugby field, I'll know him as the wonderful, down-to-earth family man and husband he is. I suspect it will be easy to forget that he even played rugby, and I'll sometimes have to remind myself that I'm sharing my life with the most capped Springbok in history, with two (hopefully three!) World Cup victories to his name.

The greatest Springbok of all time? It won't matter to Eben, and it won't matter to me, because he'll certainly be the greatest husband and dad. He will always be my and our childrens' hero, and I will just feel blessed that I'm getting to spend the rest of my life with him.

Any suggestion that I'm somehow part of something great still feels slightly unreal. I still remember being eight and getting up in the middle of the night to watch the Boks play the All Blacks with my dad and brother. We lost that game 28–0, and I was so upset, but I still wanted to wear the green and gold. That didn't look likely when I was playing in Tygerberg High

School's under–16s B team, and it's very weird to think that was only 17 years ago.

I'd have given almost anything to play just once for the Springboks, so equalling one of my heroes Victor Matfield's record of 127 caps was surreal. Rassie gave some of the guys a rest for that game against Argentina in Santiago del Estero, but he named me on the bench so that I could hopefully break the record in the return Test match in Mbombela. That was very considerate of him because it meant my family and friends could be there, including some who were planning to come over from Toulon.

I phoned my brother that week and we reminisced about supporting the Boks as kids. We thought they were the best team in the world, not just in rugby but in all of sport. However good or bad they were, we'd be glued to the TV screen for every Test match, and when we kicked a rugby ball around on the field near our house we'd pretend to be our heroes in green and gold.

Things didn't happen for Ryen as a player but he did become my number one supporter. He tells me that every time I do something big with the Boks he feels like he's in my shoes. And now I was about to become the guy who had played more games for that team than anyone else. Ryen was never an older brother that tried to push my achievements down or someone that got jealous, he was there every step of the way, just supporting me more and more as the years rolled on. He'll always be the big brother and one of my heroes.

Congratulatory messages had been rolling in all week, and

those from ex-Boks – including my fellow centurions – were particularly special. I'd never forgotten Victor's encouraging words when I was just starting out as a pro, or his warmth when he came out of retirement to play alongside me with the Boks. It didn't feel quite right that I was about to break his record.

So much had changed since I made my debut for the Boks 12 years earlier. I was still a boy back then, not long out of school and desperate to make my parents proud. And how proud they were. I so wish my dad had been there in person to see me break the record. He'd have been beaming from ear to ear. But one precious loved one had been physically replaced by another: eight months earlier, on 16 January 2024, Anlia and I had welcomed our first child into the world. We named her Elizebedi, soon shortened to Liv.

The plan was to walk out with Anlia and Liv but I had second thoughts when I saw how packed the stadium was. I usually put my phone away a few hours before kick-off but that day I sent Anlia a text from the changing room, suggesting it would be too noisy. However, I scrubbed that text and started again, reminding Anlia to put ear defenders on the little one. I'm so glad I did because those pictures of the three of us walking out together, with a big 'EBEN 128' aflame in the background, will last a lifetime. Sorry I didn't smile but I was concentrating on holding back the tears.

We still had a game to win and thankfully we won it well, clinching the Rugby Championship in the process. And while Dad wasn't in the crowd to see it, Mom was. I respect and love her so much and can speak to her about anything, so she feels as much a friend as a mom nowadays. It's impossible for me to know how she feels when she watches me play rugby for the Boks, but when my daughter started walking, Anlia and I were jumping up and down and cheering like a couple of lunatics in the playpen, so maybe Mom feels something like that. Certainly, family still comes first for her, as it does for me.

Rugby-wise, I'd like to be remembered as a hugely competitive guy who always gave it his all, never took a backwards step and was desperate to be as good as he could be for his team. But while rugby is very dear to me, I've always regarded family as the most important thing in life, as well as my faith in God.

Sure, winning things as a rugby player is incredibly rewarding, but the birth of our daughter was like winning a World Cup 10 times over. You can't prepare for that moment like you can for a rugby match, but the love I feel for my Liv is indescribable. People often talk about children changing their perspective on life and my daughter's arrival certainly made me appreciate family even more than before. But far from making me soft, it made me even more motivated to be the best I can for the Springboks for as long as possible.

I have asked myself, *Will I always be able to get myself up for yet another scrumming session? Yet another line-out session? Yet another defence session?* I must have done thousands of them down the years. And then there's all the other stuff that comes with being a Springbok: the constant travelling for club and country; not sleeping in your own bed for half the year; keeping sponsors happy; people asking for autographs, selfies and birthday messages; missing out on quality time with your family. But the very short answer is, *Yes – absolutely!* To play for the Springboks is the ultimate drive, and I want to be able to do it for a long time still. I'm aware that playing rugby is a job many people would pay to do, and I'm able to find new motivations before every season, whether it's going unbeaten on a European tour, which we did in 2024 for the first time in 11 years, or winning a Rugby Championship without losing a game, which we've never done.

I'll know when I'm not good enough, and that will be the time to stop. I'll never want to feel like I'm dragging things out and letting people down, including myself. As it is, I feel like I can push my body for a few more years. And the more I achieve, the better life I'll be able to give my family and the prouder my little girl will be of me. Maybe she'll watch me play in a World Cup final, and to have her see me winning a third title in a row would be unbelievable.

The idea of retirement doesn't scare me anyway. I'll miss game days, the competitiveness and the camaraderie, even aspects of touring that seemed like a drag at the time, but I won't sit around with a rug over my legs, dwelling on my career and wishing it could happen all over again. Why do that when the alternative is being thankful for all that rugby has given me?

Maybe I'll feel wistful when I look at all my Springbok jerseys, which I intend to stick on the walls of a special room when we move into our final family house in Cape Town; or when I'm tucking into a bowl of spaghetti bolognese, which

I've eaten before every game since I started playing senior rugby; or when I'm out for lunch with my friends and we're boring our families with stories about 'the good old days' they've heard many times already. But why want more when rugby has fulfilled me many times over?

I hope South Africa, which I truly believe is the finest country in the world, is a better place by the time I hang up my boots, but I have no control over that. What I can control is my own little family bubble, in which I am truly content.

I can see us now, gathered in our house for a matchday party: guests arriving; the girls in the kitchen drinking wine and getting the side dishes ready; the men sitting at the bar and grilling great slabs of meat on the braai; Anlia and the kids – because there will be more than one – wearing green and gold jerseys; all of us cheering on our beloved team. Only the Springboks losing could spoil that scene, but only for an hour or two. Then we'll start talking about how great they'll be next week, we'll all start smiling again, and the braai will go on.

ACKNOWLEDGEMENTS

Attempting to thank all the people who have contributed to my wonderful life so far is a daunting task for sure. However, I will give it my best shot – and for fear of forgetting anyone, I will keep it general.

The sport of rugby has provided me with so much, from the time I first picked up a ball, and I was only able to achieve my sporting dreams because of the guidance of so many fine coaches, from school to the Springboks. Thanks to all of you, but particularly Hennie Bekker and Mr Gavin Beresford, who saw something in me at a young age and believed that I could achieve something one day. Allister Coetzee, who gave me my debut for the Stormers when I wasn't long out of school; Heyneke Meyer, who first selected me for the Boks; and Rassie Erasmus and Jacques Nienaber, who transformed the Boks from underachievers to two-time world champions. Genius.

I also need to thank anyone I've played with, for school, province, clubs and country. I've made so many great friends in rugby, and while my most precious memories were made alongside my fellow Boks, I also met mates for life playing for

Tygerberg High School, the University of Cape Town Ikeys, the Stormers, NTT Docomo, Toulon and the Sharks.

A special mention must also go to the guys who got me a special gift for my 128th cap: Siya Kolisi, Handré Pollard, Damian de Allende, Jesse Kriel, Willie le Roux, RG Snyman, Lood de Jager, Frans Malherbe, Cheslin Kolbe, Faf de Klerk, Vincent Koch, Bongi Mbonambi, Franco Mostert, Steven Kitshoff, Malcolm Marx and Pieter-Steph du Toit. That was something I'll never forget and meant more than they'll ever know.

Then there are all the medics who have put me back together over the years, without whom my rugby career might have ended a long time ago; and the hundreds of backroom staff, from media officers to the people who wash the jerseys, without whom our great game would grind to a halt. Thanks to all of you.

I would also like to thank all my sponsors, past and present, for having my back and making me a part of some of the best brands in the world.

Without fans, professional rugby wouldn't exist. And South African rugby fans are among the most passionate in the world of sport. To anyone who has paid hard-earned money to watch me play or cheered me on while sat in front of their TV, your support is greatly appreciated. Long may it continue.

I didn't realise how complicated it was to write a book, so big thanks to my literary agent David Luxton and to Ben Dirs, who got my words on the page. Thanks to my editor Susannah Otter, and everyone else at Hodder & Stoughton, in the UK and Jeremy Boraine, Nicole Duncan and everyone else at Jonathan Ball in South Africa for making it happen. Also big thanks to my rugby agents Christian Abt, Hilton Houghton, Kendra Houghton and Paul van den Berg, who never stop working on my behalf and have become much more than business partners.

It's impossible to put into words how much I love my mum and dad, and I use the present tense for both because I know Dad is still with us. My brother has been the most incredible support to me throughout my rugby career and beyond, and I'm not sure it's possible for siblings to be closer. And I must mention my wife's family, who have taken me into their hearts like their own son.

To my heavenly father, who has blessed me with this talent to play rugby and who protects me every time I go onto the field. Without him, none of this would have been possible.

Finally, to Anlia, our daughter Liv, and our next child on the way: you're my main reason for living, the love I feel for all of you is like nothing I could have imagined, and I can't wait to live the rest of my life alongside you.

PICTURE ACKNOWLEDGEMENTS

Author's collection: page 1 (top, right), page 1 (middle, left), page 1 (middle, right), page 2 (middle, top right), page 5 (top, left and right), page 7 (below, left and right)

Page 1 (below, left): © Gallo Images
Page 2 (top, left): © The Asahi Shimbun via Getty Images
Page 2 (middle, below right): © Steve Haag/Gallo Images via Getty Images
Page 2 (below, left): © Gallo Images
Page 3 (top): © FRANCK FIFE/AFP via Getty Images
Page 3 (middle): © Chris Hyde/Getty Images
Page 3 (below, left): © Gallo Images
Page 4 (top, right): © Steve Haag/PA Images/Alamy.com
Page 4 (middle, left): © Gallo Images
Page 4 (below): © Ashley Vlotman/Gallo Images/Getty Image
Page 5 (below): © David Ramos – World Rugby/World Rugby via Getty Images
Page 6 (top, left and right): © Natasha Bouma
Page 6 (middle and below): © Hanri Human
Page 7 (top, left): © Gallo Images

Page 7 (middle): © Adam Pretty – World Rugby/World Rugby
  via Getty Images
Page 8 (top): © Dan Mullan/Getty Images
Page 8 (middle): © Gallo Images
Page 8 (below): © Natasha Bouma